Positive Psychology in Higher Education

Positive psychology – the scientific study of happiness – is a rapidly burgeoning field, and in no area more so than education. More departments than ever are offering courses in positive psychology, and demand for these courses is consistently high. Graduate programs offering concentrations in positive psychology have appeared at both masters and doctoral level. Educational institutions have expressed interest in using principles of positive psychology to inform institutional structure, faculty development and pedagogy.

Positive psychology has been taught and applied in higher education for almost as long as it has existed as a field, but there is little in the way of published literature that brings all of these developments together. The chapters in this volume represent the use of positive psychology at all levels of higher education – from institutional practices and curricular development to pedagogy and the teaching of positive psychology content itself. This book provides an in-depth look at this exciting area of applied positive psychology which will be relevant to educators and administrators alike.

This book is based on a special issue of *The Journal of Positive Psychology*.

Acacia C. Parks is Assistant Professor of Psychology at Hiram College, USA. She received her Ph.D. from the University of Pennsylvania's Positive Psychology Center, where she began her research program on positive psychological interventions. She is an Associate Editor of *The Journal of Positive Psychology*, and regularly teaches courses on positive, abnormal and health psychology.

Positive Psychology in Higher Education

Edited by
Acacia C. Parks

Routledge
Taylor & Francis Group

LONDON AND NEW YORK

First published 2013
by Routledge
2 Park Square, Milton Park, Abingdon, Oxon, OX14 4RN

Simultaneously published in the USA and Canada
by Routledge
711 Third Avenue, New York, NY 10017

Routledge is an imprint of the Taylor & Francis Group, an informa business

British Library Cataloguing in Publication Data
A catalogue record for this book is available from the British Library

ISBN13: 978-0-415-63129-7

Typeset in Times
by Cenveo Publisher Services

Publisher's Note
The publisher would like to make readers aware that the chapters in this book may be referred to as articles as they are identical to the articles published in the special issue. The publisher accepts responsibility for any inconsistencies that may have arisen in the course of preparing this volume for print.

Table of Contents

Citation Information

The following chapters were originally published in *The Journal of Positive Psychology*. When citing this material, please use the original issue information and page numbering for each article, as follows:

Chapter 2

Towards a positive university
Lindsay G. Oades, Paula Robinson, Suzy Green and Gordon B. Spence
The Journal of Positive Psychology, volume 6, issue 6 (November 2011) pp. 432–439

Chapter 3

Classroom assessment techniques for promoting more positive experiences in teaching and learning
Charles J. Walker
The Journal of Positive Psychology, volume 6, issue 6 (November 2011) pp. 440–445

Chapter 4

Virtues and character strengths for sustainable faculty development
Thomas V. McGovern
The Journal of Positive Psychology, volume 6, issue 6 (November 2011) pp. 446–450

Chapter 5

Incorporating positive psychology content and applications into various psychology courses
Jeana L. Magyar-Moe
The Journal of Positive Psychology, volume 6, issue 6 (November 2011) pp. 451–456

Chapter 6

Integrating research training and the teaching of positive psychology
Chu Kim-Prieto and Carianne D'Oriano
The Journal of Positive Psychology, volume 6, issue 6 (November 2011) pp. 457–462

Chapter 7

Adolescent popularity: A positive psychology course with a developmental foundation
Peter E.L. Marks
The Journal of Positive Psychology, volume 6, issue 4 (July 2011) pp. 314–319

Chapter 8

Happiness and self-knowledge: A positive psychology and judgement and decision-making hybrid course
Jaime L. Kurtz
The Journal of Positive Psychology, volume 6, issue 6 (November 2011) pp. 463–467

Preface

Two years ago, when I issued the call for proposals for the *Journal of Positive Psychology's* special issue on "Positive Psychology in Higher Education," my goal was to provide an up-to-date picture of the advancements positive psychology has made in higher education. As a graduate student at the Positive Psychology Center (PPC), I witnessed firsthand the birth and development of the Masters of Applied Positive Psychology (MAPP) program. I often heard by word-of-mouth about projects like the Geelong Grammar School and the Penn Resilience Project (both originating from the PPC), in which researchers have put positive psychology into practice in schools across the globe. I even received a few inquiries from programs hoping to use a positive psychology approach to foster personal development among students. My own experience of teaching positive psychology in various forms for 9 years cultivated a curiosity as to how others were approaching the teaching of positive psychology. The existence of six positive psychology textbooks – a staggering number given how new positive psychology is as a subarea – suggested that other teachers of positive psychology were out there, and numerous; however, I could count on one hand the number of conversations I had ever had with colleagues about teaching positive psychology. It seemed unfortunate that although positive psychology has clearly established itself in higher education, there was no forum in which to discuss what we are doing, why we are doing it, and how it well it is working.

As I began to put the special issue together a secondary goal surfaced. After the call for proposals went out, I received numerous emails, not only from potential contributors but from people looking forward to the special issue. It became clear to me that there is a thirst for information on best practices for teaching positive psychology. Anecdotal evidence from the FRIENDS-OF-PP and PSYTEACH listservs supports this impression; each time that I have offered my syllabus to one of these lists, I have received dozens and dozens of requests and questions from eager positive psychology instructors and instructors-to-be. For every instructor out there teaching positive psychology, there appear to be three more who would like to teach positive psychology, but do not know where to start.

I selected articles for the special issue, then, with two audiences in mind: *current* teachers and practitioners of positive psychology, and *potential* teachers and practitioners of positive psychology. My goal was to open up a discussion among those who are currently teaching and otherwise applying positive psychology in higher education and, in the process, to provide a resource for people who want to learn more about how positive psychology is taught, and how positive psychology might fit into their academic departments and institutions. I could not have been more satisfied with the results; the 15 articles contained in the original special issue represent the use of positive psychology in many higher education contexts – from the teaching of positive psychology content itself to institutional practices and curricular development to pedagogy.

Shortly after the special issue went into production, I was approached by Taylor & Francis to turn the special issue into this edited volume. This book is an effort on my part, and on the part of my publisher, to further disseminate the results of the special issue, and to spend additional time on a handful of topics that were not originally represented. One major omission, remedied by a new chapter, is an explicit discussion of college freshmen, and the potential role of positive psychology in facilitating the transition from high school to college. Furthermore, an introductory chapter synthesizes the contributions in this volume to create a picture of existing best practices in both teaching positive psychology and applying positive psychology in higher education settings. The work, I think, is improved by these additions.

Books are never created in a vacuum, and I am first and foremost thankful to Taylor & Francis for bringing me this opportunity, and specifically, to Emily Ross for her editorial work on the publisher side. I am grateful, too, to the contributors from the original special issue, as well as the co-authors who worked to bring together the new chapters. I want to extend special thanks to Renee Gutiérrez, Dawn Sonntag, Merose Hwang, Virginia Arreola, Cindy Pury, and Stephen Schueller for their comments, to Tom Ball for his assistance with proofreading and editing, and to my department colleagues at Hiram for their support. Lastly, I am thankful for my support system in times of frenetic writing: Amanda and Audrey, for brightening my mood via webcam; Callie, who gets stuck with my chores; and CS, who has to live with me (poor fool!).

Towards the establishment of best practices for applying positive psychology in higher education

Acacia C. Parks

Hiram College

Since its inception just over ten years ago, positive psychology (PP) has tasked itself with the scientific study of well-being – the traits and circumstances that lead to it, its benefits, and the behaviors that can be practiced in order to promote it. In that time, we have seen significant theoretical advancements, have developed myriad techniques for increasing happiness, and have made major strides in the dissemination of both research and practice to the general public. Entire volumes have been dedicated to the use of PP in coaching (e.g. Biswas-Diener, 2010) and in therapy (e.g. Magyar-Moe, 2009; O'Hanlon & Bertolini, 2012). In January 2011, *American Psychologist* dedicated a special issue to the application of positive psychology to promoting resilience in the U.S. Army (Casey, 2011). Gilman, Hubener and Furlong (2009)'s edited volume, the *Handbook of Positive Psychology in Schools*, is currently undergoing revision for a second edition, suggesting that work applying PP in K-12 is not only abundant, but ongoing.

Positive psychology has long flourished in higher education as well. Indeed, positive psychology has been taught and applied in higher education for almost as long as it has existed as a field, and yet, with few exceptions, there is little in the way of published literature that brings all of these developments together. There is, however, much to report. More departments than ever are offering courses in PP, and demand for these courses is consistently high (see Russo-Netzer & Ben-Shahar, in this volume). Graduate programs offering concentrations in positive psychology have appeared both at the masters and doctoral level. Educational institutions have expressed interest in using principles of PP to inform institutional structure, faculty development, and pedagogy. It was this observation that first motivated the special issue of the *Journal of Positive Psychology* on Positive Psychology in Higher Education, upon which this volume is based. The special issue was a first attempt to summarize the state of positive psychology in higher education. Below, you will find an overview of those articles, as well as the additional two pieces that are new to this volume. These contributions are divided into four sections: 1) institutional practices, 2) designing a positive psychology course, 3) integrating positive psychology into different courses, and 4) the ethics of teaching positive psychology.

Institutional practices

The first section of the book presents potential ways in which positive psychology can be implemented at the level of the institution – in its policies and procedures, and in the institutional culture of the faculty. In the opening piece, Lindsay G. Oades, Paula Robinson, Suzy Green, and Gordon B. Spence provide a rationale for implementing PP principles at different levels of higher education: in the classroom, in the social milieu on-campus, in the surrounding community, among the faculty and administration, and in student residential environments. Citing evidence that positive states lead to better academic outcomes, they provide specific examples of how these can be fostered through institution-level practices.

The next two chapters make suggestions for ways that faculty can integrate positive psychology into their own development and self-assessment. Charles J. Walker describes a set of techniques for assessing students' real-time experiences of two positive states – positive emotion and engagement – in the classroom. Faculty can use these types of assessments to identify in-class activities and pedagogical practices that promote and inhibit students' experiences of positive states, and in doing so may improve learning outcomes. Thomas V. McGovern provides a framework for strengths-based faculty development in which faculty can develop key strengths that are particularly useful for teaching and mentorship. Drawing from his own refashioned version of Peterson and Seligman's taxonomy of strengths and virtues, he proposes a four-module program that helps faculty explore the potential uses of each strength for the academic, intellectual, and/or social aspects of teaching. By gaining an understanding of how each of the 24 strengths can contribute to teaching and

1

learning, instructors learn how to most effectively mobilize their own strengths at work. Taken together, these pieces provide concrete ideas for how positive psychology can be used to effect change in academic institutions, and in institution-wide pedagogical practices.

Designing a positive psychology course

New PP instructors often have many questions regarding potential teaching methods and activities, as well as selection of readings and topics to cover. In this section, we turn to the question of how one might go about designing a positive psychology course, including issues of course structure, pedagogical methods, and course content. Pninit Russo-Netzer and Tal Ben-Shahar begin by sharing the thought process that went into designing Ben-Shahar's now-renowned positive psychology course that, when taught by him in 2006, was the most highly enrolled class at Harvard. Using this course as a prototype, they offer practical advice for designing a PP course. Further adding to the reader's toolbox for course design, Robert Biswas-Diener and Lindsey Patterson make an argument for the use of experiential learning in-class, through assignments practiced outside of class, and even when designing one's syllabus. Amy Kranzler, myself, and Jane Gillham describe a PP course with a major service learning component; classroom learning about resilience is paralleled and reinforced through the opportunity to teach resilience to at-risk youth in an after-school program. Marie D. Thomas and Barbara J. McPherson offer a final methodological innovation: using a positive psychology approach to team-based learning. In their course, they divide students into ongoing groups based on their character strengths, and use that group identity to structure assignments and in-class activities.

Other papers in this section provide practical advice on the selection of topics and readings in positive psychology courses. Grant Rich provides a comprehensive overview and comparison of existing PP textbooks, including a systematic review of the topics featured in each. Eranda Jayawickreme and Marie Forgeard discuss ways to dovetail more traditional readings with non-scientific materials, including popular books and self-help, as well as sources from philosophy, literature, and film. Concluding the section, Jennifer Teramoto Pedrotti offers strategies for infusing the topic of culture into PP courses, both during course design and through in-class practices.

Integrating positive psychology into existing courses

One challenge people face when trying to begin teaching positive psychology is that time, space, or resources may limit the creation of a new course. This section presents various ways in which one might bring PP into an existing curriculum, inside or outside of a psychology department.

Jeana L. Magyar-Moe discusses ways to integrate PP content into other psychology courses, emphasizing psychopathology, cultural psychology, counseling, and personality (she also offers brief suggestions for other courses, including social, health, sport, and physiological psychology). Peter E. L. Marks provides a profile of a course that revolves around popularity – which includes positive psychology topics such as friendship and pro-social behavior – while still remaining clearly seated in developmental psychology. As an example of overcoming the difficulty involved in adding a new subarea to an existing curriculum, Chu Kim-Prieto and Carianne D'Oriano describe two core psychology courses in their department – research methods and research experience – that they have infused with PP content. Jaime L. Kurtz describes her cross-disciplinary course, 'Happiness and Self-Knowledge', which tempers the science of happiness with research on judgment and decision-making; such a course could be a psychology department elective, or an offering in an interdisciplinary program – it could be easily co-taught (in the editor's opinion) with an economist or a philosopher. Most broadly, in a new contribution to the volume, I, along with Valerie Ross (director of the University of Pennsylvania's freshman writing program) write about our efforts using PP in the context of a "writing in the disciplines" first-year seminar – a pre-existing institution-wide program.

The ethics of teaching positive psychology

Dianne A. Vella-Brodrick closes this volume with a thought-provoking piece on the ethics of teaching positive psychology. Positive psychology is a field where dissemination and implementation occurs rapidly, sometimes even ahead of the science. Thus, ethical considerations are important not only as an academic topic to discuss with students in class but for us, as teachers, to consider in the design of courses and curricula. Vella-Brodrick makes a compelling case for the various ways in which ethics are relevant to PP, providing concrete ways that we can make use of these ethical concepts as instructors, and also teach ethics to our students. The issues raised by Vella-Brodrick are relevant to anyone applying positive psychology in any context; however, they are especially in higher education, as the majority of those who apply PP in other settings (in therapy, for example) are students at colleges and universities at some point.

Moving forward: Best practices in applying positive psychology in higher education

Taken together, these articles provide a snapshot of the state of positive psychology in higher education. The number of contributions in the special issue (selected from many more proposals), as well as the diversity and breadth of the articles, provides evidence that PP is taking root in many aspects of higher education. This volume provides a variety of ideas for the teaching of PP, and for the application of PP at institutions of higher education. However, to date, little or no data exists on the *effectiveness* of these practices, or on the ways in which effectiveness can be maximized. It is my hope that in the coming years, a volume like this one will be able to describe an *evidence-based* application of positive psychology in higher education, addressing questions such as: does including positive psychology in a college curriculum increase the well-being of students, and if so, does that increase lead to better objective outcomes like GPA and persistence? Does positive psychology-oriented institutional policy and faculty development have an impact on students' well-being and academic outcomes? Does the inclusion of positive psychology in a psychology department's curriculum help departments meet their educational objectives in ways that other psychology courses cannot?

To illustrate, I will give some examples of important research questions related to PP course design. There are many unanswered questions about the pedagogical utility of various approaches to teaching positive psychology. For example, there is great variation between PP sylabi in the types of sources used (see Rich, in this volume; Jayawickreme & Forgeard, in this volume), and one particularly distinctive feature of positive psychology is the widespread use of popular psychology books such as *Authentic Happiness, The Happiness Hypothesis, Positivity, The How of Happiness, Thanks!, Curious?*, and *Flourish*. Perhaps due to the inclusion of self-help under the umbrella of positive psychology (see Parks, Schueller, & Tasimi, 2013), mainstream titles appear in PP courses more so than in other areas of psychology. It is not yet been established whether the use of these books – sometimes in lieu of reading original research – bolsters pedagogy (due to their readability) or hurts it (due to their simplification for lay audiences). It is possible that in some contexts – say, a first-year seminar or freshman orientation (see Parks & Ross, in this volume) – accessibility trumps complexity, but in others – say, an advanced seminar (e.g. Kim-Prieto & D'Oriano, in this volume; Kurtz, in this volume) – it may be better to delve into research articles. Give that there is great variation from syllabus to syllabus in the breadth and depth of sources used (see Rich, in this volume; Jayawickreme & Forgeard, in this volume), an empirical examination of the impact of such variation would be worthwhile.

Many positive psychology courses are also distinctive in their emphasis on experiential learning. While previous research suggests that experiential learning is useful in any course (Clements, 1995; Poorman, 2002), positive psychology is arguably a particularly appropriate venue for hands-on activities (see Biswas-Diener & Patterson, in this volume; Kranzler, Parks & Gillham, in this volume), and many such activities exist, drawn both from research (Seligman, Steen, Park & Peterson, 2005; Emmons &

McCullough, 2003) and from teaching-related resources (e.g. see Rich, in this volume for a list of textbooks that include activities; see also Froh & Parks, 2012). Seligman et al. (2005) argue, based on their experiences teaching PP to undergraduates, that these types of activities are not only pedagogically helpful, but life changing for students. In other words, experiential learning, in the case of positive psychology, has the potential to go beyond teaching material to actually improving the everyday well-being of students. Empirical evidence of this claim – say, by making a comparison between the well-being impact of an experiential learning activity in developmental psychology and a similar activity in positive psychology – would build a powerful case for the benefits of offering PP to undergraduates.

In short, there are many opportunities to gather evidence of the benefits of positive psychology when applied in higher education, and when taught in the classroom; this book, I hope, is only the beginning of what will become an ongoing discussion about positive psychology pedagogy, course design, curricular concerns, cutting-edge teaching methods, in-class activities, faculty development, impact on student outcomes, and assessment. These conversations can happen in many contexts – on the FRIENDS-OF-PP listserv; in articles in peer-reviewed outlets such as the *Journal of Positive Psychology* and *Teaching of Psychology*; in future edited volumes; and at conferences such as the *Society for Teaching of Psychology*'s institutes at APA and SPS, and the *Positive Psychology World Congress*. It is only by accruing this evidence base that positive psychology can become its best, and in the process, break into common practice at academic institutions around the globe.

References

Biswas-Diener, R. (2010). Practicing positive psychology coaching: Assessment and strategies for success. Hoboken, NJ: Wiley.

Casey, Jr., G. W. (2011). Comprehensive soldier fitness: A vision for psychological resilience in the U.S. Army. *American Psychologist, 66,* 1–3.

Clements, A. D. (1995). Experiential-learning activities in undergraduate developmental psychology. *Teaching of Psychology, 22,* 115–118.

Emmons, R. A. (2007). *Thanks! How the new science of gratitude can make you happier.* New York, NY: Houghton-Mifflin.

Emmons, R.A. & McCullough, M.E. (2003). Counting blessings versus burdens: An experimental longitudinal investigation of gratitude and subjective well-being in daily life. *Journal of Personality and Social Psychology, 84,* 377–389.

Fredrickson, B. L. (2009). *Positivity.* New York, NY: Crown Publisher Group.

Froh, J.J. & Parks, A.C. (2012). Activities for teaching positive psychology: A guide for instructors. Washington, DC: APA Books.

Haidt, J. (2006). *The happiness hypothesis: Finding modern truth in ancient wisdom.* New York, NY: Basic Books.

Kashdan, T. B. (2009). *Curious? Discover the missing ingredient to a fulfilling life.* New York, NY: William Morrow.

Lyubomirsky, S. (2008). *The how of happiness: A scientific approach to getting the life you want.* New York, NY: The Penguin Press.

Magyar-Moe, J. L. (2009). *Therapist's guide to positive psychological interventions.* New York, NY: Academic Press.

O'Hanlon, B., & Bertolini, B. (2012). *The therapist's notebook on positive psychology: Activities, exercises, and Handouts.* New York, NY: Taylor & Francis Group.

Parks, A.C., Schueller, S.M., & Tasimi, A. (2013). Increasing happiness in the general population: Empirically supported self-help. To appear in S. David, I. Boniwell, & A.C. Ayers (Eds.), *Oxford Handbook of Happiness.* Oxford: Oxford University Press.

Poorman, B. E. (2002). Biography and role-playing: Fostering empathy in abnormal psychology. *Teaching of Psychology,* 29, 32–36.

Seligman, M. E. P. (2002). *Authentic happiness: Using the new positive psychology to realize your potential for lasting fulfillment.* New York, NY: Free Press.

Seligman, M. E. P. (2011). *Flourish: A visionary new understanding of happiness and well-being.* New York, NY: Simon & Schuster.

Seligman, M. E. P., Steen, T. A., Park, N., & Peterson, C. (2005). Positive psychology progress: Empirical validation of interventions. *American Psychologist,* 60, 410–421.

Towards a positive university

Lindsay G. Oades[a], Paula Robinson[b], Suzy Green[b] and Gordon B. Spence[a]

[a]Australian Institute of Business Wellbeing, Sydney Business School,
University of Wollongong, Sydney 2500, Australia; [b]Positive Psychology Institute, Sydney, Australia

This article explores the concept of a 'positive university'. Whilst positive education is becoming a better known concept, particularly applied to secondary schools, and positive organizational scholarship is further assisting the understanding of positive institutions, it is useful to examine the university as a special institution, in its entirety beyond a circumscribed focus on student academics (e.g. student motivation) or student well-being (e.g. well-being of medical students). In this article, we will sample the relevant evidence to date from positive psychology and positive organizational scholarship and apply it to five key environments of the university: Classroom and formal learning environments (e.g. curriculum, academic achievement), social environments (e.g. student relationships), local community and external organizations (e.g. volunteerism), faculty and administration work environments (e.g. employee stress) and residential environments (e.g. student well-being). Specific recommendations are provided for each context with reference to five routes to well-being: positive emotions, engagement, relationships, meaning and accomplishment.

Positive Education has been defined as 'education for both traditional skills and happiness' (Seligman, Ernst, Gillham, Reivich, & Linkins, 2009). We offer a broader definition as we believe that education is broader than skills, and needs to emphasize the importance of learning environments. Hence, the working definition for Positive Education for this article is 'the development of educational environments that enable the learner to engage in established curricula in addition to knowledge and skills to develop their own and others' wellbeing'. In this article, we apply the concept of positive education to the tertiary sector, the institution of the university. This includes not only the educational context, but also the generation of knowledge through research, the staff and students engaged in those endeavours, the existing organizational climate and culture, and the communities in which the organization exists. The emergence of a positive university requires an expansive systemic level understanding of tertiary institutions, one that extends beyond traditional, transactional understandings of the teacher–learner relationship.

A positive university needs to be a positive institution, insofar as its activities enable key stakeholders to utilize positive traits (e.g. strengths) in the service of individual, joint and collective goals. Furthermore, this should be done in such a way so as to increase positive emotions, meaning and engagement and decrease mental illness (e.g. stress, depression and anxiety). This is the context in which positive education will be enabled. However, as Schreiner, Hulme, Hetzel, and Lopez (2009) point out, a strengths-based educational approach at the tertiary level will quickly descend into faddism unless it is informed by relevant fields of scholarship, such as education, psychology, social work and organizational theory and behaviour.

The challenge and the opportunity

Historically, universities have sought to create cultures of excellence and peak performance. Whilst, prima facie, these would seem to be consistent with positive psychological principles and practices, in many cases, university environments continue to report significant student dropout rates and levels of psychological distress.

Some guidance for the development of positive universities can be gained from recent work conducted within the secondary school context. For example, Seligman et al. (2009) argue that well-being should be taught in secondary schools for three primary reasons: (i) as an antidote to depression, (ii) as a vehicle for increasing life satisfaction and (iii) to improve learning and generate creative thinking. We believe these reasons also have relevance in tertiary education contexts, albeit applied within an expanded systemic framework that encompasses the whole organization (i.e. staff and students).

Universities seem appropriate places to explicitly and implicitly address the well-being needs of its constituents and situate those efforts alongside its traditional teaching and research activities. The science of well-being itself is of growing scientific interest to universities. For example, Cambridge University's Institute of Well-Being is an inter-disciplinary Institute dedicated to advancing the scientific understanding of well-being and applying this new knowledge to help people and institutions develop their full potential. The Institute defines well-being as positive and sustainable characteristics which enable individuals and organizations to thrive and flourish (Well-Being Institute, University of Cambridge). Well-being is a dynamic concept that includes subjective, social and psychological dimensions as well as health-related behaviours. Universities and schools have similar capacities for cultivating prosperity, which we understand as wealth and well-being for the nation. The educational benefits of well-being seem clear (Seligman et al., 2009) and a meta-analysis of positive psychology interventions conducted by Sin and Lyubomirksy (2009; $n = 4266$) suggested that such interventions significantly enhance well-being and decrease depressive symptoms.

Given the high striving culture of most universities, it is easy for individuals (both students and staff) to neglect social relationships, emphasize extrinsic motivation (e.g. grades/promotion) over intrinsic interest (i.e. learning/innovation), work excessive hours and engage in other patterns of behaviour that diminish well-being over both the short and long term (e.g. drug use, inadequate sleep). As such, there would seem to be an opportunity for positive psychology to enhance the experience of campus life by influencing the development of a higher educational culture that understands the psychosocial determinants of well-being (e.g. positive emotions-traits-institutions) and seeks to create conditions that cultivate well-being in students and staff.

Growing evidence suggests that the cultivation of well-being might be beneficial within university environments. For example, a meta-analysis conducted by Lyubomirsky, King, and Diener (2005) suggested that happy people are more successful at work, have more satisfying relationships and better health status. Whilst most universities seek to develop the positive attributes of graduates (to equip them for life in a changing modern world), many traditional tertiary education practices are at odds with contemporary models of education and evidence emerging from the scientific study of well-being. With the increased internationalization of research and education, the tertiary context is becoming even more complex and cross-cultural considerations are becoming an increasingly important aspect of campus life.

Well-being practices

Well-being has been conceptualized in several ways, with definitions identifying an array of different facets, including emotional, subjective, psychological and social dimensions (e.g. Keyes, 2007; Rath & Harter, 2010; Ryff & Keyes, 1995). Given that there is emerging evidence of the components of well-being, such as positive emotion, engagement, relationships, meaning and accomplishment (PERMA; Seligman, 2011), it is possible to propose an initial framework for the cultivation of well-being within the university context (Table 1).

While the 'business' of universities (i.e. the production and dissemination of knowledge) is somewhat unique among organizations, their structure, cultural dynamics and basic operation make them somewhat similar to other more commercially focused organizations. As such, the organizational change and development literatures are as relevant to a university as they are to a retail bank or a transportation company. One positive organizational change and development approach reported extensively in that literature that has particular relevance to the present discussion is the appreciative inquiry (AI) approach (Srivastva & Cooperrider, 1999). AI, consistent with the philosophy of positive psychology and positive education, is encompassed by the 4-D Model (i.e. Discovery, Dream, Design and Delivery). This model is one useful starting point for any university considering the integration and application of positive psychology or positive education.

As with most organizational change, the movement towards positive education at the tertiary level would require strong, committed leadership. Most especially, this would involve some modelling of the principles underpinning the approach, including a clear direction and vision, authentic relationships, open communication and an array of other behaviours that would help to cultivate a climate of positivity across a university. In so doing, a university is more likely to be become 'positively deviant', or act in ways that substantially deviate from what is typically done to improve human experience within tertiary institutions (Cameron, Dutton, & Quinn, 2006). Should a university become a truly positive institution, the people associated with it are likely to become more engaged, make greater use of

Table 1. Well-being activities across five key contexts within universities.

	Classroom	Social	Local community	Faculty/administration	Residential
Positive emotions	• Curriculum development using PP constructs (e.g. gratitude) • Positive mood inductions (e.g. using humour at start of classes, music) • Creativity exercises	• Strengths-focused social events • Savoring activities in groups • Aspirational dinners	• Movie screenings with positive psychological content (e.g. 'Happy') • Voluntary work activities integrated into course work	• Integrate PP principles into team development activities • Run information sessions to teach staff about positivity ratios	• Implement 'strengths spotting' amongst residents • Make available cross-cultural educational material on sources of well-being
Engagement	• Teach students about flow and what promotes it • Encourage exercises that cultivate flow • Commence classes with simple mindfulness training exercises	• Support flow-inducing social groups (e.g. dance classes, chess or book clubs) • Mindfulness meditation groups	• Sponsor flow-inducing community groups (e.g. community gardens) • Run free seminars and talks on the importance of flow and absorption	• Recognize and reward workplace initiatives designed to enhance flow and engagement • Recommend practices for making meetings, seminars more engaging	• Residential events for increasing flow (e.g. African drumming) • PP information nights
Relationships	• Design strengths-based group assignments • Encourage study groups based on PP principles	• Implement programmes that encourage random acts of kindness • Positive mood inductions	• Offer parenting workshops on active constructive responding • Sponsor family days to enhance connectivity (e.g. picnic days)	• Recognize and reward work output at the team level (as opposed to the individual level)	• Celebrate national holidays to promote cross-cultural learning • Hold cultural awareness sessions • Display flags, maps, emblems of different nations
Meaning	• Develop curriculum that allows students to connect with strengths and values • Get students to contribute ideas for curriculum • Use student suggestions in curriculum development	• Assess levels of Social Capital • Develop social values from 'bottom-up' • Invite cross-campus input	• Promote the notion of the university as a virtuous organization	• Encourage job crafting to help staff develop congruent career paths • Build more flexibility and choice into job descriptions • Tap more into intrinsic motivation of staff (e.g. team innovation day)	• Enable residents to tangibly express the values of the residence
Accomplishment	• Implement assessments *for* learning, as well as assessments *of* learning	• Acknowledge individuals who positively contribute to campus life (i.e. 'positive energizers')	• Give awards for outstanding contributions to community life	• Infuse performance appraisal systems with PP approaches (e.g. AI) • Train people leaders (academics and general staff) in PP principles and coaching	• Offer evidence-based coaching to enhance academic performance • Residential goal setting in relation to enhancing life on campus • University recognition of achievements made by residents in enhancing well-being of themselves and others

their strengths, experience more positive emotion and, just as importantly, achieve higher levels of academic success (Huebner, Gilman, Reshley, & Hall, 2009).

Table 1 proposes a framework for building Positive Universities based on the PERMA model (Seligman, 2011). Five key aspects of university life are considered: (1) classroom and formal learning environments, (2) social environments, (3) local community, (4) faculty and administrative work environments and (5) residential environments. We have chosen these contexts to ensure that our recommendations are contextualized and tangible. It should be noted that the scope of this endeavour makes it difficult to rely on randomized controlled trials to validate the approach. However, enough support can be garnered from the education, positive psychology, management and positive organizational scholarship literatures to advance this as a good initial framework for the proposed endeavour.

Positive education in formal teaching environments

Formal teaching environments within the tertiary sector have significantly changed in the past 20 years. Key drivers of change include the increased internationalization of the tertiary sector, increased use of information and communication technology and competitiveness regarding teaching quality demanded by the 'student consumer'. Whilst Positive Education is on the rise in secondary schools (Seligman et al., 2009), it appears to be less present in the tertiary system. If the Australian experience is representative of global trends, then positive psychology has yet to be integrated into 'mainstream' psychology, with courses offered largely as 'special topics' at the postgraduate level.

Whilst explicit, specific activities related to positive psychology can be taught and embedded within curriculum, McGrath and Noble (2010) point out that positive teacher–student or lecturer–student relationships can contribute significantly to students' well-being, pro-social behaviours and learning outcomes. They also suggest increasing intrinsic motivation by simply having fun with students (e.g. through the use the humour or games) and by providing students with some opportunity for autonomy and choice in assignments and discussions about the way they would like their learning environment to be created.

Table 1 presents a range of simple examples of suggested activities that could be implemented in formal teaching environments that are consistent with the ethos of positive education. For brevity, only a selection of these examples is discussed in more detail.

Cultivation of positive emotion

Increases in well-being are likely to produce increases in learning because positive mood produces broader attention (Fredrickson & Branigan, 2005; Rowe et al., 2007), more creative thinking (Estrada, Isen, & Young, 1994; Isen, Daubman, & Nowicki, 1987) and more holistic thinking (Isen, Niedenthal, & Cantor, 1992). In contrast, negative mood narrows the focus of attention (Bolte, Goschke, & Kuhl, 2003) and leads to more critical and analytical thinking (Kuhl, 2000). Whilst both are important, educational institutions heavily emphasize critical (rather than creative) thinking, and the negative mood often associated with formal education settings (e.g. lecture theatres) would seem to create an imbalance towards critical thinking. There are a myriad ways to induce positive mood within these settings, including beginning lectures or tutorials with relevant musical content, using film or interesting literature to bring material 'to life', and/or through the use of humour and actively encouraging it.

Mindfulness practices

One option for enhancing the quality of student and staff experience across a university is via the use of exercises or the provision of facilities that support the cultivation of mindfulness. Mindfulness can be enhanced in many ways and practiced whilst engaged in a wide variety of personal and professional activities (for examples see Nakai & Schultz, 2000) either inside or outside formal teaching environments. Potential opportunities for developing mindfulness might include beginning lectures or tutorials with short awareness exercises (e.g. body scans, focused breathing) or providing individuals with dedicated spaces to practice more structured, formal forms of practice (e.g. 'quiet' rooms for meditation practice). Encouragingly, the philosophy, principles and practices of mindfulness are beginning to inform curriculum development at both tertiary and secondary levels. For example, in a secondary school intervention students reported reduced negative affect, greater emotional awareness and emotional regulation, along with increased feelings of calmness, relaxation and self-acceptance compared to controls (Broderick & Metz, 2009). In addition, mindfulness has been successfully incorporated into the formal training of medical students and led to a range of positive outcomes (for an example of such a programme, see Hassed, de Lisle, Sullivan, & Pier, 2008).

Strengths use in group assignments

Linley and Harrington (2006) suggest that knowing and using strengths can have a positive effect on teamwork and team outcomes. Group work assignments are often set in tertiary education based on the premise that students must learn to work together, with people from diverse backgrounds. One way to help 'scaffold' students for these tasks is to use strengths assessments such as the VIA (Peterson & Seligman, 2004) or Realise2 (CAPP, 2010) and to help students understand which strengths might be most usefully employed during group work.

Positive education and social environments

University campuses are enormously social places where very diverse groups of people come together and interact in a variety of settings (e.g. sports venues, bars, religious associations, academic clubs, bookshops). As such, there are numerous opportunities for the formation of enriching, supportive relationships, which McGrath and Noble (2010) argue can enhance educational culture (e.g. greater pro-social behaviour), student experience (e.g. increased intrinsic motivation) and lead to better academic outcomes. Given the highly social nature of university life and the strong relationship that exists between social support and well-being (Haidt, 2006; Seligman, 2002), universities seem to be ideal settings for the systematic promotion of positive relationships and generation of 'social capital'.

According to Prilleltensky and Prilleltensky (2006), social capital refers to collective resources (including civic participation, norms of reciprocity, community-focused organizations, etc.) that enhance community capacity to create structures of cohesion, support and trust. In organizational contexts, social capital is positive if it supports people to attain higher order goals that represent growth and flourishing at the individual, group and organizational level (Baker & Dutton, 2007). For example, group dynamics research suggests that interpersonal acts of generosity, kindness and other forms of positivity can create expansive emotional spaces that enhance collective effort (Losada & Heaphy, 2004).

Table 1 presents examples of campus-based activities that are consistent with the positive education ethos of increasing and teaching well-being. Some of these activities will now be discussed in more detail.

Strategies for enhancing kindness

Introducing a campus-wide kindness strategy has the potential to enhance social relationships and emotional experience. Whilst the literatures dedicated to understanding kindness and related concepts (e.g. generalized reciprocity) have yielded surprisingly few targeted interventions (Peterson & Seligman, 2004), the importance of kindness within university contexts has recently been recognized (Clegg & Rowland, 2010). According to Clegg and Rowland (2010), it is not 'out of place' to talk about kindness in higher education because the cognitive components of intellectual development are no less important than the embodied and experiential components. As such, there is an argument to be made for encouraging students and staff to look for opportunities to engage in acts of kindness or generalized reciprocity (i.e. 'paying it forward'). Buchanan and Bardi (2010) conducted an experiment designed to establish the effects of acts of kindness on life satisfaction. Participants aged 18–60 took part on a voluntary basis. They were randomly assigned to perform either acts of kindness, acts of novelty, or no acts on a daily basis for 10 days. Their life satisfaction was measured before and after the 10-day experiment. As expected, performing acts of kindness resulted in an increase in life satisfaction. It should be noted, however, that attempts to prescribe or regulate kindness are likely to diminish the impact of such acts (by making them routinized). As such, the implementation of a kindness strategy may be best addressed at the organizational level, through the adoption of values and agreed practices that increase the probability of kindness towards other people (Clegg & Rowland, 2010).

Flow-inducing social groups

Flow is prototypical of the Engaged Life and has been described as a subjective state associated with total absorption in an activity, a loss of reflective self-consciousness, temporal distortion (i.e. the subjective sense of time 'stopping') and the emerging of action and awareness (i.e. being at 'one' with the activity; Csikszentmihalyi, 1997). Importantly, flow has been associated with heightened feelings of subjective well-being (e.g. competence, satisfaction, enjoyment). Given flow research indicates that certain pre-conditions are needed for flow to occur (i.e. equilibrium between skill and challenge, short-term goals, availability immediate feedback, task choice), the theory provides practical guidance for those interested in enhancing the quality of students and staff in educational contexts. This makes the identification of 'flow-based activities' both appropriate and practical, and may involve utilising flow principles to enliven existing group activities (e.g. class debates) or to inform the introduction of novel group based activities (e.g. on-campus dance classes). Furthermore, the theory and its principles can also be used by teachers to help students take a different perspective on their learning experience and acquire knowledge that may help them to change that experience for the better.

The practical challenges of implementing a positive social agenda across campus will be broad and often unanticipated. A key way to overcome resistance and maximize autonomy will be to provide broad frameworks into which campus participants, particularly students can add to and 'color in'. Involving student organizations in these programmes from the outset will be a key implementation issue.

Positive education in the local community

The original idea of a university was to not only to produce knowledge, but also to disseminate knowledge, and not only in the classroom. That is, a university is a social institution that can and should play a significant role in the local community. The notion of a virtuous organization is particularly relevant here (Cameron et al., 2006) and based on the definition of a virtuous organization, we would propose that to claim the status of a 'positive university', a university would need to show that it: (a) is morally good, (b) has human impact and (c) creates social betterment.

Research supports the growing interest in volunteering and the associated positive benefits for those who engage in it. For example, the 'Do Good Live Well Survey' (see the report at http://www.dogoodlivewell.org, Do Good Live Will Survey, 2010) of 4582 adults (over 18 years of age) found that 41% of residents of the USA engaged in unpaid service activities (not including giving money or donations), with a quarter doing so through workplace sponsored community events. Of those who did volunteer, 68% reported that this activity has made them feel physically healthier.

A further example of a well-being initiative in the community is the Good Mood Safari (2009; see http://www.goodmoodsafari.com.au) in which the University of Wollongong and Life Line South Coast, NSW, developed a positive psychology outdoor tourist experience, which involves positive psychology experiential learning in major tourist destinations of the region. This clearly located well-being initiatives in the local community.

Faculty and administration work environments

Across universities, the focus of faculty staff may vary significantly. For instance, for some academics, the primary focus will be research, whilst for others it might be teaching, academic governance, administrative roles or some blend of these. Similarly, the roles of administrative or non-academic staff can vary greatly and range from running the university recreation and sports facilities to overseeing major capital budgets or

even dealing with the unique needs of international students. Within this context, a positive university would be proactive and responsive to its workforce, which brings the notion of a resilient organization into focus. Suttcliffe and Vogus (2006) state that the literatures that address organizational resilience are those that examine organizational learning and adaptation, dynamic capabilities and high reliability organizing. A resilient organization will flexibly rearrange or transfer knowledge and resources to deal with situations as they arise. Hence, a positive university will not only address academic and well-being issues, but the resilience of the organization as a whole. Given that universities are based on long held traditions, there may be more effort required to transform organizational cultures to those that are well-being based, unlike startup organizations well known for well-being initiatives such as Google and Zappos.

Table 1 summarizes a range of suggested activities that could be implemented in university workforces consistent with positive education principles. A notable inclusion is evidence-based coaching for the enhancement of academic performance and professional functioning more generally. The field of coaching has advanced considerably in the past decade (for a review, see Grant & Cavanagh, 2011) and recent studies indicate that evidence-based coaching is an effective means of supporting professional development within educational settings (e.g. Grant, Green, & Rynsaardt, 2010; Green, Grant, & Rynsaardt, 2007). The inclusion of evidence-based coaching in this framework is highly appropriate as it is increasingly considered a form of applied positive psychology (Grant & Cavanagh, 2011).

Positive education and the residential environments

Residential environments have been included within this article due to the central place they occupy in many students' experience of university life. Many of the world's best universities have residential facilities as central to their operations. Indeed within the Australian context, the number of residential beds aligns closely with the ranking of the quality of the university. In many ways, the original residential college drawn from Oxford and Cambridge traditions captures the essence of the university idea. Emphases of excellence, strengths and, virtue abound in these contexts, to develop individuals with meaning and purpose. With financial challenges on universities, these ideals may have been significantly diluted to cost effective student housing with few if any of the value add of the peer support and social inclusion of the residential environment. In our view, a positive university will include great emphasis on residential environments because of their ability to impact the whole student, and link alumni to the university in a life-long fashion.

Table 1 illustrates are range of suggested activities that could be implemented in residential environments that are consistent with the positive education philosophy of increasing and teaching well-being. For some residences, this will be a formalization of what already exists. For other residences, significant cultural change will be required to remove undesirable practices (e.g. the over use of alcohol) and support adjustment to the increased global student mobility diversifying the cultures represented within residence.

Implement strengths spotting amongst residents living in University housing

Through the use of strengths assessment and a strengths-discussion within the residential environment, students can be taught to cultivate the skill of identifying other residents' strengths in action. Creating social opportunities to share and complementary partner around strengths will also assist students to develop 'strengths-colored glasses' (Clifton, Anderson, & Schreiner, 2006, p. 73). This also helps to foster tolerance and an appreciation for difference, together with creating a sense of camaraderie, collaboration, teamwork and a powerful sense of relatedness and belonging.

The practical implementation of these ideas will not be without its significant challenges. Many residential environments within universities are traditional and are overseen by Boards of Directors. Dealing with these board members and explaining to them the benefits of positive education will be paramount. 'Pastoral care' is a well-known term, and in many ways positive education brings the scientific evidence base and structure to this long tradition. The creation of a positive university and the associated implementation of positive practices as outlined in this article will ultimately depend on the level of commitment by the leadership team.

A new example of a positive residence is at the University of Wollongong, NSW, Australia, where they are currently building and planning a university residence of 550 residents that is to be based entirely on positive organizational and positive educational principles. This residence (sometimes referred to as college or dormitory) is to have flourishing as its key purpose, and will include implicit and explicit education in well-being evidence. Moreover, residents will receive a *comprehensive student fitness* evaluation (examining physical and mental fitness) and also residents will receive personal flourishing coaching, which will include strengths coaching based on the Realise2 (CAPP, 2010). The use of positive computing technologies will also be implemented, and medical students will be paired with all international students as personal health mentors. The unit will include explicit use of positive leadership principles as described by Cameron (2008). Residential programming will be designed by residents within the parameters of Seligman's Well-being Theory, i.e. PERMA. Student well-being, student retention, graduate outcomes and academic performance will be benchmarked against other university students living in residence and not living in residence.

Conclusion

A sample of positive education-based evidence has been applied to key contexts of a university, using pleasure, engagement, positive relationships, meaning and accomplishment as a core organizing principle. The purpose has been to start a conversation regarding the concept of a positive university, together with expanding the concept of positive education. Different universities may select different contexts and different positive education evidence and practices to draw from. Research into positive education needs to extend to tertiary education, and not just in the formal teaching environment but include the whole organization.

References

Baker, W., & Dutton, J.E. (2007). Enabling positive social capital in organizations. In J.E. Dutton & B.R. Ragins (Eds.), *Exploring positive relationships at work* (pp. 325–346). Mahwah, NJ: Lawrence Erlbaum Associates.

Bolte, A., Goschke, T., & Kuhl, J. (2003). Emotion and intuition: Effects of positive and negative mood on implicit judgments of semantic coherence. *Psychological Science, 14*, 416–421.

Broderick, P.C., & Metz, S. (2009). *Advances in school mental health promotion* (Vol. 2). The Clifford Beers Foundation and University of Maryland, Department of Health, West Chester University of PA, USA.

Buchanan, K.E., & Bardi, A. (2010). Acts of kindness and acts of novelty affect life satisfaction. *The Journal of Social Psychology, 150*, 235–237.

Cameron, K.S. (2008). *Positive leadership: Strategies for extraordinary performance.* San Francisco, CA: Berrett-Koehler.

Cameron, K.S., Dutton, J.E., & Quinn, R.E. (Eds.) (2006). *Positive organizational scholarship.* San Francisco, CA: Berrett-Koehler.

CAPP (2010). *Technical manual and statistical properties for Realise2.* Coventry: Author.

Clegg, S., & Rowland, S. (2010). Kindness in pedagogical practice and academic life. *British Journal of Sociology of Education, 31*, 719–735.

Clifton, D.O., Anderson, C.E., & Schreiner, L.A. (2006). *StrengthsQuest: Discover and develop your strengths in academics, career, and beyond* (2nd ed.). New York, NY: Gallup Press.

Csikszentmihalyi, M. (1997). *Finding flow: The psychology of engagement with everyday life.* New York, NY: Basic Books.

Do Good Live Will Survey (2010). Retrieved from http://www.dogoodlivewell.org-/UnitedHealthcare_Volunteer Match_DoGoodLiveWell_Survey.pdf

Estrada, C.A., Isen, A.M., & Young, M.J. (1994). Positive affect improves creative problem solving and influences reported source of practice satisfaction in physicians. *Motivation and Emotion, 18,* 285–299.

Fredrickson, B.L., & Branigan, C. (2005). Positive emotions broaden the scope of attention and thought-action repertoires. *Cognition and Emotion, 19,* 313–332.

Good Mood Safari (2009). Retrieved from http://www.goodmoodsafari.com.au

Grant, A.M., & Cavanagh, M.J. (2011). Coaching and positive psychology. In K.M. Sheldon, T.B. Kashdan, & M.F. Steger (Eds.), *Designing positive psychology: Taking stock and moving forward* (pp. 293–309). New York, NY: Oxford University Press.

Grant, A.M., Green, S., & Rynsaardt, J. (2010). Developmental coaching for high school teachers: Executive coaching goes to school. *Psychology Journal: Practice and Research, 62,* 151–168.

Green, S., Grant, A.M., & Rynsaardt, J. (2007). Evidence-based life coaching for senior high school students: Building hardiness and hope. *International Coaching Psychology Review, 2,* 24–32.

Haidt, J. (2006). *The happiness hypothesis.* New York, NY: Basic Books.

Hassed, C., de Lisle, S., Sullivan, G., & Pier, C. (2008). Enhancing the health of medical students: Outcomes of an integrated mindfulness and lifestyle program. *Advances in Health Science Education, 14,* 387–398.

Huebner, E.S., Gilman, R., Reshley, A.L., & Hall, R. (2009). Positive psychology on campus. In S.J. Lopez, & C.R. Snyder (Eds.), *Oxford handbook of positive psychology* (2nd ed., pp. 561–568). New York, NY: Oxford University Press.

Isen, A.M., Daubman, K.A., & Nowicki, G.P. (1987). Positive affect facilitates creative problem solving. *Journal of Personality and Social Psychology, 52,* 1122–1131.

Isen, A.M., Niedenthal, P.M., & Cantor, N. (1992). An influence of positive affect on social categorization. *Motivation and Emotion, 16,* 65–78.

Keyes, C.L.M. (2007). Promoting and protecting mental health as flourishing: A complementary strategy for improving national mental health. *American Psychologist, 62,* 95–108.

Kuhl, J. (2000). A functional-design approach to motivation and self-regulation: The dynamics of personality systems and interactions. In M. Boekaerts, P.R. Pintrich, & M. Zeidner (Eds.), *Handbook of self-regulation* (pp. 111–169). San Diego, CA: Academic Press.

Linley, P.A., & Harrington, S. (2006). Strengths coaching: A potential-guided approach to coaching psychology. *International Coaching Psychology Review, 1,* 37–46.

Losada, M., & Heaphy, E. (2004). The role of positivity and connectivity in the performance of business teams: A nonlinear dynamics model. *The American Behavioral Scientist, 47,* 740–765.

Lyubomirsky, S., King, L.A., & Diener, E. (2005). The benefits of frequent positive affect. *Psychological Bulletin, 131,* 803–855.

McGrath, H., & Noble, T. (2010). Supporting positive pupil relationships: Research to practice. *Educational and Child Psychology, 27,* 79–90.

Nakai, P., & Schultz, R. (2000). *The mindful corporation: Liberating the human spirit at work.* Los Angeles, CA: Leadership Press.

Peterson, C., & Seligman, M.E.P. (2004). *Character strengths and virtues: A classification and handbook.* New York: Oxford University Press/Washington, DC: American Psychological Association.

Prilleltensky, I., & Prilleltensky, O. (2006). *Promoting well-being: Linking personal, organizational, and community change.* Hoboken, NJ: John Wiley & Sons.

Rath, T., & Harter, J.K. (2010). *Wellbeing: The five essential elements.* New York, NY: Gallup Press.

Rowe, G., Hirsh, J.B., & Anderson, A.K. (2007). Positive affect increases the breadth of attentional selection. *Proceedings of the National Academy of Sciences, USA, 104,* pp. 383–388.

Ryff, C.D., & Keyes, C.L.M. (1995). The structure of psychological well-being revisited. *Journal of Personality and Social Psychology, 69,* 719–727.

Schreiner, L.A., Hulme, E., Hetzel, R., & Lopez, S. (2009). Positive psychology on campus. In S. Lopez & C.R. Snyder (Eds.), *Oxford handbook of positive psychology* (2nd ed., pp. 569–578). New York, NY: Oxford University Press.

Seligman, M.E.P. (2002). *Authentic happiness.* Sydney: Random House.

Seligman, M.E.P. (2011). *Flourish: A visionary new understanding of happiness and wellbeing.* New York: Simon & Schuster.

Seligman, M.E.P., Ernst, R.M., Gillham, J., Reivich, K., & Linkins, M. (2009). Positive education: Positive psychology and classroom interventions. *Oxford Review of Education, 35,* 293–311.

Sin, N.L., & Lyubomirsky, S. (2009). Enhancing well-being and alleviating depressive symptoms with positive psychology interventions: A practice-friendly meta-analysis. *Journal of Clinical Psychology, 65,* 467–487.

Srivastva, S., & Cooperrider, D.L. (1999). *Appreciative management and leadership: The power of positive thought and action in organization* (Revised ed). Cleveland, OH: Lakeshore Communications.

Sutcliffe, K., & Vogus, T. (2006). Organizing for resilience. In K.S. Cameron, J.E. Dutton, & R.E. Quinn (Eds.), *Positive organizational scholarship* (pp. 94–110). San Francisco, CA: Berrett-Koehler.

Classroom assessment techniques for promoting more positive experiences in teaching and learning

Charles J. Walker

Department of Psychology, St. Bonaventure University, St. Bonaventure, NY 14778, USA

Two classroom assessment techniques (CATs) for promoting more positive teaching and learning experiences in classrooms are described. Derived from research on psychological well-being, these CATs put into practice what is taught in courses on positive psychology. Both techniques are best used during a course; however, they could be used as end-of-the-semester assessment tools. The first technique assesses student anxiety, dejection, calmness, and enthusiasm. High scores on any of these emotions prescribe specific interventions to increase enthusiasm for learning. The second CAT, for exploring classroom flow experiences, assesses not only when flow occurs, but also why it occurs. Its results suggest feasible things that can be done to increase the frequency and intensify classroom flow experiences. Both assessment techniques are designed to be used by a single instructor; however, with modifications, they could also be used by institutional researchers to explore student learning in curricula throughout an institution.

Introduction

What do students take with them when they graduate? Do they have the knowledge we worked so long and hard to convey? Have we touched their hearts as well as their heads? Has our passion for learning been infectious? And what has our relationship with them done to us? Are we more generative? Are we more vital? These are the kinds of questions positive classroom assessment attempts to answer. There is a large and growing research literature that supports the proposition that positive classroom climates enhance the learning of students (Benson, Cohen, & Buskist, 2005) as well as strengthen the vitality of teachers (Walker & Hale, 1999). Positive classroom climates make teaching and learning more enjoyable by providing an environment that supports autonomy and liberates creativity in the pursuit of challenging, meaningful learning goals. However, currently, in higher education, we more vigorously and confidently assess knowledge and skill than the emotions accompanying learning experiences (Suskie & Banta, 2009). The psychological well-being of students and instructors is easy to overlook, not because it is unimportant, but because it is difficult to assess and promote.

In this article, I propose two new ways to assess how students feel about their learning experiences. These classroom assessment techniques (CATs) should be of particular interest to college instructors who desire to create more positive learning climates in their classrooms, not only for the psychological well-being of their students, but also for themselves.

Discovering and promoting enthusiasm for learning

The first assessment tool I propose, the *Enthusiasm for Learning Classroom Assessment Technique* (ELCAT) has been derived from the circumplex model of affect. This adaptation has been shaped by the results of many years of research on human emotions and performance (Diener & Lucas, 1999; Posner, Russell, & Peterson, 2005; Remmington, Fabrigar, & Vissar, 2000; Warr, 1999). The ELCAT assumes that students experience emotions while they are learning and that emotions like enthusiasm, anxiety, dejection, and boredom validly reflect the state and quality of their learning experience. Moreover, it assumes that enthusiasm and excitement are preferred emotional conditions for learning and teaching. Described below is a graphic form of the ELCAT that I have found is most preferred by instructors and their students. Interested readers can download a copy of the ELCAT at the website address http://wellbeingincollege.org/faculty-resources.

ELCAT scores

According to past research (Remington et al., 2000) and from the results of test trials, the ELCAT yields several useful scores:

(1) The frequencies of the words students use to describe their emotions during learning render a vivid picture of the emotional climate of a course or other units of learning experience (e.g. course sequences, majors, or degree programs). These data become particularly rich when student supplied examples of specific learning experiences are included.

(2) The average percentage time reported feeling an emotion assigned to cell *A*, for *anxiety*, is an index of the proportion of learning moments that students may not have sufficient control of a learning situation, yet where the learning is likely to be perceived as important.

(3) The average percentage assigned to cell *C*, for *calmness*, indicates the proportion of learning moments in which students are experiencing positive outcomes, but may be at risk of being bored or understimulated.

(4) The cell *D* score, for *dejection*, estimates the percentage of learning moments, wherein students lack sufficient control of an uninteresting, negative experience.

(5) In contrast, the cell *E* score, for *enthusiasm*, estimates the percentage of moments in which students feel in control of a provocative, meaningful learning experience.

(6) Combining the scores of cells *A* and *D* gives an instructor an index of the amount of moments that students are having an unpleasant experience while learning, whereas the total of cells *C* and *E* estimates the percentage of learning moments associated with positive feelings.

(7) The combined average total of cells *A* and *E* estimates the percentage of learning moments in which students find their learning experience to be stimulating, whereas the total of cells *D* and *C* gages the learning moments associated with insufficient stimulation.

(8) Positivity ratios can also be calculated, *Positivity ratio* $= (E+C)/(A+D)$, for individuals, assignments, courses, sequences, departments, colleges, or schools. Ratios of 3:1 or greater identify learning conditions that should support the flourishing of students (Fredrickson & Losada, 2005).

ELCAT administration

The administration of the ELCAT is similar to that of other course evaluation instruments: to obtain more honest and useful feedback, students should be anonymous and the ELCAT form should be delivered by a neutral third party. However, unlike traditional course evaluations which are given at the end of courses, the ELCAT is a course-embedded tool. The best results are achieved when it is given mid-semester or at other times while a course is in progress. This is suggested because the results can be shared with students for the purposes of clarification and to involve them in the implementation of course changes compelled by the results.

Interpreting the results

High scores in cells *A*, *D*, and *C* have implications for changes in learning and teaching (Table 1). Instructors with high student dejection scores (cell *D*) may be creating a learning environment that does not have enough meaning and is difficult for students to control (Figure 1). These instructors are probably trying to challenge students, but unfortunately are doing it in a way that suppresses the will to learn. Excessively difficult grading systems, arbitrary assignments that are indifferent to student needs and interests, and unfair performance evaluation are conditions likely to be associated with high dejection scores. On the other hand, high contentment scores (cell *C*) may signal a lack of motivation because students have too much control (i.e. the course is too easy). Simply increasing the amount of work required or, more preferably, slightly raising the level of difficulty of the work, should regain more optimal levels of student arousal. Finally, high anxiety scores (cell *A*) are likely to be found in courses where the work is meaningful and the goals of the course are important, but students are asked to do too much work or work beyond their skill levels. Decreasing the amount, but not the challenge, of the work while helping students to acquire the skills and knowledge they need to gain more control of the learning environment should improve this situation.

Feedback session suggestions

Between class meetings, I urge instructors to review the mean percentage of emotion scores, the frequencies of emotion words selected, and the lists of students' examples of alleged causes of their emotions. Special attention should be given to their suggestions for increasing enthusiasm for learning. The results of this assessment technique must be shared with students soon after it is administered. After the results are shared with your students, I recommend that you give an immediate reaction and begin a class-level discussion on what you and your students might do to improve their learning. If you disagree with your students, tell them why, or if it is simply unfeasible to implement their suggestions, explain your position.

Table 1. Possible causes of high emotion scores and suggestions for reactions of instructors and students.

Strongest score[a]	Possible causes	What instructors might do	What students might do
*A*nxiety	Insufficient student control of the learning of important course contents.	• Reduce quantity but not challenge of learning tasks. • Offer more choice in assignments and grading procedures. • Teach course-specific learning skills.	• Develop new meta-cognitive skills. • Invest more time and effort in course work. • Study and work with others.
*C*almness	Too much control of acceptable but not inspiring course contents. Also may indicate a safe, stress-free classroom climate.	• Increase the level of challenge. • Assess student interests and adjust course contents and assignments. • Increase pre-class student work and preparations.	• Participate more in class. • Elect learning that is more intrinsically interesting. • Increase the quality of work. • Increase challenge.
*D*ejection	Insufficient student control of irrelevant, arbitrary, unimportant course contents.	• Assess grading procedures. • Assess student interests. • Seek ideal levels of challenge by reducing amount of student work and maybe difficulty of work.	• Give constructive, useful feedback to the instructor. • Embrace changes in course contents and procedures. • Study with others.
*E*nthusiasm	Ideal student control of interesting, important and relevant course contents. Ideal classroom social climate.	• Transfer techniques, methods, and insights to other courses. • Do additional assessments to gain insight into one's success.	• Transfer and apply insights and meta-cognitive skills to other courses. • Give constructive feedback to other instructors.

Note: [a]Comparison data: The ELCAT was given to 56 seniors (29 women). They were asked to complete the assessment tool with either the best or worst college course they had taken in mind. To refresh their memories, first they were instructed to write a summary of the syllabus, assignments, grading procedures, instructor traits, and style of instruction. Then, with order counterbalanced, they described their emotional experiences while learning in their best and worst courses (Figure 1).

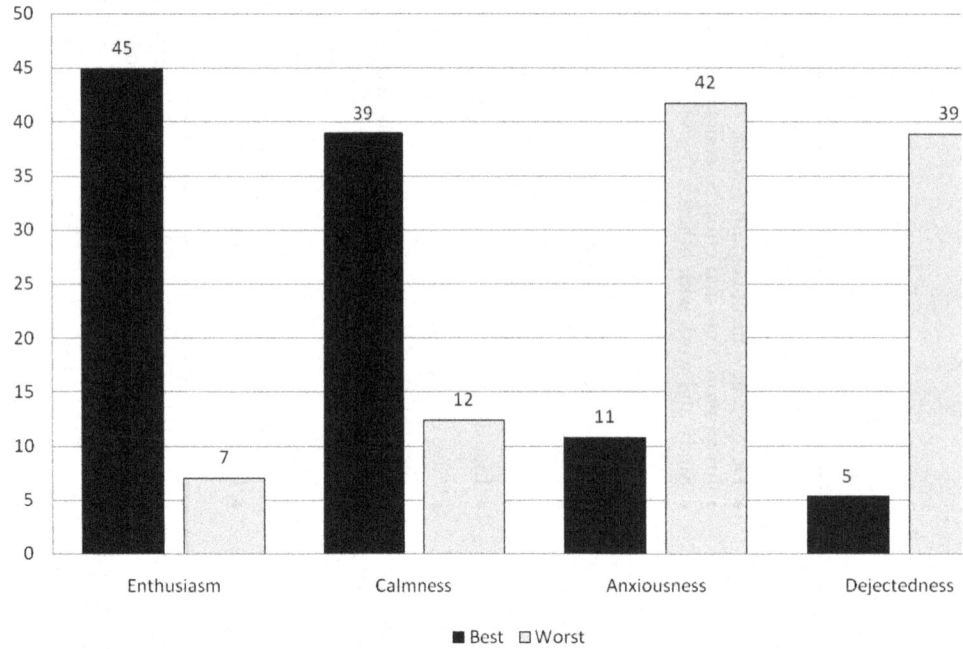

Figure 1. Percentage of time students estimated feeling emotions during their best and worst courses.

You may want to give yourself a day or two before giving them your final reaction. Sometimes, student feedback can be overwhelming or upsetting and you may need more time to reflect and consider your options *and* their options. If you administer the ELCAT at the end of the semester, you will avoid these awkward conversations with students, but also lose the benefits of their collaboration.

Curriculum assessment and other applications

The ELCAT is a context-free, content-free, tool. This technique can be used in almost any learning situation and at any point in time. It is not biased for or against any specific academic discipline. The present instructions describe its use at mid-term in a typical college-level course. However, with minor modifications, the technique can be applied at other grade levels (e.g. K-12). It should be of value to educational institutions that wish to complement performance measures with emotion assessment, that is, institutions that want their students to be not only more skilled and knowledgeable, but also more enthusiastic about learning itself.

When the instructions on the ELCAT are modified for administering it at the end of courses or at other terminal points in learning (e.g. capstone courses), the data can be aggregated and statistically analyzed to render the topography of the emotions of an entire curriculum or institution. In the hands of teams of instructors, these data can elucidate curriculum-based

strengths, guide change, and stimulate positive developments in teaching and learning.

Discovering and promoting moments of flow in the classroom

The second assessment tool I propose has been derived from basic and applied research on creativity and absorption or what is called flow (Csikszentmihalyi, 1990; M. Csikszentmihalyi & I. Csikszentmihalyi, 1988; Nakamura & Csikszentmihalyi, 2003). When award-winning college instructors were asked to recall their best moments in the classroom, the majority vividly described flow experiences (Froh, Menges, & Walker, 1993). Interestingly, of these best moments, the ones they said were the best of the best were mutual flow experiences or what is now called *social flow* (Walker, 2010). I designed the *Flow Moment Classroom Assessment Technique* (FMCAT) to help college instructors capture and replicate illusive, but wonderful, moments in education when teachers and students are in a state of mutual flow. A copy of the FMCAT can be downloaded from the website address http://wellbeingincollege.org/faculty-resources.

FMCAT administration

Like all other CATs, the FMCAT is course embedded. It is best used at the end of a specific class day while a course is in progress. However, with minor changes in the instructions, it could be also used at the end of a semester. The FMCAT invites teachers and students to engage in a collaborative form of action research (McIntyre, 2008). The results of test trials suggest that class time spent to discover and promote flow is class time well spent. Nonetheless, some instructors may not have the interest or time to do this kind of classroom research. For instructors who can commit a couple of class days to do this research, for the best results, they should acquaint their students with flow theory (Csikszentmihalyi, 1990) and classroom assessment (Angelo & Cross, 1993). The FMCAT is a complex but useful assessment technique. Instructors and their students must first learn how to administer it, then cooperatively interpret and apply its results.

FMCAT scores

The FMCAT generates two kinds of data on flow experiences in the classroom: (1) qualitative data that identify flow and non-flow moments and (2) quantitative data that measure the conditions for flow. Data from the first page of the FMCAT help instructors and students develop a consensus on when flow happens, whereas data from the second page provide insights on why it happens. Because students and instructors are agents of their own and each other's flow experiences, the FMCAT also yields data on individual flow and social flow experiences.

Interpreting the results

The instructions on first page of the FMCAT ask students to identify the four most common flow or non-flow moments in a certain class day. However, even after students have become good observers and coders of flow moments, sometimes they may not sufficiently agree with each other. If you are concerned about the reliability of the data, I recommend analyzing only those results where there is at least 60% agreement among students, treating the rest as "outliers". On the other hand, if the unique flow experiences of individuals are of interest, establishing reliability may not be relevant or worthwhile.

On the second page of the FMCAT, students are asked to rate how confident and certain they are that the conditions for flow or non-flow were present during a specific class day. Minimally, simple descriptive statistics should be calculated on these data. However, if you are doing a series of studies in a program of classroom research, you may need to use inferential statistics (e.g. to contrast the ratings on teachers vs students, or to test the effectiveness of alternative methods of teaching between or within instructors).

Interpreting the results

Based on the past research (Csikszentmihalyi, 1990; M. Csikszentmihalyi & I. Csikszentmihalyi, 1988), all the results have implications for adjustments in teaching and learning. For example, frequent reports of anxiety by either an instructor or his students suggest that the level of challenge of a class activity is too high. This conclusion should be supported by the ratings on challenge on the second page of the FMCAT. In this case, flow theory prescribes increasing skills, reducing challenge or both to achieve optimal experience. Frequent reports of boredom suggest that the challenge is too low and that the challenges in future classes should be increased. If apathy is consistently reported, this finding indicates that challenge and skill are not only too low, but also the learning activity may be uninteresting and not meaningful. Instructors interested in advancing from low flow to high flow should closely examine the ratings on speed of the passage of time, distractions, self-awareness, and absorption, to gain insights on how they might intensify and stabilize flow. If the focus of a particular class activity is only on the instructor (e.g. when she has prepared and delivered a new lecture), or if the work of just the students is emphasized (e.g. when debates or group exercises are used), the data on instructor dominated flow or student dominated flow should be given special attention. However, considering the finding that the very best learning and teaching involves social flow, both students and instructors should try to discover the ingredients of these ideal moments in education. Then, *together*, they should attempt to make social flow experiences more likely in future classes. Results of laboratory and classroom research suggest that social flow is more attainable when all the conditions for individual flow are met and (1) both instructors and students energetically plan and prepare for a class, (2) the learning activity selected demands cooperation and coordination, and (3) during the class, emotions are openly expressed and contagiously shared (Walker, 2010).

Caveats and summary remarks

The science of positive psychology can inform both what and how we teach. At best, it is inconsistent to ask students to learn about intriguing topics such as flow or signature strengths, then to teach them in a way that is boring and disengaging. The first place we should apply positive psychology is in our own classrooms. Because of the time required, it may be easy to view classroom assessment as an unnecessary interruption of one's teaching, especially when the emotions of students are being measured. However, instructors who regularly used classroom assessment reported that they became more effective and satisfied teachers precisely because they discovered new ways to increase student learning and engagement (Angelo, 1998). But to create more positive learning experiences, classroom assessment must monitor emotions. Recent research strongly suggests that classroom climate and the rapport instructors have with students are necessary conditions for better learning (Benson et al., 2005; Keeley, Smith, & Buskist, 2006). This finding should come as no surprise to practitioners of positive psychology. To become a more effective college instructor, you have to touch the hearts as well as heads of students. The ELCAT and EMCAT are two ways to discover how to touch more hearts and heads. While assessment techniques like the ELCAT and FMCAT are not without flaws, in the hands of conscientious instructors, they hold the promise of increasing enthusiasm for learning not only during college days, but also after graduation. Is there any more positive effect of the generativity of a teacher than this?

References

Angelo, T.A. (1998). Classroom assessment and research: An update on uses, approaches and research findings. *New directions for teaching and learning* (Vol. 75). San Francisco, CA: Jossey-Bass.

Angelo, T., & Cross, P. (1993). *Classroom assessment techniques: A handbook for college teachers* (2nd ed.). San Francisco, CA: Jossey-Bass.

Benson, T.A., Cohen, A.L., & Buskist, W. (2005). Rapport: Its relation to student attitudes and behaviors toward teachers and classes. *Teaching of Psychology, 32*, 237–239.

Csikszentmihalyi, M. (1990). *Flow: The psychology of optimal experience.* New York, NY: Harper & Row.

Csikszentmihalyi, M., & Csikszentmihalyi, I. (Eds.) (1988). *Optimal experience: Psychological studies of flow in consciousness.* New York, NY: Cambridge University Press.

Diener, E., & Lucas, R.E. (1999). Personality and subjective well-being. In D. Kahneman, E. Diener, & N. Schwarz (Eds.), *Well-being: The foundations of hedonic psychology* (pp. 213–229). New York, NY: Russell Sage Foundation.

Fredrickson, B.L., & Losada, M.F. (2005). Positive affect and the complex dynamics of human flourishing. *American Psychologist, 60*, 678–686.

Froh, R.C., Menges, R.J., & Walker, C.J. (1993). Revitalizing faculty work through intrinsic rewards. In R. Diamond (Ed.), *New directions in higher education* (Vol. 81, pp. 87–95). San Francisco, CA: Jossey-Bass.

Keeley, J., Smith, D., & Buskist, W. (2006). The teacher behaviors checklist: Factor analysis of its utility for evaluating teaching. *Teaching of Psychology, 33*, 84–90.

McIntyre, A. (2008). *Participatory action research.* London: Sage Publications.

Nakamura, J., & Csikszentmihalyi, M. (2003). The construction of meaning through vital engagement. In C. Keyes & J. Haidt (Eds.), *Flourishing: Positive psychology and the life well-lived* (pp. 83–104). Washington DC: American Psychological Association.

Posner, J., Russell, J.A., & Peterson, B.S. (2005). The circumplex model of affect: An integrative approach to affective neuroscience, cognitive development, and psychopathology. *Developmental Psychopathology, 17*, 715–734.

Reminington, N.A., Fabrigar, L.R., & Vissar, P.S. (2000). Reexamination of the circumplex model of affect. *Journal of Personality and Social Psychology, 79*, 286–300.

Suskie, L., & Banta, T.W. (2009). *Assessing student learning: A common sense guide* (2nd ed.). San Francisco, CA: Jossey-Bass.

Walker, C.J. (2010). Experiencing flow: Is doing it together better than doing it alone? *The Journal of Positive Psychology, 5*(1), 3–11.

Walker, C.J., & Hale, N.M. (1999). Faculty vitality and well-being. In R. Menges (Ed.), *Professors in new jobs: Mastering academic work* (pp. 216–240). San Francisco, CA: Jossey-Bass.

Warr, P. (1999). Well-being and the workplace. In D. Kahneman, E. Diener, & N. Schwarz (Eds.), *Well-being: The foundations of hedonic psychology.* New York, NY: Russell Sage Foundation.

Virtues and character strengths for sustainable faculty development

Thomas V. McGovern

New College of Interdisciplinary Arts and Sciences, Arizona State University, West Phoenix, AZ, USA

For this special issue about teaching Positive Psychology, I show how the virtues and character strengths are at the heart of an interdisciplinary faculty development program. They can be pragmatic responses to the critical incidents encountered during a semester, and serve as stimuli for continuing reflection and sustained renewal. First, I synthesize research on faculty development, teacher behaviors, and re-define the virtues and character strengths to apply directly to learning and teaching. Second, I describe a four-module program with reflective exercises that can be delivered in face-to-face workshops, via guided self-instruction, and in online formats.

Before reading the Positive Psychology literature, I conducted continuing education workshops, sponsored by the American Psychological Association (APA), on 'Thinking about Learning/Learning about Teaching' for new and experienced teachers. The topics included composing philosophy of teaching statements and linking them to strategies for designing effective syllabi, identifying student learning outcomes, choosing effective pedagogical and assessment strategies for these outcomes, and constructing post-semester evaluation methods. I recognized, however, that after the behavioral skills of effective teaching had become well-practiced, faculty turned to larger 'why-questions' about their identities as academics and how to adapt to changes in the populations and environments of higher education. How they could use 'signature strengths every day in the main realms of your life to bring abundant gratification and authentic happiness' (Seligman, 2004, p. 161) became the bridge to Dahlsgaard, Peterson, and Seligman's (2005) and Peterson and Seligman's (2004) work on virtues and character strengths.

In a special issue of *Teaching of Psychology* on the Scholarship of Teaching and Learning, McGovern and Miller (2008) first re-defined the 24 character strengths to be directly applicable to learning and teaching. For example, Peterson and Seligman (2004, pp. 29–30) use the following definitions:

Creativity [*originality, ingenuity*]: Thinking of novel and productive ways to conceptualize and do things; includes artistic achievement but is not limited to it.

Citizenship [*social responsibility, loyalty, teamwork*]: Working well as a member of a group or team; being loyal to the group; doing one's share.
Gratitude: Being aware of and thankful for the good things that happen; taking time to express thanks.

In McGovern and Miller (2008, p. 282), we adapted these three original definitions:

Creativity and ingenuity: Constructs novel and innovative conceptualizations of student learning and pedagogy.
Citizenship and teamwork: Builds collaborative communities of learners rather than solely rewarding individual achievements.
Gratitude: Appreciates and responds to being graced by the profound and simple gifts found in the classroom and its diverse participants.

With adapted definitions of the virtues and strengths as core concepts, we designed a faculty development workshop to explore a life story model of identity (McGovern, 2006) and critical questions that emerged from teaching, research, and citizenship activities. Workshop participants generated, in small groups, critical incidents that could be addressed effectively by a single or multiple character strengths.

I delivered a keynote address in 2009 to the Association for Psychological Science/Society for the Teaching of Psychology and an introductory 2-h workshop to 30 international psychology faculty in 2010. Based on positive responses at these annual teaching institutes and feedback from other university colleagues who reviewed the workshop materials, I created a more thoroughly integrated faculty development program that could be delivered in face-to-face workshops, by guided self-instruction, or via online courses (McGovern, 2011a).

Faculty virtues and character strengths for sustainable development

If faculty construe their role to be as a sage on the stage, being knowledgeable is valued above all else. Yet, the landscape in higher education has changed and psychologists now understand student learning in more complex ways. In the summary chapter from a national conference on undergraduate education in psychology handbook, McGovern (1993) proposed this interactive set of questions:

> What kind of *outcomes* can be achieved with
> What kind of *students* taught by
> What kind of *faculty* using
> What type of *teaching methods* as part of
> What kind of *curriculum*? (p. 218; italics in original)

This formula remained valid for the study groups at the University of Puget Sound national conference who produced a new blueprint for the future of undergraduate psychology (Halpern, 2010). As a participant and group leader at the 2008 conference, I was struck by how many of the issues being studied by academic faculty psychologists could be integrated with the virtues and character strengths. A chapter on 'psychologically literate citizens' (McGovern et al., 2010) as a desired learning outcome for all students taking psychology courses led to my chapter on 'virtues and character strengths of psychologically literate faculty' (McGovern, 2011b).

To more effectively synthesize the Positive Psychology objectives about virtues and strengths leading to gratification and authentic happiness, and the longer tradition of faculty development in behalf of teaching and learning, I revised all of the character strength definitions. They are shown in Table 1.

I re-designed the original workshop structure and handbook materials. After a brief introduction to Positive Psychology tenets and the intellectual and empirical bases for the virtues and character strengths, and my application of them to learning and teaching, there are four distinct modules.

- Module 1 on *Core Virtues* introduces participants to all six virtues and their broad applications to learning and teaching.
- Module 2 on *Thinking about Learning* explores the virtues of Wisdom and Knowledge and Humanity and how character strengths intersect with the philosophical assumptions for learning and teaching held by participants.
- Module 3 on *Learning about Teaching* evaluates how the virtues of Justice, Temperance,

and Courage are integral to the management of critical incidents.
- Module 4 on *Sustainable Renewal and Strategic Planning* probes how the virtue of Transcendence is a capstone for the reflective exercises and becomes the platform for strategic planning for growth and sustained renewal.

The actual workshop delivery depends on audiences and time availability. With 35 doctoral students planning academic careers, I delivered Module 1 and exercises from Modules 2–4 in a 3-h session in spring 2011. I constructed an online Blackboard-based course using the same handbook in order to continue discussions with this same group through the academic year 2011–2012, as they finish their doctoral programs and begin new teaching appointments. I will deliver a 7-h session with exercises from all four modules to doctoral candidates and new and seasoned faculty members as an APA Continuing Education Workshop in summer 2011.

In the following sections, I offer a synopsis of all the modules and some of the exercises.

Module 1: Core virtues

Beginning with a guided fantasy exercise about a past teacher's ideal qualities, faculty members explore all six virtues' applications to learning and teaching. The module stimulates participants' focusing on their assumptions about exemplary teaching, but they learn to use the vocabulary of the virtues to articulate their understandings. Roundtable discussions foster the evaluation of past experiences, as they discover common denominators fostered by interpreting diverse episodes as the displayed qualities of various virtues.

Module 2: Thinking about learning (Wisdom and Knowledge and Humanity)

Planning a semester begins with identifying required learning outcomes and then scripting pedagogical strategies to accomplish them. I ask participants to match their current syllabi outcomes with the character strengths of wisdom and knowledge and humanity. Interdisciplinary doctoral students in a recent workshop discovered that objectives from diverse curricula (e.g., anthropology, marketing, and mathematics) came together as liberal arts outcomes when construed as modeling character strengths like *critical thinking* or *love of learning*. From the virtue of humanity, they evaluated how tending and befriending strengths like *social and emotional intelligence* captured the types of interpersonal relationships they hoped to have with students and their faculty mentors,

Table 1. Virtues and character strengths for learning and teaching.

WISDOM AND KNOWLEDGE: Cognitive strengths used to acquire and create knowledge
Creativity and Ingenuity: Construct original and innovative strategies for learning and teaching
Curiosity and Openness to New Experiences: Examine processes as well as outcomes of learning and teaching; find gratification in the mundane phenomenology of required tasks and topics
Critical Thinking, Judgment, and Open-Mindedness: Seek and evaluate evidence fairly, and respond differentially, even when contrary to personal beliefs or perspectives
Love of Learning: Pursue new discoveries and methods in the world of ideas, systematically, and appreciate serendipity
Perspective and Wise Counsel: Provide wise counsel to students and teachers, grounded in reflected experience, and with empathy for diverse ways of seeing and being in the world

HUMANITY: Interpersonal strengths that involve tending and befriending
Care, Compassion, Generosity, Kindness, and Nurturance: Contribute ethically and responsibly to the welfare of others despite a breadth or depth of differences
Social/Emotional Intelligence: Attend to subtle cues in teacher and student and colleague relationships and group dynamics; able to use one's emotions as part of problem solving
Love: Create safe-havens in the classroom that foster reciprocal relationships of support and respect; demonstrate cognitive and affective acceptance of others

JUSTICE: Civic strengths that contribute to diverse and healthy communities
Citizenship, Loyalty, and Teamwork: Build collaborative communities of learners rather than solely rewarding individual achievements or solo performances; foster effective group dynamics
Fairness: Develop nuanced capacity to identify biases in our perspectives; reason, make judgments, and implement ethical actions
Leadership: Facilitate the task demands and interpersonal dynamics of learning environments

TEMPERANCE: Discipline that protects against excess in our relationships with students, faculty colleagues, and administrators
Forgiveness and Mercy: Diminish anger with empathy; sustain and renew relationships despite setbacks that derive from others' shortcomings or mistakes
Humility and Modesty: Communicate genuine self-assessments of strengths and limitations, valuing multiple perspectives and outcomes
Discretion and Prudence: Take care in daily choices; promote measured balance and harmony in the pursuit of intended goals
Self-Control and Self-Regulation: Manage initial reactions to consider and implement disciplined responses, especially in difficult, 'no-win' classroom and professional situations

COURAGE: Emotional strengths to accomplish goals despite internal or external obstacles
Bravery and Valor: Act with conviction, despite risks and dangers; to 'bear witness'
Authenticity, Integrity, and Honesty: Declare clear principles and values; present oneself sincerely and act genuinely, modeling how this quality is essential for trusting relationships
Persistence and Perseverance: Sustain effort despite obstacles, boredom, or frustration, and without apparent rewards; find pleasure in completing tasks
Enthusiasm, Vitality, and Zest: Show a passion for teaching, learning, and deliberate practices for well-being; demonstrate a focused sense of priorities

TRANSCENDENCE: Strengths that forge connections to the larger universe and meanings
Appreciation of Beauty and Excellence, Awe, and Wonder: Recognize and take pleasure in others' and one's own talents and creativity, and especially in the splendid discoveries of students
Gratitude: Be thankful for grace of both simple and profound gifts from learning and teaching
Hope and Optimism: Respond to successes and adversities with an open-minded perspective tempered by humility and wisdom; expect the best and work to achieve it
Humor and Playfulness: Approach life with a playful recognition of incongruities and circumstances beyond our control
Spirituality, Faith, and Purpose: Foster inquiry about higher purposes and meanings; enable students to genuinely grapple with mystery and what is sacred in their life experiences

---

Source: Adapted by McGovern (2011a) from Peterson and Seligman (2004).

whether teaching French, electrical engineering, or behavioral neuroscience.

The in-depth program available with more time, via guided instruction, or online in an interactive format, probes all 24 character strengths for all six virtues. For example, in the module on thinking about learning, wisdom's cognitive character strengths include *creativity, curiosity, critical thinking, love of learning* and *wise counsel or perspective*. The following are examples of stimulus prompts from these five character strengths to illustrate how they can inspire the content and

processes we script into our syllabi even before a first class meeting.

- How do I conform AND vary from traditional ways to create a course and its potential for learning? The topics covered? Innovative pedagogical strategies?
- What do I assume about how my students learn?
- How do I motivate students to be amiable skeptics in thinking critically about different points of view?

- What are my cues for feeling 'in a rut' about my subject matter or my methods?
- Who are the types of individuals who seek my counsel and the perspectives they seem most apt to explore with me?

Humanity's tending and befriending strengths include *care and compassion*, *social/emotional intelligence*, and *love*. Sample prompts to explore these character strengths include:

- How do I communicate my accessibility and a willingness to listen to more than what has already been spoken? Do students or peers feel 'safe' with me?
- What evokes 'noise' in my interpersonal relationships and disrupts my empathy?
- How do I fulfill my needs for intimacy and community by the work that I do and with the colleagues who share the same academic life?

Module 3: Learning about teaching (Justice, Temperance, Courage)

In order to diversify how we learn about teaching, critical incidents exercises (e.g., creating collaborative learning environments; disruptive student reacting to a hot topic; sagging attendance and diminished performance) connect the virtues of justice, temperance, and courage with their respective character strengths.

Justice is practiced when we use civic character strengths – *loyalty and teamwork, fairness, leadership* – that teach students how to contribute to a healthy community life. This virtue connects directly to the new concept of psychologically literate citizens (McGovern et al., 2010). Sample prompts include:

- How do I facilitate both the achievement of independent learning and the communitarian skills formed by collaborative learning?
- How does someone 'fail' in my classes? Do I allow students to choose to fail? How much responsibility am I willing to take for *not* letting someone fail?
- How do I adapt my leadership ethic for the dynamics of specific environments and diverse populations of students or faculty colleagues?

Temperance protects us against excess in our relationships with students, colleagues, and administrators. Its character strengths include *humility and modesty, forgiveness and mercy, discretion and prudence*, and *self-regulation and self-control*. The following prompts and others for temperance's strengths help faculty consider alternative strategies:

- What is my genuine appraisal of my subject matter expertise and how well I teach it?

- What is my calculus for balancing mercy with justice in conflicted situations?
- What are my 'go-to strategies' for clear and authentic responses as I try to balance long-term outcomes with short-term demands to take immediate action?
- What have I learned are my low and high thresholds for anger, frustration, sadness and disappointment, need for recognition and reward, fatigue?

Students' post-semester missives frequently recall situations when our displays of temperance's character strengths had long-lasting value. Their recollections about 'What would my professor do in this situation?' offer inspiration about alternative responses to tough situations.

Contemporary college classrooms increasingly call upon us to practice the virtue of Courage as we use emotional character strengths to accomplish goals despite internal or external obstacles. Courage's character strengths include *bravery and valor, authenticity and integrity, perseverance*, and *enthusiasm and zest*. A sampling of prompts includes:

- What has been my experience(s) of danger or risk? Hostile student? Unpredictable or ill-tempered colleague/administrator? What have I feared most in such interactions?
- What single principle about authentic learning and teaching do I stand by – across diverse students, situational contexts, and my years in academic life?
- What are the roots and fruits of my being careless from time to time?
- How do I set my priorities for an academic year, and what calculus do I use to evaluate or recalibrate their importance as time goes on?

Module 4: Sustained renewal (Transcendence and Strategic Planning)

Having drawn inspiration from the memories of ideal teachers, scripted desired cognitive and emotional learning outcomes, and navigated critical incidents, we reach the end of a semester's work. Student ratings of instruction or a peer review of our performance provides us with food for thought about its quality. Why return to do battle again? How do we savor the pleasures of learning and teaching and situate the failures in a larger perspective? The virtue of transcendence helps forge connections between recent experiences and a larger universe of meanings. Its character strengths include *appreciation of excellence and awe, gratitude, hope and optimism, humor and playfulness*, and *spirituality or sense of faith and purpose*.

In McGovern (2006), I explored how important it was to evaluate our learning and teaching as part of a longer narrative of an academic career. Our answers to 'why-questions' inspire sustained commitment and renewal of a teaching life. The prompts for Transcendence also synthesize what participants have learned about the other five virtues' strengths.

- How do I appreciate the many acts of COURAGE demonstrated by students who return to school each year despite economic or emotional adversity?
- How can I express my gratitude for HUMANITY'S tending and befriending acts offered me by my students and colleagues?
- Hope springs from environments of JUSTICE – safe places where others can be trusted and unanticipated things learned. Do I create spaces where hope flourishes?
- How do I recognize my limitations in moments that call for TEMPERANCE, learning from students' playfulness and being able to laugh at my own foibles?
- How have my students affirmed my faith in WISDOM and KNOWLEDGE this past year, and my commitment to the power of learning and teaching?

These prompts consolidate understanding of the inter-relationships among the virtues and their character strengths. A subtext for sustainable faculty development, via these reflections on the virtue of transcendence, is to consider what remains to be added in future chapters of an academic life narrative. The synthesis questions from transcendence provide the experiential conclusion to the workshop. A final roundtable discussion focuses on developing a strategic plan as the pragmatic conclusion to the exercises.

Final thoughts

The work of a teacher – exhausting, complex, idiosyncratic, never twice the same – is, at its heart, an intellectual and ethical enterprise. Teaching is the vocation of vocations, a calling that shepherds a multitude of other callings. It is an activity that is intensely practical and yet transcendent, brutally matter-of-fact, and yet fundamentally a creative act. Teaching begins in challenge and is never far from mystery (Ayers, 2001, p. 122).

Faculty members are storytellers who have academic degrees. The virtues and character strengths have high value as stimuli for the gathering of insight-laden stories about learning and teaching. They have even higher value as the sources for faculty members' sustainable growth and renewal as they build academic communities of psychologically literate citizens where virtue is learned by being practiced.

References

Ayers, W. (2001). *To teach: The journey of a teacher*. New York, NY: Columbia University Teacher's College Press.

Dahlsgaard, K., Peterson, C., & Seligman, M.E.P. (2005). Shared virtue: The convergence of valued human strengths across culture and history. *Review of General Psychology, 9*, 203–213.

Halpern, D.F. (2010) (Ed.). *Undergraduate education in psychology: A blueprint for the future of the discipline*. Washington, DC: American Psychological Association.

McGovern, T.V. (1993). Transforming undergraduate psychology for the next century. In T.V. McGovern (Ed.), *Handbook for enhancing undergraduate education in psychology* (pp. 217–238). Washington, DC: American Psychological Association.

McGovern, T.V. (2006). Self-evaluation: Composing an academic life narrative. In P. Seldin & Associates (Eds.), *Evaluating faculty performance: A practical guide to assessing teaching, research, and service* (pp. 96–110). Bolton, MA: Anker.

McGovern, T.V. (2011a). Faculty virtues and character strengths: Reflective exercises for sustained renewal. Workshop handbook available from the author at thomas.mcgovern@asu.edu

McGovern, T.V. (2011b). Virtues and character strengths of psychologically literate faculty. In J. Cranney & D. Dunn (Eds.), *Psychologically literate citizenship: Foundations and global perspectives* (pp. 449–461). Oxford: Oxford University Press.

McGovern, T.V., Corey, L., Cranney, J., Dixon Jr, W.E., Holmes, J.D., Kuebli, J.E.,..., Walker, S.J. (2010). Psychologically literate citizens. In D.F. Halpern (Ed.), *Undergraduate education in psychology: A blueprint for the future of the discipline* (pp. 9–27). Washington, DC: American Psychological Association.

McGovern, T.V., & Miller, S.L. (2008). Integrating teacher behaviors with character strengths and virtues for faculty development. *Teaching of Psychology, 35*, 278–285.

Peterson, C., & Seligman, M.E.P. (2004). *Character strengths and virtues: A handbook and classification*. New York, NY: Oxford University Press.

Seligman, M.E.P. (2004). *Authentic happiness: Using the new positive psychology to realize your potential for lasting fulfillment*. New York, NY: Free Press.

Incorporating positive psychology content and applications into various psychology courses

Jeana L. Magyar-Moe

Department of Psychology, University of Wisconsin-Stevens Point, Science Building Room D240, Stevens Point, WI 54481, USA

Courses devoted to the subject of positive psychology are becoming more common in colleges and universities throughout the United States and beyond, however, there are still many schools that do not have a positive psychology course as part of the psychology curriculum. This article was designed for instructors in such settings who desire to teach positive psychology, but do not have access to a course specifically on this topic or for those who already teach a positive psychology course but desire to implement positive psychology topics into other psychology courses as well. Although the recommendations in this article are not exhaustive in terms of covering all psychology courses and all aspects of positive psychology that have applications to these courses, the material provided should stimulate thinking about the various ways in which positive psychology can be infused into courses that are not entirely dedicated to the topic.

Although courses devoted to the subject of positive psychology are becoming more common in colleges and universities throughout the United States and beyond, there are still many schools that do not have a positive psychology course as part of the psychology curriculum. This article was designed for instructors in such settings who desire to teach positive psychology, but do not have access to a course specifically on this topic or for those who already teach a positive psychology course but desire to implement positive psychology topics into other psychology courses as well. The following sections include examples of ways in which positive psychology can be infused into courses in psychology such as Abnormal Psychology, Psychological Assessment, Multicultural Psychology, Counseling Skills and Techniques, Personality Psychology, and more.

Positive psychology in courses on abnormal psychology and psychological assessment

There are numerous components of positive psychology that have direct relevance to courses in abnormal psychology and psychological assessment. On the surface, this may seem counterintuitive, given that positive psychology is about optimal human functioning whereas abnormal psychology is about pathology and psychological assessment is often utilized for identifying psychopathology. The reality is that positive psychology can be infused into courses on psychopathology and psychological assessment in order to create more balance in the ways that students conceptualize people with mental illness, thereby destigmatizing disorders and enhancing empathy for those who experience such disorders.

Within abnormal psychology and assessment courses, much of the content taught revolves around diagnostic labels derived from the *Diagnostic and Statistical Manual of Mental Disorders* (*DSM*; American Psychiatric Association, 2000). Such diagnoses are considered by most to be negative, as they represent problems or deficits in functioning. Labels are very powerful in general, but they are especially so when they are negative and when they are applied to people.

Perhaps the most problematic aspect of negative labels is that they lead to deindividuation, which results in the creation on in-groups and out-groups and fosters the development of prejudices as instructors and students focus on symptoms of psychopathology, label people as part of a group based on those symptoms, and then assign different, negative behaviors to people in that in-group versus those who are part of the out-group (Wright & Lopez, 2002). Indeed, the process of deindividuation may lead to dehumanization, whereby the client with a mental illness diagnosis is seen as being equivalent to the disorder label.

In addition, members of the out-group (i.e., clinicians/instructors/psychology students) are more likely to pathologize the experiences of members of the in-group (i.e., clients/patients) and to ignore the role of environmental factors in contributing to the perceived problems of the in-group. Furthermore, information that is consistent with the deviant label (i.e., that which is negative) may be highlighted while that which is not consistent (i.e., that which is positive) is overlooked.

Various positive psychology concepts and models can be utilized in the classroom to offset these biases associated with negative labeling. More specifically, people-first language (i.e., 'a client with anorexia' versus 'an anorexic') can be implemented throughout one's teaching and can also be expected of students (both in oral and written communication) in an effort to help offset the potential problems related to the dehumanizing power of negative labels. Indeed, lack of people-first language suggests that the only thing that is important about the client is his or her pathology. In addition to using people-first language, students should be taught about the power of positive labels and encouraged to look for client strengths as well. By explicitly naming human strengths, the person labeled as well as those who are informed of his or her label come to find merit in the label. Human strengths become salient when named (Snyder et al., 2003). Similarly, self-fulfilling prophecies may come into play when people are labeled as having talents, strengths, abilities, and positive resources. Just as people who are labeled with disorders may come to internalize their negative labels, so too may people come to internalize positive labels. Just as clinicians may inadvertently change the way they treat a client based on the diagnostic label applied, so too may a clinician change the way the client is treated based on the strength label applied. Such a process may serve to further enhance the labeled strengths and the client may become more cognizant of his or her potential, more interested in nurturing these talents and strengths, and more confident in utilizing these skills and positive resources to manage areas of weakness or deficit.

Given the power of labels, it is imperative that instructors point out strengths and resources in addition to signs of pathology in any case studies, video examples, or case examples used when teaching about abnormal psychology or the assessment of psychopathology. Likewise, including strengths and resources within case studies that one develops for assignment or exam purposes is also in line with a positive psychology perspective. Students should also be required to include information on strengths within any assessment reports written and exposing them to strengths measures, such as the Satisfaction with Life Scale (Diener, Emmons, Larsen, & Griffen, 1985), the Adult Trait Hope Scale (Snyder et al., 1991), or the

Values in Action Strengths Survey (Peterson & Seligman, 2004; see Lopez & Snyder, 2003, for examples of more strengths measures) is also suggested. Finally, reviewing the Values in Action Classification of Character Strengths (Peterson & Seligman, 2004) and highlighting how this manual was developed in order to be an adjunct to the *DSM* allows students to develop a broader strengths lexicon while also enhancing their sense of appreciation for the importance and legitimacy of attending to strengths in all people, including those with psychopathology.

Additional models of positive psychology that foster balanced perspectives of people with pathology and enhance student empathy for those with mental illness include the four-front approach to client assessment (Wright & Lopez, 2002), the complete state model of mental health (Keyes & Lopez, 2002), and the seven-axis system of positive psychological assessment (Magyar-Moe, 2009). Briefly, the four-front assessment approach entails purposeful attending to, gathering of, and reporting of information on (a) client strengths/assets; (b) client deficiencies/undermining characteristics; (c) environmental resources; and (d) environmental deficits (Wright & Lopez, 2002). The complete state model of mental health defines mental health and mental illness as existing on two separate continuums such that the absence of mental illness is not equal to the presence of mental health. Rather, clients are assessed according to the degree of symptoms of mental illness they experience (high to low), as well as the degree of symptoms of well-being they experience (high to low). Combining these continua together, a client can be conceptualized as: (1) completely mentally healthy or flourishing (low symptoms of mental illness and high symptoms of well-being); (2) completely mentally ill or floundering (high symptoms of mental illness and low symptoms of well-being); (3) incompletely mentally healthy or languishing (low symptoms of mental illness and low symptoms of well-being); or (4) incompletely mentally ill or struggling (high symptoms of mental illness and high symptoms of well-being; Keyes & Lopez, 2002). The seven-axis system of positive psychological assessment entails a few simple changes or additions to the current *DSM* five-axis assessment system (Lopez, Snyder, & Rasmussen, 2003; Magyar-Moe, 2009). These changes include (a) broadening Axis IV to include not only psychosocial and environmental *problems* but also psychosocial and environmental *resources*; (b) broadening Axis V to include two global assessment of functioning scales with one focused on symptoms of mental illness (i.e., global assessment of *negative* functioning) and the other on symptoms of well-being (global assessment of *positive* functioning; Magyar-Moe, 2009); (c) adding an Axis VI in which positive and negative aspects of the client's cultural identities are documented (D.S. Sue, D.W. Sue, &

S. Sue, 2006); and (d) adding an Axis VII in which the personal strengths and facilitators of growth of clients are documented (Snyder et al., 2003).

Positive psychology in multicultural psychology courses

Positive psychology can be applied within courses on multiculturalism to highlight the strengths that come from understanding and appreciating the various cultural identities of self and others. While it is essential that students understand negative issues related to culture such as racism, prejudice, White privilege, gender privilege, heterosexual privilege, ageism, classism and more, failing to address the positive aspects of culture can leave students with a false perception that culture is bad, frightening, or something to be ignored or avoided. One way to achieve a balanced perspective on culture is to discuss with students the cultural values, beliefs, and practices that moderate racial stress, such as collectivism, racial and ethnic pride, spirituality, religion, holistic health, and family and community importance. In addition, attending to the skills and strengths that have developed through overcoming adversity such as racism, prejudice, or oppression can also lead to important discoveries about culturally sensitive optimal human functioning (Constantine & Sue, 2006).

Sue (2003) notes that some of the skills or strengths that may develop for people who overcome racial or cultural adversity include heightened perceptual wisdom (i.e., the ability to correctly perceive underlying motives, intentions, and meanings of others), the ability to rely on non-verbal or contextual meanings, and bicultural flexibility (i.e., openness to multiple worldviews, sensitivity to other's viewpoints, and behavioral flexibility). Such flexibility often leads to a broadened world view, an appreciation for the strengths and weaknesses of all people, comfort with cultural differences and better effectiveness in relating to those of diverse backgrounds, an enhanced sense of self-fulfillment, and a sense of connection and commitment to better citizenship and social responsibility.

Positive psychology can also be applied within courses on multiculturalism through such exercises as having students examine all aspects of their own cultural identities via use of the ADDRESSING model (Hays, 1996, 2001). ADDRESSING is an acronym, with each letter representing one aspect of culture as follows: *A*ge and generational influences, *D*isability status (developmental), *D*isability status (acquired), *R*eligion and spiritual orientation, *E*thnicity, *S*exual orientation, *S*ocioeconomic status, *I*ndigenous heritage, *N*ational origin, and *G*ender. Students should be challenged to consider what

personal strengths, interpersonal supports, culturally-related knowledge and skills, and environmental strengths have developed for them due to their cultural make-up.

Positive psychology in introduction to counseling skills and techniques courses

Positive psychology can be incorporated into counseling skills courses in some of the same ways as previously noted within the contexts of abnormal psychology or psychological assessment classes. More specifically, people-first language, the four-front assessment approach (Wright & Lopez, 2002), and the complete state model of mental health (Keyes & Lopez, 2002) are all applicable to counseling. Several other concepts from positive psychology also have applicability when it comes to teaching students basic counseling skills, including active-constructive responding (Gable, Reis, Impett, & Asher, 2004), positive empathy (C.W. Conoley & J.C. Conoley, 2009), and highlighting client strengths and resources throughout the counseling process.

According to Gable et al. (2004), there are four possible ways in which one can respond to the good events in the lives of those with whom one interacts: (1) active-constructive (responding enthusiastically); (2) passive-constructive (happy, but downplayed); (3) active-destructive (pointing out the downside); (4) passive-destructive (lacking interest). Of the four styles, only the active-constructive style benefits both the individual one is interacting with, as well as the relationship between the two parties. Students should be exposed to the idea of active-constructive responding and encouraged to respond in this manner to the good news, positive experiences, and victories that they hear in the stories that their clients tell. Indeed, responding in this manner serves to strengthen the ever-important working alliance within the therapeutic relationship.

Positive empathy can also be taught to supplement training in general empathy. Empathy is typically defined as the ability to understand and enter into another's feelings, emotions, and experiences and is a hallmark of the counseling process. Rogers (1957) notes that traditional empathy typically focuses on deep client experiences of pain, fear, or anger. Indeed, when empathy is taught to students who are learning to be helpers, the focus of the empathic responses tends to revolve around negative issues. For instance, an empathic response to a client who says 'I have tried, and tried, and tried to figure out a way to get my son to listen and behave appropriately and nothing works' might be 'You are feeling frustrated and worn out because nothing you try seems to be working. That can really be energy-depleting'. While this response may be validating and help the client to feel understood, it emphasizes the negative and has the potential to increase a sense of hopelessness. In contrast, a positive empathy response would entail validation of the experience while also attending to the positive aspects of the story, with the focus being on the client's deep experiences of hope and desire (C.W. Conoley & J.C. Conoley, 2009). In this case, a positive empathic response would be 'although you are feeling some frustration, it is apparent that you are really committed to your son and getting through to him because it is very important to you that your son learns to make good choices. Your persistence is a strength that will help you to reach your parenting goals.' Pointing out the parental commitment of this client as well as his or her personal strength of perseverance versus the parental failures can make a world of difference in terms of the client's levels of hope and motivation, as well as how the client views him or herself. In addition, positive empathy is likely to strengthen the therapeutic alliance.

Finally, encouraging students to be vigilant of signs of client strengths and abilities, as well as indicators of psychosocial and environmental resources, and to point these out to clients as they arise is recommended. Students typically do not miss the weaknesses or struggles that clients report, but often overlook entirely positive functioning, assuming that the goals of therapy are to address issues or problems that clients have identified. Teaching them right from the start that the positive is just as important as the negative is essential. Indeed, from a positive psychological perspective, doing therapy without attending to the positive is just as ludicrous as doing therapy without attending to the negative. The goal is to strike a balance, and helping students to understand this in the early phases of learning to be a helper is crucial.

Positive psychology in personality psychology courses

Positive psychology can be applied within the context of courses on personality when reviewing humanistic theories. Indeed, positive psychology has many roots in humanistic psychology (Seligman & Csikszentmihalyi, 2000). More specifically, the humanistic tenets that people are basically good and that they naturally strive toward personal growth, full functioning, and self-actualization fit very well with the premises of positive psychology.

Although they are not identical, Maslow's (1970) concept of peak experiences is related to Csikszentmihalyi's (1990) flow theory. Peak experiences are defined as especially joyous and exciting moments in life, involving sudden feelings of intense happiness and awe that are often inspired by deep meditation, intense feelings of love, exposure to great art or music, or the overwhelming beauty of nature.

When peak experiences are especially powerful, the sense of self dissolves into an awareness of a greater unity (Maslow, 1970). Flow, also referred to as optimal experience, is defined as a psychological experience in which one is fully immersed in what he or she is doing. In order for flow to occur, one must perceive a challenge or opportunity for action that stretches (without overmatching or underutilizing) his or her existing skill level. This is referred to as the challenge-skills balance (Jackson & Csikszentmihalyi, 1999). In addition, flow becomes more likely when such challenging activities are intrinsically rewarding, require concentration, and have clear goals coupled with immediate feedback on progress. Under these conditions, people often enter into a subjective state in which there is a merging of action and awareness, deep, effortless involvement in the task at hand, intense focus in the moment, a loss of self-consciousness, a sense of control, and distortion of time (Jackson & Csikszentmihalyi, 1999). While peak and flow experiences can be one in the same, flow experiences require a challenge-skills balance, whereas peak experiences do not. Likewise, peak experiences are often achieved via extraordinary life moments, whereas flow can be achieved through more routine activities (Jackson & Csikszentmihalyi, 1999).

Positive psychology can also be applied within personality psychology courses when addressing the concept of emotional affectivity. Discussion of the valance of emotions and the utility of both negative and positive emotions can be enhanced through incorporation of the broaden and build theory of positive emotions (Fredrickson, 1998, 2001). Indeed, many students recognize the value of negative emotions such as fear, anger, and sadness but fail to see the value of positive emotions beyond the fleeting good feelings they provide. Through review of the broaden and build model, students are able to see how positive emotions can lead to survival through broadening thought-action repertoires and building enduring personal resources (i.e., social, psychological, intellectual, and physical), while also undoing lingering negative emotions and fueling psychological resilience (Fredrickson, 2001).

Finally, when reviewing trait theories, incorporation of the VIA Strengths Survey (Peterson & Seligman, 2004) affords students the opportunity to assess personality in terms of strengths of character in addition to the more traditional trait measures.

Positive psychology in other common psychology courses

In addition to the information provided thus far, there are applications of positive psychology to other common psychology courses including social psychology (e.g., positive romantic illusions, Murray & Holmes, 1997; egotism and empathy motives for altruistic, grateful, and forgiving behaviors, Snyder & Lopez, 2007; the feel-good, do-good phenomenon, Salovey, Mayer, & Rosenhan, 1991; and the broaden and build theory of positive emotions, especially as it relates to the building of social resources, Fredrickson, 1998, 2001), health psychology (e.g., the link between health outcomes and optimism, Curbow, Somerfield, Baker, Wingard, & Legro, 1993; Fitzgerald, Tennen, Affleck, & Pransky, 1993), sport psychology (e.g., the role of optimism and hope in sports performance, Curry & Snyder, 2000; Seligman, Nolen-Hoeksema, & Thornton, 1990; flow in sports, Jackson & Csikszentmihalyi, 1999), developmental psychology (e.g., fostering secure attachments, Snyder & Lopez, 2007; successful aging, Valliant, 2002), research methods (e.g., using research studies on positive psychology topics as examples of qualitative versus quantitative designs, to demonstrate survey designs versus quasi-experimental designs, or to demonstrate experience sampling and the differences between prospective, retrospective, and current-moment assessments), theories of counseling and psychotherapy (e.g., Quality of Life Therapy, Frisch, 2006; Positive Psychotherapy, Rashid, 2008; Seligman, Rashid, & Parks, 2006; Strengths-based Counseling, Smith, 2006), career development courses (e.g., strengths theory, Clifton & Nelson, 1992; gainful employment, Snyder & Lopez, 2007; StrenghtsQuest, Clifton & Anderson, 2002); and physiological psychology (e.g., neural correlates of well-being, Urry et al., 2004) just to name a few. Indeed, one would be hard pressed to find a psychology course in which one or more concepts or findings from positive psychology could not be applied. This makes sense, given that the hope of those who spear-headed the positive psychology movement was that someday positive psychology would not be a special subfield within psychology, but that it would cut across and inform all aspects of the discipline (Seligman & Csikszentmihalyi, 2000).

Although the recommendations in this article are not exhaustive in terms of covering all psychology courses and all aspects of positive psychology that have applications to these courses, the material provided should serve to stimulate thinking about the various ways in which positive psychology can be infused into courses that are not entirely dedicated to the topic. Indeed, if one desires to teach about positive psychology, there are many ways in which this can be done even in the absence of a dedicated positive psychology course. Based upon personal experiences over the past decade with teaching positive psychology within a dedicated course and within the context of other psychology courses, students typically demonstrate a lot of enthusiasm and excitement when learning about

positive psychology topics, regardless of the course in which the material is incorporated.

References

American Psychiatric Association (2000). *Diagnostic and statistical manual of mental disorders* (4th ed., text revision). Washington, DC: American Psychiatric Association.

Clifton, D.O., & Anderson, E.C. (2002). *StrengthsQuest: Discover and develop your strengths in academics, career, and beyond.* Washington, DC: The Gallup Organization.

Clifton, D.O., & Nelson, P. (1992). *Soar with your strengths.* New York, NY: Dell.

Conoley, C.W., & Conoley, J.C. (2009). *Positive psychology and family therapy: Creative techniques and practical tools for guiding change and enhancing growth.* Hoboken, NJ: John Wiley & Sons.

Constantine, M.G., & Sue, D.W. (2006). Factors contributing to optimal human functioning in people of color in the United States. *The Counseling Psychologist, 34*, 228–244.

Csikszentmihalyi, M. (1990). *Flow: The psychology of optimal experience.* New York, NY: Harper & Row.

Curbow, B., Somerfield, M.R., Baker, F., Wingard, J.R., & Legro, M.W. (1993). Personal changes, dispositional optimism, and psychological adjustment to bone marrow transplantation. *Journal of Behavioral Medicine, 16*, 423–443.

Curry, L.A., & Snyder, C.R. (2000). Hope takes the field: Mind matters in athletic performances. In C.R. Snyder (Ed.), *Handbook of hope: Theory, measures, & applications* (pp. 243–260). San Diego, CA: Academic Press.

Diener, E., Emmons, R.A., Larsen, R.J., & Griffin, S. (1985). The satisfaction with life scale. *Journal of Personality Assessment, 49*, 71–75.

Fitzgerald, T.E., Tennen, H., Affleck, G., & Pransky, G.S. (1993). The relative importance of dispositional optimism and control appraisals in the quality of life after coronary artery bypass surgery. *Journal of Behavioral Medicine, 16*, 25–43.

Fredrickson, B.L. (1998). What good are positive emotions? *Review of General Psychology, 2*, 300–319.

Fredrickson, B.L. (2001). The role of positive emotions in positive psychology: The broaden-and-build theory of positive emotions. *American Psychologist, 56*, 218–226.

Frisch, M.B. (2006). *Quality of life therapy: Applying a life satisfaction approach to positive psychology and cognitive therapy.* Hoboken, NJ: John Wiley & Sons.

Gable, S.L., Reis, H.T., Impett, E.A., & Asher, E.R. (2004). What do you do when things go right? The intrapersonal and interpersonal benefits of sharing positive events. *Journal of Personality and Social Psychology, 87*, 228–245.

Hays, P.A. (1996). Addressing the complexities of culture and gender in counseling. *Journal of Counseling and Development, 74*, 332–338.

Hays, P.A. (2001). *Addressing cultural complexities in practice.* Washington, DC: American Psychological Association.

Jackson, S.A., & Csikszentmihalyi, M. (1999). *Flow in sports: The keys to optimal experiences and performances.* Champaign, IL: Human Kinetics Books.

Keyes, C.L.M., & Lopez, S.J. (2002). Toward a science of mental health: Positive directions in diagnosis and intervention. In C.R. Snyder & S.J. Lopez (Eds.), *Handbook of positive psychology* (pp. 45–62). New York, NY: Oxford University Press.

Lopez, S.J., & Snyder, C.R. (2003). *Positive psychological assessment: A handbook of models and measures.* Washington, DC: American Psychological Association.

Lopez, S.J., Snyder, C.R., & Rasmussen, H.N. (2003). Striking a vital balance: Developing a complementary focus on human weakness and strength through positive psychological assessment. In S.J. Lopez & C.R. Snyder (Eds.), *Positive psychological assessment: A handbook of models and measures* (pp. 3–20). Washington, DC: American Psychological Association.

Magyar-Moe, J.L. (2009). *Therapist's guide to positive psychological interventions.* San Diego, CA: Elsevier Academic Press.

Maslow, A. (1970). *Religion, values and peak experiences.* New York, NY: Viking Press.

Murray, S.L., & Holmes, J.G. (1997). A leap of faith? Positive illusions in romantic relationships. *Personality and Social Psychology Bulletin, 23*, 586–604.

Peterson, C., & Seligman, M.E.P. (2004). *Character strengths and virtues: A handbook and classification.* New York, NY: Oxford University Press.

Rashid, T. (2008). Positive psychotherapy. In S.J. Lopez (Ed.), *Positive psychology: Exploring the best in people* (Vol. 4, pp. 187–217). Westport, CT: Praeger.

Rogers, C. (1957). The necessary and sufficient conditions of therapeutic personality change. *Journal of Consulting Psychology, 21*, 95–103.

Salovey, P., Mayer, J.D., & Rosenhan, D.L. (1991). Mood and helping: Mood as a motivator of helping and helping as a regulator of mood. In M.S. Clark (Ed.), *Prosocial behavior* (pp. 215–237). Newbury Park, CA: Sage.

Seligman, M.E.P., & Csikszentmihalyi, M. (2000). Positive psychology: An introduction. *American Psychologist, 55*, 5–14.

Seligman, M.E., Nolen-Hoeksema, S., & Thornton, N. (1990). Explanatory style as a mechanism of disappointing athletic performance. *Psychological Science, 1*, 143–146.

Seligman, M.E.P., Rashid, T., & Parks, A.C. (2006). Positive psychotherapy. *American Psychologist, 61*, 774–788.

Smith, E. (2006). The strengths-based counseling model. *The Counseling Psychologist, 34*, 13–79.

Snyder, C.R., Harris, C., Anderson, J.R., Holleran, S.A., Irving, L.M., Sigmon, S.T., . . . , Harney, P. (1991). The will and the ways: Development of an individual-differences measure of hope. *Journal of Personality and Social Psychology, 60*, 570–585.

Snyder, C.R., & Lopez, S.J. (2007). *Positive psychology: The scientific and practical explorations of human strengths.* Thousand Oaks, CA: Sage.

Snyder, C.R., Lopez, S.J., Edwards, L.M., Pedrotti, J.T., Prosser, E.C., Walton, S.L., . . . , Ulven, J.C. (2003). Measuring and labeling the positive and the negative. In S.J. Lopez & C.R. Snyder (Eds.), *Positive psychological assessment: A handbook of models and measures* (pp. 21–40). Washington, DC: American Psychological Association.

Sue, D.W. (2003). *Overcoming our racism: The journey to liberation.* San Francisco, CA: Jossey-Bass.

Sue, D.S., Sue, D.W., & Sue, S. (2006). *Understanding abnormal behavior* (8th ed.). Boston, MA: Houghton Mifflin.

Urry, H.L., Nitschke, J.B., Dolski, I., Jackson, D.C., Dalton, K.M., Mueller, C.J., . . . , Davidson, R.J. (2004). Making a life worth living: Neural correlates of well-being. *Psychological Science, 15*, 367–372.

Valliant, G.E. (2002). *Aging well: Surprising guideposts to a happier life.* Boston, MA: Little Brown.

Wright, B.A., & Lopez, S.J. (2002). Widening the diagnostic focus: A case for including human strengths and environmental resources. In C.R. Snyder & S.J. Lopez (Eds.), *The handbook of positive psychology* (pp. 26–44). New York, NY: Oxford University Press.

Integrating research training and the teaching of positive psychology

Chu Kim-Prieto and Carianne D'Oriano

Department of Psychology, The College of New Jersey, Ewing, NJ 08628, USA

Faculty hoping to add a Positive Psychology course into the undergraduate curriculum as a regularly taught stand-alone course may face multiple hurdles: finding the time to develop the course, and once it is developed, attaining approval by departmental level as well as college level curriculum committees. In addition, even after the approval process, faculty might find that the ability to regularly offer the course may be limited due to the demand for the teaching of other basic courses. On the other hand, most undergraduate Psychology curriculums require students to successfully complete at least one course on research methodology. We describe two courses, a 200-level and an upper-level course, that integrates positive psychology topics into the teaching of research methods and hands-on research experience.

The American Psychological Association's guidelines for the undergraduate psychology major (APA, 2007) identifies understanding and being able to apply basic research methodology in psychology as a key goal for attaining knowledge and skills that are consistent with understanding of psychology as a science. Proposed benchmarks for assessing quality of undergraduate programs include the teaching of psychology as a discipline grounded in science (Dunn, McCarthy, Baker, Halonen, & Hill, 2007; see also McGovern, Furumoto, Halpern, Kimble, & McKeachie, 1991).

In line with these goals, research methodology courses as well as courses that incorporate hands-on research experience are frequent requirement for students completing their undergraduate programs in psychology in the United States. National survey of undergraduate psychology departments and programs found that 73% of the programs surveyed required at least one course in research methodology (Messer, Griggs, & Jackson, 1999). A more recent survey by Perlman and McCann (2005) of research requirements at undergraduate psychology departments and programs found that of the 203 departments and programs that responded, 79% required research experience as a degree completion requirement. In addition, research methodology courses not only fulfill the goal of understanding and learning how to apply scientific methods, but also teach critical thinking, written and oral communication skills, as well as information literacy. Of course, while above-mentioned skills are elements that can be successfully integrated into many different courses, they are a natural fit for research methodology courses because critiquing of research methodologies, conducting library research, and literature reviews, along with critically analyzing different methodologies and assessing research claims, are elements found in many research methods courses and textbooks.

However, in spite of the discipline's focus on scientific methodology and research experience, student interest in research methodology courses or research experience has remained consistently low. In their investigation of undergraduate psychology majors, Vittengl et al. (2004) found that students' self-reported mean level of interest in research was at 1.67, on a scale of 0 (not at all) to 4 (extremely). In addition, Sizemore and Lewandowski (2009) found that while students gain research knowledge at the completion of a research and statistics course, attitudes toward research either showed no change or significant declines in favorability. Indeed, the lack of student interest in research methodology has resulted in the development of a wide range of teaching tools devoted to whetting student interest in research: using astrology, handedness, yearbook pictures or tendency to smile to teach research methodology or research design, or the usage of single-case designs, to name just a few (Grahe, Williams, & Hinsz, 2000; Johnson, 1996; Lipsitz, 2000; Morgan, 2009; Ward & Grasha, 1986).

In contrast, courses in positive psychology, happiness, and subjective well-being are widely popular (Max, 2007). Many students find the topic to be intrinsically interesting and relevant at an intuitive level – something that they perhaps do not experience with research methodology courses. However, because the field of positive psychology is relative new, faculty who are interested in teaching such a course can face multiple hurdles. Creating a new course from the ground up can be time consuming. Developing the syllabus, choice of articles or textbooks, creating exercises and assignments, in addition to the development of lecture materials, are all tasks that take considerable time, in spite of access to high quality resources and examples. Furthermore, in addition to the time necessary to devote to creating a course, the faculty member may also need to gain the approval of curriculum committees that oversee the development of new courses. Indeed, many academic institutions have a multi-layered approval process, necessitating approval at not just the departmental level, but at the school, college, and/or at the institution level. Even after these hurdles, faculty may find that being able to regularly offer a course in positive psychology to be a challenge due to staffing demands. This last constraint may be especially pertinent at smaller psychology departments and primarily undergraduate institutions, where faculty members may be expected to teach five or six different courses every year in order to insure that students are exposed to a wide range of different course topics, as well as teach courses in the methodological core, such has research methods and statistics. Furthermore, students eager to complete their education with the requisite basic set of courses found in most departments (and expected by most graduate programs) may not have the room in their schedule for a specialized course in a relatively novel topic.

Thus, while positive psychology is a potentially popular course topic, such a course may lack necessary resources that would allow it to be offered with regular frequency. On the other hand, while research methodology courses already exist and are a requirement in most undergraduate psychology departments – considered fundamental to learning of psychology as a science – it suffers from low interest and perceptions of irrelevance from the students. We propose that by integrating the topic content area of positive psychology into the teaching of research methodology and research laboratory courses, faculty and psychology departments can tap into the benefits posed by each, while ameliorating the negatives of both.

We present two different ways in which topics on positive psychology can be integrated into research methodology and research laboratory courses by providing a detailed description of two different courses at The College of New Jersey (TCNJ, 2009) that have successfully integrated these two topics. One is a 200-level research methodology course that is a requirement for the major (*Research Seminar*), and a second, at the 300-level (*Lab Learning*), that students can choose from a menu of different upper-level courses. In both of these courses, topics relevant to positive psychology are woven into the curriculum, such that students learn about positive psychology topics through their research activities.

Research seminar: Happiness in a research methodology course

At TCNJ, psychology majors are required to satisfactorily complete a three-course methodology core sequence. The initial course in the curriculum is a 100-level research methodology course, designed as an introduction to research methodology. In this course, students can choose to participate in research as research participants in the departmental subject pool, but do not conduct independent research. Psychology majors generally take this course immediately after their introductory psychology course, usually during the first year of their undergraduate career. This course is followed by a statistics course, in which students learn basic statistical methods. The last course in the three-course sequence is a 200-level research methodology course, *Research Seminar*. Within this semester-long course, students develop an idea, derive a testable research hypothesis, test the hypothesis, and present their findings through an oral presentation and a written report. In addition, because writing is taught across the curriculum at TCNJ, this research methodology course also serves as the mid-level writing intensive course for the students. As a writing intensive course, students engage in iterative writing assignments throughout the semester, culminating in a 15–20 page research report at the end of the semester.

Topic choice and introduction to happiness

In order to insure that students are able to conceive and complete a research project within the span of a semester, topic choice and research idea development begins during the first week of classes. Students are provided with a brief lecture of the topic, along with a short and accessible reading assignment during the first week of classes.

The introductory lectures provide a broad overview of positive psychology, focusing on happiness. The lecture begins with definitions of subjective well-being and discussion of eudemonic versus hedonic differences in defining the meaning of happiness (for review, see Kahneman, 1999; Ryan & Deci, 2001). This allows students to conceptualize the science of happiness as encompassing not just the subjective evaluation of affective states, but also as encompassing meaning, goals, and self-realization. Allowing for a more broad definition allows students to find a subtopic within the topic area of happiness that they are interested in. Providing this introduction during the first day of classes (after syllabus review) is useful, as it allows for immediate immersion into the topic. Next two class periods are devoted to two different topics – predictors of happiness and outcomes of happiness. In discussing predictors, inclusion of various demographic variables, such as income, sex, and age are helpful because students often default to descriptive demographic research questions in their attempts to derive their own research questions (e.g., Are female college students happier than male college students? Are wealthy people happier than those less wealthy?). By providing a summary of the research on demographic variables that indicate the statistically significant but limited predictive power of demographic variables, students can be encouraged to focus on process variables and ask questions such as 'how' or 'why.' In addition to demographic variables, it is also helpful to review variables such as goals, motivation, flow, and positive affect as predictors of subjective well-being. In lecturing on the outcomes of happiness, the work done by Lyubomirsky, King, and Diener (2005) is especially useful. Thus, providing a review of the variables that predict happiness, as well as the variables that result from our attainment of happiness gives students a wide range of variables and research questions that they then can pursue as they formulate their own research hypothesis.

In addition, a class period devoted to discussing various methodologies for assessing happiness has also been beneficial for the students, as it provides them with a starting ground for thinking about possible methodologies as the students develop their own research question and consider various ways for them to test their hypotheses. This information is usually incorporated into discussion held with each of the separate research groups as the students begin work on planning their methodology. Discussion of possible methodologies to consider include self-report measures, including ecological momentary assessment and daily dairy assessment (for review, see Scollon, Kim-Prieto, & Diener, 2003; Stone, Shiffman, & DeVries, 1999) as well as a discussion of specific measures, such as the Subjective Well-Being Scale (Diener, Emmons, Larsen, & Griffin, 1985) and the Fordyce Happiness Measure (Fordyce, 1988). Discussions have also included concerns regarding accessibility of information, conversational norms, reliability, and validity (for review, see Larsen & Fredrickson, 1999; Schwarz & Strack, 1999). Because this course is capped at 15 students, who are divided into four groups, tailoring the methodology content for separate groups is a manageable solution. However, in larger courses, or in settings where each student develops individual projects, instructors may find it more useful to lecture on different types of methodologies. Another advantage of such as lecture would be that it could include discussions of biological measures and behavioral measures, both of which are typically beyond the scope of feasibility within the context of an undergraduate research method course.

In addition to these content-based lectures and discussions, students are assigned readings that provide a broad overview of positive psychology, and specifically, happiness. Examples of readings that are accessible to intermediate-level psychology undergraduates include introductory chapters from traditional textbooks such as Baumgardner and Crothers (2009), or review articles such as Kim-Prieto, Diener, Tamir, Scollon, and Diener (2005). In addition to these articles and chapters, instructors might also find it useful to use popular press articles to whet students' appetites and introduce them to the science of happiness; examples include an extensive review of George Valiant's Harvard Study of Adult Development in *The Atlantic* (Shenk, 2009), as well as *Time* magazine's review of positive psychology (Wallis, 2005). While these popular press articles do not provide the rigor that would be expected of academic texts, they provide students an opening through which they can develop their interest and begin their research inquiry. Other options include more accessible evidence-based books written for a lay audience, such as *How of Happiness* (Lyubomirsky, 2007).

Students are encouraged to choose their topic and research interest early in the semester through a homework assignment given out during the first class meeting. This assignment requires students to identify a broad topic of interest, or a broad question that they would like to find out more information about. Students are encouraged to use a wide array of possible sources, such as an article of interest in a newspaper or a magazine, an observation of an interpersonal interaction, or introspection. This assignment can be tailored to be as broad or as narrow as needed. Instructors might leave the topic broad as 'anything to do with happiness,' or provide greater focus by specifying a more narrow topic, such as 'meaning in life,' 'experiencing joy,' or 'demographics of happiness.' These initial lay ideas that the students identify are then used as a springboard for the next assignment, in which students conduct a preliminary literature search on the broad topic. The preliminary literature search is used to allow students to identify a review article that discusses the phenomenon that they may have identified in their initial homework assignment. Students are expected to find a review article on their topic because it provides them with a useful reference list that becomes a starting point for a more extensive literature search, and because being able to identify a review article on the topic signals that the topic choice is appropriate. If the student cannot find a review article, then the topic choice may be too narrow for a comprehensive review, or too broad to fit into a single review article.

Research design and hypothesis

Next set of assignments and classroom learning objectives require students to identify and gather empirical articles on their research topic, and answer specific set of questions about the articles in order to help the students develop a hypothesis. For example, students are asked to identify the hypothesis of an empirical article, the research design that was used, and a threat to validity that might result in a viable alternative explanation for the results. Students are also asked to identify any follow-up questions that the research findings bring up. Through this process, students learn about the different research designs, such as experimental, quasi-experimental, and correlational. In addition, students learn about the strengths and weaknesses of different designs, as well as the types of research questions that are possible to answer through the different designs. In addition, students also become familiar with different types of validity, and the various threats that are posed by violations of validity. Finally, in designing the methodology, students are again referred to the empirical articles that they have collected in order to find measures and manipulations. By doing so, they become familiar with different types of measures (self-report, observations, etc.), as well as different types of experimental manipulations. It should be noted, however, that most students need extensive initial guidance in being able to identify the above noted elements, and multiple practices in class with sample articles may be needed. Instructors may find the measurement chapter of Baumgardner and Crothers (2009) useful as a starting point. However, using the empirical articles themselves that discuss the findings related to the topic of students' interest has been useful in having students realize the impact of different methods on research findings.

Data collection and statistical analysis

Because our department's participant pool is set up to allow students in this course access to the pool, students may design a small scale study that allows them to test their hypothesis using the participant pool. However, in most departments, undergraduate student access to the participant pool is limited. Topics on happiness and well-being are especially well suited for departments with limited student access to the participant pool because large-scale data sets on happiness and well-being, such as the General Social Survey, are readily available to students. Using archival datasets are also attractive because it allows faculty to devote

more class time to the specific content area, rather than manage student data collection.

Written report

As noted earlier, this 200-level course is a writing intensive course, with students expected to write a 15–20 page research report in APA style. The articles that they have read and annotated previously in developing the research hypothesis, as well as designing the research methodology, are expected to form the backbone of the literature review section. Students are also expected to refer to the methods sections of the articles as useful samples in developing their own methods sections. Students find the writing of the report onerous; however, the emphasis on the topic of happiness, as well as a sense of ownership of the research project, appear to make the process more manageable.

Evaluation of the course

Student perception and self-rated evaluation of the course have been in general positive. Anonymous course evaluations have included comments such as 'this class turned out to be a lot better than I thought,' 'It wasn't an easy class but I feel very accomplished.' In addition, students have also expressed genuine enjoyment of the course and the research process: 'I really enjoyed the class!'

Lab learning: Happiness in an advanced research laboratory course

In addition to the 200-level research methodology course, which is a requirement for the major, advanced psychology students also have the option of enrolling in a faculty-led research laboratory course. These Lab Learning courses may be taken as a 300-level upper level course, or as a 400-level Senior Capstone course. Within this context, the Lab Learning course allows students to study a topic within the given subject area over multiple semesters.

Research activities engaged in by the students include creation and evaluation of measures, pilot testing of manipulations, brainstorming sessions, data entry and data collection, as well as data analysis and data presentation. Students also take an active role in presenting the research at undergraduate student conferences as well as at regional psychology conferences.

In addition to the research activities noted above, students are expected to attain additional learning goals. Because the ratio of new students to returning students changes from semester to semester, the list of reading assignments has also changed. However, broad upper-level overview articles, such as Diener, Suh, Lucas, and Smith (1999), Ryan and Deci (2001), Kim-Prieto et al. (2005), or Lyubomirsky, King, and Diener (2005) are possible articles that can be used. Because some of the readings are more appropriate for more advanced undergraduate students, the initial choice of readings should depend on the student composition of the course in any given semester. For example, Diener et al. (1999) and Kim-Prieto et al. (2005) would be more appropriate for use with less advanced students, whereas Ryan and Deci (2001), Lyubomirsky et al. (2005) or Diener, Oishi, and Lucas (2003) would be more appropriate for junior or senior level students due to greater statistical complexity and/ or length. In addition, when the majority of the students in the Lab Learning course are students who are already familiar with the topic, overview articles have been dispensed with.

In addition to the review articles, students also spearhead the article selection and discussion throughout the semester. Each student chooses the article on a topic relevant to the research project that the lab is focused on, provides a brief presentation of the article, and leads the class in discussing the article. Through these weekly critiques, students hone their critical thinking and analytic skills that they first developed in their 200-level research methodology course. For example, when evaluating articles, students often fall for the relatively easy critique of sample size, or lack of generalizability due to the sample population of college students. However, being able to expand on this discussion to be able to understand the concept of statistical power, or when generalizability may or may not be of concern, is helpful for the students. For example, in discussing Lyubomirsky, Sousa, and Dickerhoof (2006), students questioned the generalizability of the findings because of the large percentage of females in the sample. Through extended discussion, students were encouraged to further consider ways in which sex of the participant may or may not have impacted the results. Students were encouraged to expand their critical analysis to determine whether the supposed fault was in actually a fault at all or not. For example, students were asked to consider whether sex of the participants might have been a confounding variable, and how the results might have differed if such were the case. In another example, in discussing Carver, Sinclair, and Johnson (2010), students questioned the small sample size, but were able to realize that the small sample size should not be a cause for concern if it does not pose a threat to the validity of the study.

Evaluation of the course

Student evaluations of the course have been positive over multiple semesters: Overall course rating means of instructor related items is 4.89 out of 5 over the course of eight semesters that the course has been taught, and range from 4.64 to 5. In addition, as noted above, students often choose to re-enroll in the course, sometimes extending their enrollment over four semesters, even after they can no longer apply the credits earned toward the major. Open-ended comments have often provided qualitative evidence of students' enjoyment of research methodology and research in general. Comments from anonymous feedback forms have included such as, 'awesome class – lots of fun and helped me hone my research skills,' 'great class – learning a lot of valuable skills,' and 'this course has given me such an excellent real-world research experience.' Thus, students equate research experience with valuable skills that have real-world implications, as well as fun and enjoyment.

Discussion

Providing research training to undergraduate psychology majors and instilling lasting interest in research can be challenging. Psychology majors are more frequently interested in the applied clinical or therapeutic aspect of psychology, and do not view research as relevant or interesting. However, by integrating the teaching of research methodology as well as research experience to a topic of intrinsic interest to many students, student interest in research methodology can be maintained, and continued involvement in psychology research developed. Feedback from course evaluations shows that students are finding psychological research to be enjoyable, and that they are finding it to be relevant to their daily lives. While evaluations for the upper-level course are in general more positive in terms of enjoyment of research compared to the 200-level course, students in the mid-level course nevertheless do express a sense of accomplishment and learning.

References

APA (2007). *APA guidelines for the undergraduate psychology major*. Washington, DC: Author.

Baumgardner, S.R., & Crothers, M.K. (2009). *Positive psychology*. Upper Saddle River, NJ: Prentice Hall.

Carver, C.S., Sinclair, S., & Johnson, S.L. (2010). Authentic and hubristic pride: Differential relations to aspects of goal regulation, affect, and self-control. *Journal of Research in Personality, 44*, 698–703.

Diener, E., Emmons, R.A., Larsen, R.J., & Griffin, S. (1985). The satisfaction with life scale. *Journal of Personality Assessment, 49*, 71–75.

Diener, E., Oishi, S., & Lucas, R. (2003). Personality, culture, and subjective well-being: Emotional and cognitive evaluations of life. *Annual Review of Psychology, 54*, 403–425.

Diener, E., Suh, E., Lucas, R., & Smith, H. (1999). Subjective well-being: Three decades of progress. *Psychological Bulletin, 125*, 276–302.

Dunn, D.S., McCarthy, M.A., Baker, S., Halonen, J.S., & Hill, G.W. (2007). Quality benchmarks in undergraduate psychology programs. *American Psychologist, 62*, 650–670.

Fordyce, M. (1988). A review of results on the happiness measures: A 60-second index of happiness and mental health. *Social Indicators Research, 20*, 355–381.

Grahe, J.E., Williams, K.D., & Hinsz, V.B. (2000). Teaching experimental methods while bringing smiles to your student's faces. *Teaching of Psychology, 27*, 108–111.

Johnson, D.E. (1996). A "handy" way to introduce research methods. *Teaching of Psychology, 23*, 168–170.

Kahneman, D. (1999). Objective happiness. In D. Kahneman, E. Diener, & N. Schwarz (Eds.), *Well-being: The foundations of hedonic psychology* (pp. 3–25). New York, NY: Russell Sage Foundation.

Kim-Prieto, C., Diener, E., Tamir, M., Scollon, C., & Diener, M. (2005). Integrating the diverse definitions of happiness: A time-sequential framework of subjective well-being. *Journal of Happiness Studies, 6*, 261–300.

Larsen, R.J., & Fredrickson, B.L. (1999). Measurement issues in emotion research. In D. Kahneman, E. Diener, & N. Schwarz (Eds.), *Well-being: The foundations of hedonic psychology* (pp. 40–60). New York, NY: Russell Sage Foundation.

Lipsitz, A. (2000). Research methods with a smile: A gender difference exercise that teaches methodology. *Teaching of Psychology, 27*, 111–113.

Lyubomirsky, S. (2007). *How of happiness: A scientific approach to getting the life you want.* New York, NY: Penguin Press.

Lyubomirsky, S., King, L., & Diener, E. (2005). The benefits of frequent positive affect: Does happiness lead to success? *Psychological Bulletin, 131*, 803–855.

Lyubomirsky, S., Sousa, L., & Dickerhoof, R. (2006). The costs and benefits of writing, talking, and thinking about life's triumphs and defeats. *Journal of Personality and Social Psychology, 90*, 692–708.

Max, D.T. (2007, January 7). Happiness 101. *New York Times Magazine.* Record number: 2007-01-07-911305.

McGovern, T., Furumoto, L., Halpern, D., Kimble, G., & McKeachie, W. (1991). Liberal education, study in depth, and the arts and sciences major: Psychology. *American Psychologist, 46*, 598–605.

Messer, W.S., Griggs, R.A., & Jackson, S. (1999). A national survey of undergraduate psychology degree options and major requirements. *Teaching of Psychology, 26*, 164–171.

Morgan, D.L. (2009). Using single-case design and personalized behavior change projects to teach research methods. *Teaching of Psychology, 36*, 267–269.

Perlman, B., & McCann, L.I. (2005). Undergraduate research experiences in psychology: A national study of courses and curricula. *Teaching of Psychology, 32*, 5–14.

Ryan, R.M., & Deci, E.L. (2001). On happiness and human potentials: A review of research on hedonic and eudaimonic well-being. *Annual Review of Psychology, 52*, 141–166.

Schwarz, N., & Strack, F. (1999). Reports of subjective well-being: Judgmental processes and their methodological implications. In D. Kahneman, E. Diener, & N. Schwarz (Eds.), *Well-being: The foundations of hedonic psychology* (pp. 61–84). New York, NY: Russell Sage Foundation.

Scollon, C., Kim-Prieto, C., & Diener, E. (2003). Experience sampling: Promises and pitfalls, strengths and weaknesses. *Journal of Happiness Studies, 4*, 5–34.

Shenk, J.W. (June, 2009). What makes us happy? *The Atlantic Magazine, 43*, 36–41, 44, 46–48, 50–53.

Sizemore, O.J., & Lewandowski, G.W. (2009). Learning might not equal liking: Research methods course changes knowledge but not attitudes. *Teaching of Psychology, 36*, 90–95.

Stone, A.A., Shiffman, S.S., & DeVries, M.W. (1999). Ecological momentary assessment. In D. Kahneman, E. Diener, & N. Schwarz (Eds.), *Well-being: The foundations of hedonic psychology* (pp. 40–60). New York, NY: Russell Sage Foundation.

TCNJ (2009). *Fact Book 2009.* TCNJ Office of Institutional Research & Assessment: Author.

Vittengl, J.R., Bosley, C.Y., Brescia, S.A., Eckardt, E.A., Neidig, J.M., Shelver, K.S., & Sapenoff, L.A. (2004). Why are some undergraduates more (and others less) interested in psychological research? *Teaching of Psychology, 31*, 91–97.

Wallis, C. (2005, January 9). The new science of happiness. *Time, 165*, A2–9.

Ward, R.A., & Grasha, A.F. (1986). Using astrology to teach research methods to introductory psychology students. *Teaching of Psychology, 13*, 143–145.

Adolescent popularity: A positive psychology course with a developmental foundation

Peter E.L. Marks

Department of Psychology, Reed College, Portland, OR 97202, USA

Because positive psychology is still an emerging subfield, it can often be difficult to fit dedicated positive psychology courses into academic curricula, particularly at small colleges. This article describes 'Adolescent Popularity', a Special Topics course with a 'balanced' view of peer interactions that can fit naturally within the developmental offerings of most colleges. The course curriculum focuses on popularity-relevant issues of measurement (both quantitative and qualitative), social behaviors/characteristics (e.g., prosocial behavior, physical attractiveness, athletic achievement, and aggression), and peer relationships (including friendships, romantic relationships, and social groups). Suggested primary readings and course assignments are outlined. Ultimately, the goal of this course is for students to gain a deep understanding of popularity and peer relations during adolescence, as well as a general appreciation for the importance of researching positive aspects of human behavior.

Introduction to popularity

As discussed by both Kim-Prieto (this issue) and Magyar-Moe (this issue), one of the major challenges of teaching courses in positive psychology, especially within small psychology departments, is fitting such courses within the normal structure of departmental offerings. This article discusses a course in Adolescent Popularity – a positive psychology course that doubles as a Topics course within developmental psychology.

The study of child and adolescent popularity represents an emerging area of focus within psychology. Although most popularity study is being conducted by peer relations researchers, the topic should also be of great interest to researchers (and students) who wish to focus on positive aspects of human interaction. Indeed, the study of popularity emerged partly as a reaction to the focus on peer rejection prominent during the 1980s and 1990s. As Cillessen and Marks (2011, p. 28) note, 'The zeitgeist [during this period] was to focus on children with problems in the behavioral and relationship domains and to design and test successful methods of preventing these problems'. Through the early 1990s, 'popularity' was usually measured using sociometric methods (i.e., methods that require adolescents to nominate peers who fit a certain criteria) and asking participants to name the peers that they 'like the most' and 'like the least'. In 1998, however, Parkhurst and Hopmeyer noted that adolescents, themselves, did not use the term 'popularity' in a way that was synonymous with liking/disliking; rather, adolescents used 'popularity' to denote status. Currently, researchers differentiate between *acceptance* (liking), *rejection* (disliking), *preference* (quantified as liking – disliking), and *popularity* (Cillessen & Marks, 2011; see also Cillessen & Rose, 2005, for a concise review of the preference/ popularity distinction). *Popularity*, under this definition, is a status term defined subjectively by adolescents themselves, and (usually) quantified by asking adolescents to nominate the peers in their class/ grade 'who are most popular'.

Over the course of the past decade, researchers using this new operationalization of popularity have documented a complex profile for high-status youth: popular adolescents are socially skilled, savvy, and knowledgeable individuals whose place within the social hierarchy is valued and respected by many of their peers. Often, popular adolescents are capable leaders who bring groups together and channel the group needs. On the other hand, many adolescents seem to combine aspects of leadership and aggression/ manipulation in their peer interactions, leading to ambivalent views of popular adolescents reflected in such films as *Heathers* and *Mean Girls*. Thus, the topic of adolescent popularity is ideal for instructors and researchers who want to take a 'balanced' view of human behavior (Seligman, Parks, & Steen, 2005) by acknowledging and attending to negative implications, while still fully considering and exploring positive aspects of peer relationships and interactions.

Course overview and topics

A course on adolescent popularity allows for a great deal of freedom in terms of analytic assignments, and lends itself to assigning readings from across a variety of fields, particularly psychology, sociology, and anthropology. Discussions of multicultural issues, gender differences, and Western pop culture will be common. More than anything, though, an examination of popularity will draw upon the personal experiences of every student in the class – whether they were popular, unpopular, or nonpopular in high school and beyond, they all have experience with social status and social systems. Because the literature on popularity is so recent, students can easily form novel hypotheses based on their individual experiences, and can propose (or even conduct) small-scale studies that have never been conceived.

Students should emerge from the course having carefully considered the following questions: Is popularity novel to American adolescents? What is the meaning of popularity to adolescents? And most importantly: Is popularity entirely a good thing? Is it, indeed, a reflection of social skill? And can we, as adults and educators, mitigate the 'dark side' of popularity and channel adolescents toward benevolent, thoughtful, and prosocial group leadership?

The course being described was initially taught as a Special Topics course in the child psychology department of a large, Midwestern university. The course met weekly for 2.5 h. Topics were structured so that history, methods, and foundational information were discussed at the beginning, aspects of status (dominance/visibility/preference) were in the middle, and correlates of popularity (aggression, attractiveness) were at the end. All course readings were primary sources or chapters; the majority of the assigned readings are cited below. The course could alternately be taught with a required text – the recently released *Popularity in the Peer System* (Cillessen, Schwartz, & Mayeux, 2011) would be ideal. In this case, the readings cited below would serve as excellent supplementary readings and prep materials.

The history of popularity

The first full class session focused on the history of popularity, both as a term and a concept. This topic serves as an ideal starting point for discussion of popularity because it allows students to consider their lay views of popularity and its uses in terms of the ways that adolescents and adults discussed popularity decades or centuries ago. Students should be challenged to look for similarities and differences between old popularity writings and their current everyday experiences with interpersonal status. In seeing, for example, how important adolescents considered popularity to be in the 1930s, students will hopefully gain an appreciation of a shared, universal adolescent experience that provides a foundation for their consideration of popularity throughout the semester.

When I taught this course, I assigned a number of short articles and snippets to give students a flavor for old discussions of popularity. The poem by Dodd (1767; available on Google Books) and the essay by Taunton (1936), both titled *Popularity*, provide a good starting point. Writings by or about adolescents from the early twentieth century, including advice columns by Blake (1914, 1936; the Anne Landers of her day) really show the struggle that adolescents faced to gain popularity. In addition, the wonderfully titled 'Must I Pet to Be Popular?' (1932) concisely and dramatically illustrates the struggle for popularity in the 1930s, and serves as a surefire conversation-starter in class.

Sociometric research

After the more 'lay' discussion of the first week, the second week dove headlong into a discussion of research methods. Sections from Terry (2000) and Cillessen (2009), both of which provide overlapping discussions of sociometric methods, were assigned readings. The discussion focused on different types of sociometric measurement (e.g., peer nominations vs. ratings vs. rankings), psychometric properties of peer nominations (e.g., issues of validity and reliability; Cillessen & Marks, 2011), and ethical issues surrounding the use of peer reports (e.g., is it wrong to ask kids to name peers they dislike? Will it make some kids sad, or increase rejection? See Babad, 2001; Bell-Dolan, Foster, & Sikora, 1989). Although admittedly one of the more 'dry' topics in the course, this discussion (along with the methodological content of the following 2 weeks) provided students the necessary background for reading (and, later, proposing) quantitative studies on popularity and peer relationships.

Measuring popularity and preference

In this class session, students should get their first understanding of the distinction between measuring popularity and preference from the introduction to Babad (2001) and through the review of Cillessen and Rose (2005). The central topic for discussion, however, should be acceptance and rejection, the combination of acceptance and rejection scores in creating social preference and social impact scores, and the concept of sociometric status groups (Coie, Dodge, & Coppotelli, 1982). Discussions may be somewhat conceptual, but should be anchored in measurement and operationa-lization of the variables. During this class session, a small-group activity required students to come up with one character from popular media (fiction or nonfic-tion) for each of Coie et al.'s (1982) sociometric status group. Students then argued about which character fits best into each grouping – this served as a boisterous discussion in which students were required to leverage and utilize their understanding of the operationalized social categories. For example, although everyone agreed that Eeyore was a perfect example of a 'neglected' (low-impact, neither liked nor disliked) character, students argued over whether Lindsay Lohan or Harry Potter served as appropriate 'contro-versial' (both liked and disliked) characters.

Qualitative methods

With the previous 2 weeks focusing on quantitative methods, the readings for this session should provide a stark contrast for students. There are many qualitative sources to choose from, but I assigned Ostermeier and Eicher (1966) and Merten (1997), as well as a chapter from Eder (1995). Each of these sources discusses peer relationships and status, and each provides an excellent example of qualitative research. I would also highly recommend the first chapter of Adler and Adler (1998), which provides a fantastic discussion of the challenges of conducting qualitative research using one's own children as the research subjects. In-class discussion can focus on comparing qualitative and quantitative approaches to studying popularity. How do students (particularly psych majors) react to reading well-done sociological inquiry (in my experience, some students appreciate the depth and descriptive nature of quali-tative work, while others consider it to be inherently biased and unreplicable). How would the claims in these qualitative studies be tested by quantitative researchers?

Status and dominance

This class session should be dedicated to discussing general aspects of dominance and power. Although I assigned adolescent-relevant dominance readings by Pellegrini (2002) and Milner (2004) as readings for this class session (along with Silk's, 2002, research on primate aggression), I think it would have been more interesting to assign more anthropological and etho-logical readings, and include a class discussion focusing on the relative merits of looking across cultures and species when considering behavior. Retaining Silk (2002), I might also add Itani (1961) and/or sections from Bernstein (1981) for a perspective based on research with primates, and provide classic anthro-pological/sociological perspectives on sources and uses

of power from Lippitt, Polansky, Redl, and Rosen (1960) and French and Raven (1959).

Social visibility, coolness, and style

This week considered an aspect of status that comple-ments dominance: social visibility. How does notoriety impact one's place in the popularity hierarchy? Readings were sections from Canaan (1987) and Milner (2004) focusing on what it means to be visible (or well known) in middle and high school. How do popular adolescents work to increase their visibility, and why do unpopular (particularly bullied) adoles-cents sometimes work to make themselves invisible? In addition, a short section on 'Coolness' from Adler and Adler (1998) provided a basis for a discussion about the differences between being cool and being popular, and drew upon students' own understanding of what would be considered 'cool'. A small-group activity required students to describe and debate the stereo-typical physical appearances and styles of 'popular', 'unpopular', and 'cool' boys and girls. Not being a fashion expert, myself, I found it entertaining (and educational) to see the variety and specificity of appearance stereotypes!

Youth culture, social groups, and conformity

This one is all about the writings of Bradford Brown (Brown, Lohr, & Trujillo, 1990; Brown, Mory, & Kinney, 1994), who is probably the foremost expert on studying peer subcultures ('preppies', 'druggies', etc.) from a psychological perspective. Discussion can focus on students' personal experiences with social groups during adolescence. Most schools have 'nerds' and 'jocks', but the variety of groupings (and bases for groupings) that students can share, even in a small class, is fascinating. The discussion may also consider a two-dimensional view of status, with a horizontal dimension indicating social groups and lifestyles, and a vertical dimension locating each individual *and group* in terms of their overall levels of social status (Brantlinger, 1993; Schwartz & Merten, 1967). Even if all jocks are more popular than all nerds, is it better to be the most popular nerd or the least popular jock?

Correlates of popularity

This 3-week block was divided into *Extracurricular Activities, Athletics, and Cheerleading* (Readings: Holland & Andre, 1995; Snyder & Spreizer, 1987; sections from Eder, 1995; Gordon, 1957), *Aggression and Deviance* (Readings: Andreou, 2006; Crick, Murray-Close, Marks, & Mohajeri-Nelson, 2009; see also Prinstein & Cillessen, 2003), and *Physical Attractiveness* (Readings: Cross & Cross, 1971;

Goldman & Lewis, 1977; Landy & Sigall, 1974; Wang, Houshyar, & Prinstein, 2006). Each session discussed operationalization and measurement of the relevant variables as well as the meanings of these variables to adolescents. These 3 weeks allowed for discussions about the positive *and* negative consequences of status, both for popular and unpopular adolescents. How do things we value (popularity, attractiveness, and athletics) allow and pull for *both* prosocial *and* antisocial behaviors?

Popularity and relationships

The following 2-week block focused on relationships and relationship-relevant behavior. *Friendship and Prosocial Behavior* (Reading: Bukowski, Motzoi, & Meyer, 2009) looked at the importance of friendships during adolescence, particularly in relation to peer relationships, and discussed prosocial behaviors (i.e., sharing, helping, cooperation, leadership, etc.). *Romantic Relationships and Sexual Behavior* involved both classic and modern takes on romantic relationships and status (see sections from Adler & Adler, 1998; Folsom, 1934; Waller, 1938) as well as direct relations between sexual activities and adolescent popularity (Prinstein, Meade, & Cohen, 2003). In both cases, the operationalization, measurement, and developmental significance of friendships and romantic relationships were discussed, as well as the reasons that adolescents choose to begin relationships with each other.

Popularity across contexts

The final class session of the year focused primarily on cross-cultural differences in popularity. Students should be challenged to consider whether popularity is, in fact, a universal adolescent construction of status, and whether there are American (or Western) aspects of popularity that do not translate into other cultures. Can we say that popularity in the USA is identical to popularity in The Netherlands, where adolescents use two separate terms to describe popular peers (i.e., they distinguish between prosocial and antisocial popular peers in their everyday language; de Bruyn & Cillessen, 2006), or in China, where adolescent status reflects intelligence more than athletic ability (Dong, Weisfeld, Boardway, & Shen, 1996)?

Assignment structure

I utilized a fairly standard assignment structure in teaching this course, with requirements including an integrative response paper, weekly discussion points, and a multi-stage (topic statement, bibliography, first draft, final draft) research proposal as the final paper.

The other major assignment for the course was the 'Popularity in Popular Culture' paper, which required students to select a film and write about its portrayal of status and peer relationships in terms of course readings and discussions. Choices included *Heathers*, *She's All That*, and *The Breakfast Club*. A variation of this assignment could require students to read and comment upon a young adult novel featuring popularity (e.g., the *Gossip Girl* or *Clique* series).

Two variations of other assignments that I used in a recent course on adolescent development would also fit perfectly into this assignment structure. The first requires students to comment upon a book of advice written for preteens – a number of good advice books are available, and many of them discuss popularity, friendships, conformity/peer pressure, sexuality, and other group processes (e.g., Borden, Miller, Stikeleather, Valladares, & Yelton, 2005; Erlbach, 2003; and several of the advice books under the *American Girls* imprint). Students must discuss advice in terms of research findings discussed in the course, and should suggest ways that the advice and/or topic coverage might be improved.

The second assignment requires students to attend a midnight showing of the *Rocky Horror Picture Show*, and write a paper about how the behavior and appearance of adolescent (and young adult) attendees reflect aspects of subculture, peer norms, style, conformity, sexuality, and deviance. *Rocky Horror* is, in many ways, a quintessentially adolescent experience. In attending the show, students enter a ritualized context that may be completely foreign and may reflect values they do not share. Obviously, this assignment is only feasible if the course is being taught in or near a city in which *Rocky Horror* showings are weekly or semi-weekly; however, variations of the assignment will work (heavy metal concerts, comic cons, etc.) as long as they encourage students to observe a uniquely adolescent subcultural experience.

Feedback on course structure and assignments

At the end of the semester, students were asked to respond to an anonymous 'Unofficial Course Evaluation' (UCE). Out of the 15 students enrolled in the initial course, 14 completed these UCEs. Responses indicated that students' favorite topics were attractiveness, romantic relationships, aggression, and the history of popularity. Their least favorite topics were the weeks on methodology, which they felt were dry. On the other hand, UCEs explicitly asked students to comment on the structure of the semester, and all 14 respondents expressed approval for the structure that had been used, providing comments like 'very necessary to have the basics covered first' and 'glad we got the boring stuff out of the way'.

Feedback regarding course assignments indicated that the 'Popularity in Popular Culture' paper was well-received; the response paper and research proposal (unsurprisingly) received mixed reviews. UCEs also revealed that requiring four weekly discussion questions/comments was effective (if not particularly original) – 11 out of 14 students stated that they completed more of the readings because of the requirement than they otherwise would have.

Conclusion

A course on adolescent popularity will engage students in terms of their experiences and cultural understanding, while also providing a broad and in-depth consideration of an emerging topic within psychology. The popularity literature is complex yet approachable, comprehensive yet incomplete. Students will leave the course with questions that have never been addressed, but will also have the background and tools to investigate those questions in future research. And ultimately, a course on adolescent popularity serves as an ideal vehicle for bringing the positive psychology perspective into psychology departments, within the bounds of pre-set course structures that may not allow for the implementation of an exclusively 'pos psych' course.

Acknowledgments

The author would like to thank Peter Adler, Antonius Cillessen, and Nicki Crick for providing consultation and suggestions during the initial design of the course described in this paper, and Acacia Parks for guidance and edits regarding this manuscript.

References

Adler, P.A., & Adler, P. (1998). *Peer power: Preadolescent culture and identity.* New Burnswick, NJ: Rutgers University Press.

Andreou, E. (2006). Social preference, perceived popularity and social intelligence: Relations to overt and relational aggression. *School Psychology International, 27,* 339–351.

Babad, E. (2001). On the conception and measurement of popularity: More facts and some straight conclusions. *Social Psychology of Education, 5,* 3–29.

Bell-Dolan, D.J., Foster, S.L., & Sikora, D.M. (1989). Effects of sociometric testing on children's behavior and loneliness in school. *Developmental Psychology, 25,* 306–311.

Bernstein, I.S. (1981). Dominance: The baby and the bathwater. *Behavioral and Brain Sciences, 4,* 419–457.

Blake, D. (1914, September 5). Doris Blake says. *Chicago Daily Tribune,* p. 14.

Blake, D. (1936, April 28). Making aim at popularity is disillusioning. *Chicago Daily Tribune,* p. 14.

Borden, S., Miller, S., Stikeleather, A., Valladares, M., & Yelton, M. (2005). *Middle school: How to deal.* San Francisco, CA: Chronicle Books.

Brantlinger, E.A. (1993). *The politics of social class in secondary school: Views of affluent and impoverished youth.* New York, NY: Teachers College Press.

Brown, B.B., Lohr, M.J., & Trujillo, C. (1990). Multiple crowds and multiple life styles: Adolescents' perceptions of peer-group stereotypes. In R.E. Muuss (Ed.), *Adolescent behavior and society: A book of readings* (pp. 30–36). New York, NY: McGraw-Hill.

Brown, B.B., Mory, M.S., & Kinney, D. (1994). Casting adolescent crowds in a relational perspective: Caricature, channel, and context. In R. Montemayor, G.R. Adams, & T. Gullotta (Eds.), *Personal relationships during adolescence* (pp. 123–167). Thousand Oaks, CA: Sage.

Bukowski, W.M., Motzoi, C., & Meyer, F. (2009). Friendship as process, function, and outcome. In K.H. Rubin, W. Bukowski, & B. Laursen (Eds.), *Handbook of peer interactions, relationships, and groups* (pp. 217–231). New York, NY: Guilford Press.

Canaan, J. (1987). A comparative analysis of American suburban middle class, middle school, and high school teenage culture. In G. Spindler & L. Spindler (Eds.), *Interpretive ethnography of education: At home and abroad* (pp. 385–406). Hillsdale, NJ: Lawrence Erlbaum Associates.

Cillessen, A.H.N. (2009). Sociometric methods. In K.H. Rubin, W. Bukowski, & B. Laursen (Eds.), *Handbook of peer interactions, relationships, and groups* (pp. 82–99). New York, NY: Guilford Press.

Cillessen, A.H.N., & Marks, P.E.L. (2011). Conceptualizing and measuring popularity. In A.H.N. Cillessen, D. Schwartz, & L. Mayeux (Eds.), *Popularity in the peer system* (pp. 25–56). New York, NY: Guildford Press.

Cillessen, A.H.N., & Rose, A.J. (2005). Understanding popularity in the peer system. *Current Directions in Psychological Science, 14,* 102–105.

Cillessen, A.H.N., Schwartz, D., & Mayeux, L. (Eds.). (2011). *Popularity in the peer system.* New York, NY: Guildford Press.

Coie, J.D., Dodge, K.A., & Coppotelli, H. (1982). Dimensions and types of status: A cross-age perspective. *Developmental Psychology, 18,* 557–570.

Crick, N.R., Murray-Close, D., Marks, P.E.L., & Mohajeri-Nelson, N. (2009). Aggression and peer relationships in school-aged children: Relational and physical aggression in group and dyadic contexts. In K.H. Rubin, W. Bukowski, & B. Laursen (Eds.), *Handbook of peer interactions, relationships, and groups* (pp. 287–302). New York, NY: Guilford Press.

Cross, J.F., & Cross, J. (1971). Age, sex, race and the perception of facial beauty. *Developmental Psychology, 5,* 433–439.

de Bruyn, E.H., & Cillessen, A.H.N. (2006). Popularity in early adolescence: Prosocial and antisocial subtypes. *Journal of Adolescent Research, 21,* 607–627.

Dodd, W. (1767). Popularity: A thought from Shenstone. In *Poems by Dr. Dodd* (p. 190). London: D. Leach.

Dong, Q., Weisfeld, G., Boardway, R.H., & Shen, J. (1996). Correlates of social status among Chinese adolescents. *Journal of Cross-Cultural Psychology, 27*, 476–493.

Eder, D. (1995). *School talk: Gender and adolescent culture.* New Brunswick, NJ: Rutgers University Press.

Erlbach, A. (2003). *The middle school survival guide.* New York, NY: Walker.

Folsom, J.K. (1934). *The family: Its sociology and social psychiatry.* New York, NY: John Wiley & Sons.

French Jr, J.R.P., & Raven, B. (1959). The bases of social power. In D. Cartwright (Ed.), *Studies in social power* (pp. 150–167). Ann Arbor, MI: Institute for Social Research.

Goldman, W., & Lewis, P. (1977). Beautiful is good: Evidence that the physically attractive are more socially skilled. *Journal of Experimental Social Psychology, 13*, 125–130.

Gordon, C.W. (1957). *The social system of the high school.* Glencoe, IL: Free Press.

Holland, A., & Andre, T. (1995). Prestige ratings of high school extracurricular activities. *The High School Journal, 78*, 67–72.

Itani, J. (1961). The society of Japanese monkeys. *Japan Quarterly, 8*, 421–430.

Landy, D., & Sigall, H. (1974). Beauty is talent: Task evaluation as a function of the performer's physical attractiveness. *Journal of Personality and Social Psychology, 29*, 299–304.

Lippitt, R., Polansky, N., Redl, F., & Rosen, S. (1960). The dynamics of power. In D. Cartwright & A. Zander (Eds.), *Group dynamics* (2nd ed., pp. 745–765). Evanston, IL: Row, Peterson.

Merten, D.E. (1997). The meaning of meanness: Popularity, competition, and conflict among junior high school girls. *Sociology of Education, 70*, 175–191.

Milner, M. (2004). *Freaks, geeks, and cool kids.* New York, NY: Routledge.

Must I pet to be popular? (1932, January). *Ladies' Home Journal, 49*(1), 7, 84, 86.

Ostermeier, A.B., & Eicher, J.B. (1966). Acceptance of adolescent girls. *MSU Quarterly Bulletin, 48*, 431–436.

Parkhurst, J., & Hopmeyer, A. (1998). Sociometric popularity and peer-perceived popularity: Two distinct dimensions of peer status. *Journal of Early Adolescence, 18*, 135–144.

Pellegrini, A.D. (2002). Affiliative and aggressive dimensions of dominance and possible functions during early adolescence. *Aggression and Violent Behavior, 7*, 21–31.

Prinstein, M.J., & Cillessen, A.H.N. (2003). Forms and functions of adolescent peer aggression associated with high levels of peer status. *Merrill-Palmer Quarterly, 49*, 310–342.

Prinstein, M.J., Meade, C.S., & Cohen, G.L. (2003). Adolescent oral sex, peer popularity, and perceptions of best friends' sexual behavior. *Journal of Pediatric Psychology, 28*, 243–249.

Schwartz, G., & Merten, D. (1967). The language of adolescence: An anthropological approach to the youth culture. *American Journal of Sociology, 72*, 453–468.

Seligman, M.E.P., Parks, A.C., & Steen, T. (2005). A balanced psychology and a full life. In F. Huppert, N. Baylis, & B. Keverne (Eds.), *The science of well-being* (pp. 275–283). New York, NY: Oxford University Press.

Silk, J.B. (2002). Practice random acts of aggression and senseless acts of intimidation: The logic of status contests in social groups. *Evolutionary Anthropology, 11*, 221–225.

Snyder, E.E., & Spreitzer, E. (1987). Change and variation in the social acceptance of female participation in sports. In A. Yiannakis, T.D. McIntyre, M.J. Melnick, & D.P. Hart (Eds.), *Sport sociology: Contemporary themes* (3rd ed., pp. 133–137). Dubuque, IA: Kendell/Hunt.

Taunton, W.E. (1936). Popularity. *Oxford English prize essays* (Vol. 1, pp. 294–317). Oxford: D. A. Talboys.

Terry, R. (2000). Recent advances in measurement theory and the use of sociometric techniques. In A.H.N. Cillessen & W.M. Bukowski (Eds.), *Recent advances in the measurement of acceptence and rejection in the peer system. New directions for child and adolescent development* (Vol. 88, pp. 27–53). San Francisco, CA: Jossey-Bass.

Waller, W. (1938). *The family: A dynamic interpretation.* New York, NY: Dryden Press.

Wang, S.S., Houshyar, S., & Prinstein, M.J. (2006). Adolescent girls' and boys' weight-related health behaviors and cognitions: Associations with reputation- and preference-based peer status. *Health Psychology, 25*, 658–663.

Happiness and self-knowledge: A positive psychology and judgment and decision-making hybrid course

Jaime L. Kurtz

Department of Psychology, James Madison University, Harrisonburg, VA 22807, USA

This chapter describes an undergraduate positive psychology course that specifically focuses on the construct of happiness, or subjective well-being. Judgment and decision-making research is used to understand the processes involved in making decisions with the goal of promoting happiness. The course heavily focuses on methodology and recent empirical research. However, students are also given hands-on activities and are encouraged to consider the relationship between happiness, self-knowledge, and decision-making processes in their own lives.

As aptly noted by the economist March (1978), 'All decisions are based on a prediction of future tastes and feelings'. Implicit in this is the notion that decision making is inherently affective and relies on questions like, 'Will this make me happy?' and 'Will I like this better than the alternatives?'. Therefore, to be both applicable and comprehensive, a positive psychology course must at least give a nod to the question of how people make decisions. A course that goes beyond this, incorporating the literature on judgment and decision-making topics such as hedonic adaptation, affective forecasting, memory biases, and temporal construal, can lead to stimulating discussions about the nature of happiness, the feasibility of lasting happiness, and strategies one should adopt to live a happier life.

My upper-level undergraduate course, Happiness and Self-Knowledge, considers these questions by examining empirical research in social, cognitive, and positive psychology. At this time in their lives, students are on the verge of major life decisions: whether to go to graduate school or to enter the workforce; whether to seek novelty and excitement or comfort and familiarity; or whether to stay with a current romantic partner or open oneself up to future possibilities. Students may initially feel alone in these struggles and are surprised to see their existential questions recast in the form of empirical research on happiness and decision making. Below are two examples of the sort of accessible and applicable research discussed in this course.

The study of Schwartz (2004) on 'the paradox of choice' finds that, contrary to popular belief, having more choice options is often detrimental to good decision making. For example, most people would prefer to shop in a grocery store that has 20 different types of cereal rather than just five. However, choosing one cereal from an array of 20 is more difficult, and people tend to be less happy with the choice they eventually make. This is especially true for maximizers, who tend to seek out 'the best' and therefore find it difficult to manage a large array of choice options. This topic is consistently appealing to students. Most of them can readily call to mind examples of times when they maximized, be it in the college search process, while shopping for a new gadget, or in their dating lives. Some staunchly adhere to the belief that maximizing is a superior decision-making strategy, despite the research findings we discuss. This leads to fun and stimulating in-class discussions and hits on the disconnect between self-knowledge and effective decision making.

A second example comes from the hedonic adaptation literature (Brickman, Coates, & Janoff-Bulman, 1978; Diener, Lucas, & Napa Scollon, 2006), which states that, over time and through repeated exposure, people, places, and experiences that initially brought pleasure or pain gradually and naturally cease to do so. Once again, students can quickly get their minds around the concept of adaptation by reflecting on their arrival at college: the campus was so imposing, the array of extracurricular activities limitless, and their new freedom a source of constant excitement. However, those positive attributes quickly became a part of their everyday lives and ceased to bring them the constant pleasure they initially experienced.

While applying material to their own lives and learning to make better decisions are certainly favorable outcomes of this course, my primary objectives are to expose students to a wide variety of empirical research, teach them to critically read, to consider issues of measurement, to gain a deeper understanding of good methodology, and to improve their written and oral communication. The subject matter makes these goals more feasible, because the broad concepts we discuss are highly relatable and students tend to be intrinsically motivated by a desire to understand the nature of happiness.

Specific course structure

Judging by the list of publicly available syllabi available on the University of Pennsylvania's Positive Psychology Center website, most positive psychology courses take a different approach than mine, examining the emerging field more broadly and including topics such as strengths and virtues, optimism, creativity, spirituality, and resilience. My course is different from most positive psychology courses in that, rather than being an overview of positive psychology, I focus solely on the causes and correlates of *happiness*. This is partially for pragmatic reasons. Currently, there is little research at the intersection of decision making and other variables of interest within positive psychology (cf. Schwartz & Sharpe, 2006). However, I also focus primarily on happiness because there is sufficient research on the construct to allow for a semester-long, in-depth analysis.

Happiness and Self-Knowledge is divided into three broad units. The first, Conceptual and Methodological Background, begins with a presentation on the field of positive psychology with a particular emphasis on the nature of happiness, or subjective well-being (SWB). We consider whether happiness is a desirable goal and read the influential work of Fredrickson (2001) on the broaden-and-build model of positive emotions. We also devote a class to issues of measurement. Students take a variety of global, retrospective measures of SWB measures on their own, and then we discuss and contrast them with 'online' or momentary measures such as experience sampling (Csikszentmihalyi, 1990) and the Day Reconstruction Method (Kahneman, Krueger, Schkade, Schwarz, & Stone, 2004). We also discuss the specific biases inherent in self-reported global measures of SWB (Schwarz & Strack, 1999). This naturally leads to discussions of the nature of happiness, and how operationally defining and measuring it a certain way might lead to very different conclusions. This section lays a necessary groundwork

for the rest of the course, and the readings discussed here come up again and again in future weeks.

The second unit of the course, Challenges to Happiness, delves into topics related to decision making. We read and discuss the classic study of lottery winners and paraplegics (Brickman et al., 1978) and consider recent revisions to the hedonic treadmill argument (e.g. people do not always adapt to major life events such as divorce or unemployment; Diener et al., 2006). We transition into a discussion of affective forecasting (Wilson & Gilbert, 2005) and the reasons why we are often inaccurate at predicting our future feelings – one being that we fail to accurately anticipate adaptation. In this unit, we also discuss anticipated, experienced, and recalled emotional experience, and why the three do not always align. For example, we tend to recall certain types of experiences as more positive than they really were in the moment, which can certainly lead to suboptimal decision making when considering whether to do something similar in the future (Loewenstein, 1996; Mitchell, Thompson, Peterson, & Cronk, 1997; Wirtz, Kruger, Napa Scollon, & Diener, 2003). This topic nicely draws on the previous discussion of online *versus* global, retrospective measures of SWB. Another relevant topic, one that is a perennial favorite of students, is choice and maximizing tendencies, as described above (Schwartz, 2004). This unit also leads to interesting discussions on how to spend money and structure one's life to make it more likely to provide happiness (Csikszentmihalyi, 1990; Dunn, Aknin, & Norton, 2008). In fact, we end this unit with a discussion of this nature, before segueing into the final unit, Enhancing Happiness.

By this point in the course, there may be a feeling of pessimism about the likelihood of making any lasting changes to one's happiness. After all, if we do adapt to our life circumstances, inaccurately recall past affective experiences, and are so poor at anticipating our future emotional states, how can we hope to make choices that promote our future well-being? I counter these questions by beginning this third unit with the finding that it actually *is* possible to make sustainable increases in happiness, despite hedonic adaptation, memory biases, and other imperfections in the decision-making process (Lyubomirsky, Sheldon, & Schkade, 2005; Sheldon & Lyubomirsky, 2006). In the classes to follow, we discuss what has been shown to work. We consider social support and interpersonal relationships as key predictors of happiness (Myers, 1999; Putnam, 2000). We discuss the importance of life experiences rather than material possessions (Van Boven & Gilovich, 2003); and of mindsets such as flow (Csikszentmihalyi, 1990), mindfulness (Brown & Ryan, 2003), and appreciation (Emmons & McCullough, 2003). Having already discussed topics such as hedonic adaptation and memory biases, we can engage in engaging and informed discussions of why things like interpersonal relationships and exciting life experiences may be resistant to adaptation and more likely to promote lasting happiness. With a background in research on self-knowledge, discussions of these topics inevitably gravitate to questions like, 'Do people *know* that quality relationships are so central to happiness?', 'In the evenings, why do we often choose to passively watch TV rather than pursue an engrossing hobby, join a community organization or socialize with friends?' and 'Why do we choose to spend our money on material possessions rather than on rich life experiences?'

The course wraps up broadly, with a discussion of application and implications for public policy. For instance, if we are less than perfect at making decisions to promote happiness, and given that psychologists and economists have a wealth of knowledge about what actually *does* make people happy, is there a responsibility associated with this? Should happiness be a concern of policymakers, and exactly what measures should be taken to promote enhanced well-being? Thaler and Sunstein (2008) have recently stated that this body of research should be used by policy-makers to 'nudge' people to make decisions that maximize health and happiness, an argument that we discuss and debate. We also consider the argument of Diener and Seligman (2004) for directly measuring national indicators of well-being, rather than using *per capita* income as a proxy. This study can lead to broad discussions not only about the disconnect between happiness and income, and the idea of using happiness to inform public policy, but also about the responsibility of researchers and the relationship between academia and the world outside of it.

Journal assignments

In addition to more traditional assignments (e.g. a literature review and research proposal on an area of interest), before most classes, students are asked to complete a hands-on activity and corresponding journal assignment. These assignments are designed to help students apply the readings to their own lives. As mentioned above, early in the course, students are instructed to complete the Positive and Negative Affect Schedule (Watson, Clark, & Tellegen, 1988), the Subjective Happiness Scale (Lyubomirsky & Lepper, 1999), and the Satisfaction with Life Scale (Diener, Emmons, Larson, & Griffin, 1985) and comment on their results. They are also asked to reflect on how each measure operationally defines happiness, report which scale they think is the 'best', and suggest other ways in which psychologists could better measure happiness. This activity allows students to think about methodological and measurement issues while also learning about frequently used measures of

happiness, which we continue to discuss throughout the course.

As another example, for the class on affective forecasting, students are given the following prompt: 'Describe a time when you made an inaccurate affective forecast. Why do you think you were so inaccurate? Did you learn from the experience and avoid making a similar inaccurate forecast in the future? If yes, why? If no, why not?'

Early in the course, students design and attempt to live a perfect day (although they are somewhat limited by their schedules and circumstances). They write a reflection on this day. For the final journal assignment, they reflect on this perfect day and describe what they would change, given what they have learned in the course. This activity is certainly enjoyable. After all, students are granted the opportunity to create an optimally enjoyable experience, for a class assignment. However, it also reinforces what they have learned throughout the semester, and highlights particular lapses in self-knowledge. It also raises interesting points, such as the fact that constantly assessing happiness levels is actually detrimental to happiness, and its often better to just relax and 'go with the flow' (Schooler, Ariely, & Loewenstein, 2003).

Students are not required to share specifics of these assignments in class, but they are welcome to do so, and these real-life examples often provide a useful starting point for class discussions. Sometimes, they even lead to empirical questions that are extensions of the research read for the day's class.

Adapting the course

I have taught this class at both a large research university and a small liberal arts college. In both settings, students were primarily junior and senior undergraduates (ranging between 12 and 20 students) and the class size was small, which is important for creating a sense of interpersonal comfort and giving everyone a chance to participate. The course is generally thought of as a 'capstone', one of the final classes students take in the psychology major.

Ideally, the course will be taught using empirical journal articles as the primary reading material. However, for these articles to be read critically and understood in a way that allows for fruitful discussion, students should be fairly advanced in psychology major, having had courses in statistics and research methods. This is not essential, however, and the class could be adapted for less-advanced psychology majors and non-majors. This approach could rely primarily on popular books (e.g. Gilbert, 2007; Schwartz, 2004; Thaler & Sunstein, 2008) and the occasional brief research report. Also, although I did not give exams, they could easily be constructed.

Course evaluations and conclusions

Although I did not collect objective indicators of student learning, end-of-semester course evaluations indicate that students both greatly enjoyed and learned a good deal in this course. Averaging across multiple semesters, at a large research university, mean ratings on the item 'This course taught me a lot' were 4.54 ($SD = 0.55$), where $1 =$ poor and $5 =$ excellent. At a small liberal arts college, ratings were similar ($M = 4.67$, $SD = 0.55$). Representative, anonymous comments included, 'The course really challenged me to think carefully about social psychology concepts and applying them to the real world.' 'I learned a lot from this course that I can apply both to the study of psychology and to my everyday life. That, to me, is the mark of a great class.' 'I have never enjoyed a class more than this one, and this class has definitely helped me realize that I made a right decision in becoming a psychology major. I learned many things that I can apply to improve my life and other people's lives.' The class is extremely popular and has been enrolled to capacity every time it has been offered.

While it may lack the breadth of other positive psychology courses, this approach to studying happiness in the context of decision making has proven effective and interesting to students. The subject matter touches on or applies to various subfields of psychology, appealing to students who have a wide variety of interests within psychology (e.g. social, cognitive, clinical, and industrial-organizational). The course is also useful to students going on to research-oriented graduate programs, careers in counseling, or into business or industry. As an upper-level psychology course, it reinforces methodology and focuses on empirical research on a topic that is of particular interest to students. Finally, it exposes them to empirically validated techniques for enhancing decision making at a critical juncture in their lives.

References

Brickman, P., Coates, D., & Janoff-Bulman, R. (1978). Lottery winners and accident victims: Is happiness relative?. *Journal of Personality and Social Psychology, 36*, 917–927.

Brown, K.W., & Ryan, R.M. (2003). The benefits of being present: Mindfulness and its role in psychological well-being. *Journal of Personality and Social Psychology, 84*, 822–848.

Csikszentmihalyi, M. (1990). *Flow: The psychology of optimal experience*. New York, NY: Harper & Row.

Diener, E., Emmons, R.A., Larson, R.J., & Griffin, S. (1985). The satisfaction with life scale. *Journal of Personality Assessment, 49*, 71–75.

Diener, E., Lucas, R.E., & Napa Scollon, C. (2006). Beyond the hedonic treadmill: Revising the adaptation theory of well-being. *American Psychologist, 61*, 305–314.

Diener, E., & Seligman, M.E.P. (2004). Beyond money: Toward an economy of well-being. *Psychological Science in the Public Interest, 5*(1), 1–31.

Dunn, E.W., Aknin, L.B., & Norton, M.I. (2008). Spending money on others promotes happiness. *Science, 319*, 1687–1688.

Emmons, R.A., & McCullough, M.E. (2003). Counting blessing versus burdens: An experimental investigation of gratitude and subjective well-being in daily life. *Journal of Personality and Social Psychology, 84*, 377–389.

Fredrickson, B.L. (2001). The role of positive emotions in positive psychology: The broaden-and-build theory of positive emotions. *American Psychologist, 56*, 218–226.

Gilbert, D.T. (2007). *Stumbling on happiness*. New York, NY: Knopf.

Kahneman, D., Krueger, A.B., Schkade, D., Schwarz, N., & Stone, A.A. (2004). A survey method for characterizing daily life experiences: The day reconstruction method. *Science, 306*, 1776–1780.

Loewenstein, G. (1996). Out of control: Visceral influences on behavior. *Organizational Behavior and Human Decision Processes, 65*, 272–292.

Lyubomirsky, S., & Lepper, H.S. (1999). A measure of subjective happiness: Preliminary reliability and construct validation. *Social Indicators Research, 46*, 137–155.

Lyubomirsky, S., Sheldon, K.M., & Schkade, D. (2005). Pursuing happiness: The architecture of sustainable change. *Review of General Psychology, 9*, 111–131.

Mitchell, T.R., Thompson, L., Peterson, E., & Cronk, R. (1997). Temporal adjustment of the evaluation of events: The rosy view. *Journal of Experimental Social Psychology, 33*, 421–448.

Myers, D. (1999). Close relationships and the quality of life. In D. Kahneman, E. Diener, & N. Schwarz (Eds.), *Well-being: The foundations of hedonic psychology* (pp. 376–393). New York, NY: Russell Sage Foundation.

Putnam, R.D. (2000). *Bowling alone: The collapse and revival of American community*. New York, NY: Simon & Schuster.

Schooler, J.W., Ariely, D., & Loewenstein, G. (2003). The pursuit and assessment of happiness can be self-defeating. In I. Brocas & J.D. Carrillo (Eds.), *The psychology of economic decisions. Vol. 1: Rationality and well being* (pp. 41–70). New York, NY: Oxford University Press.

Schwartz, B. (2004). *The paradox of choice: Why more is less*. New York, NY: Ecco.

Schwartz, B., & Sharpe, K.E. (2006). Practical wisdom: Aristotle meets positive psychology. *Journal of Happiness Studies, 7*, 377–395.

Schwarz, N., & Strack, F. (1999). Reports of subjective well-being: Judgment processes and their methodological implications. In D. Kahneman, E. Diener, & N. Schwarz (Eds.), *Well-being: The foundations of hedonic psychology* (pp. 61–84). New York, NY: Russell Sage Foundation.

Sheldon, K.M., & Lyubomirsky, S. (2006). Achieving sustainable gains in happiness: Change your actions, not your circumstances. *Journal of Happiness Studies, 7*, 55–86.

Thaler, R.H., & Sunstein, C.R. (2008). *Nudge: Improving decisions about health, wealth, and happiness.* New Haven, CT: Yale University Press.

Van Boven, L., & Gilovich, T. (2003). To do or to have? That is the question. *Journal of Personality and Social Psychology, 85,* 1193–1202.

Watson, D., Clark, L.A., & Tellegen, A. (1988). Development and validation of brief measures of positive and negative affect: The PANAS scales. *Journal of Personality and Social Psychology, 54,* 1063–1070.

Wilson, T.D., & Gilbert, D.T. (2005). Affective forecasting: Knowing what to want. *Current Directions in Psychological Science, 14,* 131–134.

Wirtz, D., Kruger, J., Napa Scollon, C., & Diener, E. (2003). What to do on spring break? The role of predicted, on-line, and remembered experience in future choice. *Psychological Science, 14,* 520–524.

'Learning from success': A close look at a popular positive psychology course

Pninit Russo-Netzer[a] and Tal Ben-Shahar[b]

[a]Department of Counseling and Human Development, University of Haifa, Mount Carmel, Haifa 31905, Israel;
[b]Interdisciplinary Center (IDC), Herzliya, P.O. Box 167, Herzliya 46150, Israel

This article is a case study of an undergraduate course in positive psychology taught by Dr Tal Ben-Shahar. The course has been taught three times between 2004 and 2008 in the Department of Psychology at the Harvard University. It is currently being taught at the School of Psychology, 'Interdisciplinary Center', Herzliya (one of Israel's leading colleges), in both English and Hebrew. The course's main emphasis is on transformation rather than information, while exploring the main question: 'How can we help ourselves and others – individuals, communities, and society – to become happier?' The course was innovative in its content as well as in its teaching methods. When taught, it was the most popular course at Harvard with the largest attendance in the history of the psychology department – with enrollment reaching over 855 students (about one out of every seven undergraduate students). Understanding the uniqueness of this course could contribute to the development of teaching the popular and broad field of positive psychology at the undergraduate level and to varied populations.

Teaching positive psychology – The message and the messenger

The growing interest in positive psychology in academia has been demonstrated by the increasing number of courses and programs offered in leading universities and colleges worldwide at the undergraduate and graduate levels (e.g., Linley, Joseph, Harrington, & Wood, 2006; Seligman, Steen, Park, & Peterson, 2005). A large part of this phenomenon is rooted in the field's unique emphasis on the science of happiness, flourishing life, and well-being rather than on stress, trauma, and dysfunction (Keyes & Haidt, 2003). This science, which promotes 'that which makes life worthwhile', has the potential of building bridges, specifically between the 'Ivory Tower' and Main Street, i.e., practitioners, organizations, and the general public.

The objective of the course discussed in this case report emphasizes the importance of this potential to bridge the empirical foundation of academic research and the accessibility of the 'self-help' movement. Combining action and reflection, theory and practice, is especially important in an applied field such as positive psychology, aiming to implement principles and tools of positive human functioning and flourishing into practice in various professional domains – for individuals, groups, organizations, and society. Understanding the material is not enough. The message should be personally relevant to the life of the teacher as well as to that of his or her students. Furthermore, it has to motivate the students to actively practice the principles learned in their lives.

In order to achieve these goals, the course was constructed based on a cross-disciplinary selection of topics that are central and important psychological aspects of a fulfilling and flourishing life. This interdisciplinary and integrated approach is manifested in the incorporation of topics that are at the core of the positive psychology field (e.g., Carr, 2003), such as happiness, gratitude, flow, relationships, strengths, humor, mindfulness, and optimism, together with various topics that touch on other areas in the science of psychology but are relevant to the human pursuit for a life of meaning, fulfillment, and happiness (such as self-esteem, creativity, perfectionism, goal setting, and the mind–body connection). The integration of topics covered under the holistic umbrella of mind, body, and social environment and physical environment (Baylis, 2004) has the potential of contributing to a broader and enriched understanding of well-being and a thriving life.

We recommend that while constructing a positive psychology course, the instructor should take some time to reflect and engage in a personal process, applying the methodology of appreciative inquiry (AI; e.g., Cooperrider & Whitney, 2005) into personal values, vision, and mission. The AI method is based on the fact that questions tend to focus attention and therefore exploring and learning from past success and present potential ('what works'), both personal and others. This in turn enables inspiration and positive energy that may contribute to gaining more clarity on possible course goals and guiding principles that both the instructor and the students can benefit from. It is suggested that the process would include questions that cover aspects of content and method, such as:

> What are the things I've learned or done that had made me happy and contributed to my well-being? What have I learned from other teachers and courses I have taken? What was most meaningful for me? What did I want to learn as a student? What motivates me to teach this kind of course? What important messages do I want my students to remember from this class? If I could put together the class that I would have loved to have taken as a student, what would it look like and how can I construct it?

This guideline in constructing the course itself as a whole is congruent with the statement of Carl Rogers, 'What is most personal is most general', and Maslow's 'Knowledge of one's own deep nature is also simultaneously knowledge of human nature in general'. The passion derived from selecting the topics that are most relevant to the teacher, the kind of issues that he or she would have liked to study as a student, is contagious and attracts students. If the material relates to the teacher personally, it is more likely that other people, i.e., students, will also benefit from this, especially if the material presented is based upon personal experiences.

The importance of designing and exploring the contents covered in the course (the 'What') highlights the prominence of the teacher, the facilitator and the messenger of the message (the 'How'). How can the teacher be an effective messenger of that message? This article addresses the domain of positive psychology teaching methods in general, considering the course's 'building blocks' in particular. The objective of the teacher in this course is not merely to inform students about research in the field, but additionally to transform the way the students see the world. As Shakespeare said, 'There is nothing either good or bad, but thinking makes it so'. Happiness is very much about how we perceive the world.

We shall first present the pedagogical principles upon which the course is based. Next, we shall discuss the teacher's role as the facilitator of the materials in positive psychology, especially in view of their personal and sometimes intimate nature. Lastly, we shall propose some useful methods that were identified as effective teaching instruments and used in the course both in the United States and in Israel.

Pedagogical principles

The course's curriculum is mainly based upon a fundamental principle, namely the combination of *action and reflection.* The class is taught on two interconnected and yet distinct levels. The first level is similar to any other psychology class. Students read seminal academic papers and studies available in the field. They write papers that must be based upon academic research and they are tested in exams. However, there is also a second level that aims at encouraging application to their personal lives. The constant integration of these two levels emphasizes that a good theory is something that works in practice. As Alfred North Whitehead notes, 'The careful shielding of a university from the activities of the world around us is the best way to chill interest and to defeat progress. Celibacy does not suit a university. It must mate itself with action'.

Application is where *theory and practice* create a positive reinforcing spiral. For healthy growth, action must intertwine with reflection, acting upon our reflections and reflecting on our actions. Reflection as a self-analysis and meaning-making skill is considered to be a key component in learning (e.g., McKillop, 2005). Reflection is important, especially in a class such as positive psychology, where personal growth is a central concern both as part of the content studied in class and also for students' self-development, based on experience and implementation.

Works of Pennebaker and Seagal (1999) and King (2001) emphasize the importance of writing, specifically for increasing positive emotion. Based on the suggestions from King (2001) and others (e.g., Lyubomirsky, Sousa, & Dickerhoof, 2006), students are encouraged to keep an ongoing journal throughout the course, documenting personal experiences, aspirations, and goals, as well as issues that were added by the instructor, such as meaningful insights, personal failures, or challenges. Other than improving the students' well-being and personal development, reflection has the potential of improving retention. Active reflection is important to increase learning from experience (e.g., Keeton, Sheckley, & Griggs, 2002). Hence, it can make a significant difference both pedagogically and personally for the students.

In addition to the journals, students are required to complete experiential exercises, namely written response papers, every week throughout the course with the goal being to apply the material to their lives. The response papers are graded pass/fail, and students pass if they hand them in. The objective of these papers is to enable students to meaningfully experience the material first-hand and deepen their understanding and internalization. Integrating exercises that include intense reflection about ideas discussed in class and direct experience with key concepts as part of course requirements has the potential to enliven teaching and enrich learning. Reflection activities enable students to gain 'a sense of agency' (Eyler, 2002) and develop meta-cognitive skills. These promote active learning (Bransford, Brown, & Cocking, 2002) and empower the students to take responsibility for their own learning experience (A.Y. Kolb & D.A. Kolb, 2005). The method of structured reflection, aiming to foster connections between the material and practice, is one of the important dimensions constructing the response papers used in the course. Each response paper usually includes three parts: a personal reflection, an action component, and an open introspection in reference to the weekly reading list. The first part includes guided questions, instructions, or sentence completion, with the intention of providing the students with the opportunity to reflect on the subject or issue they have learned during the last week in class. The reflection is followed by exercises to put the ideas into practice in the students' lives, i.e., to explore different dimensions or aspects of the subject discussed in action and to report them – what they did and how it impacted them. The final part usually instructs the students to identify one 'pearl' from the weekly reading, i.e., an interesting idea, a useful tool, or an insightful comment/quote, and to write a couple of sentences about it at the end of the response paper.

The students indicated that they were intrinsically motivated to complete the assignments since they challenged them to address essential and relevant concerns in their personal lives and explore issues they care about. In some cases, it was the first time they were asked explicit questions concerning issues of self-development and growth, such as, what is really important for them or what they really would like to do with their lives. The opportunity to examine and explore values, experiences, beliefs, and worldviews regarding major life concerns, such as happiness, relationships, and success, can serve as a critical component of identity exploration, especially during emerging adulthood developmental stage (e.g., Arnett, 2000).

The final project integrates these processes based on the course's objective of bridging the Ivory Tower with Main Street. The students are required to prepare a 20–30 min PowerPoint presentation on any topic within the field of positive psychology. As modeled in the lectures throughout the course, the students' presentation should synthesize research-grounded information (based on empirical readings covered in class and additional resources) with accessibility and actionable messages (using stories, film excerpts,

exercises of their choice, etc.). The students are instructed that with research as the foundation, they can use their ideas and experiences creatively to illustrate their claims and make their presentation more effective and interesting. Each student is required to present his/her project to a group of at least four people they choose (friends, colleagues, students, employees, community members, etc.) before the project is due, who in turn complete a peer evaluation form for feedback following the presentation. The final project includes submission of the following components: a written text – the presentation script (10–15 pages), including references and one-page handout that was given to audience members concerning key points and suggestions for application; printed slides that were used in the presentation; and four completed evaluation forms and a one-page summary explaining how the student integrated the feedback received and lessons learned from the experience into the final project (which includes a broad description of the project's chosen topic, objectives, thesis, recommendations, etc.).

This assignment serves as a way of passing on the messages of positive psychology as well as a method of learning through teaching others (see e.g., Falchikov, 2001). The many diverse and innovative examples of ideas and presentations conducted by students reflected creativity and deep engagement in the process, indicating that the students were living the philosophy as they taught it. Also, many of the students chose to share their presentation, as well as ideas and insights, with broader circles beyond formal requirements.

The teacher

This section presents a two-part principle which can be seen as carrying complementary facets concerning the importance of the teacher to the learning process.

'*Know thyself*': Effective teaching is based upon knowing one's strengths and preferences, upon authenticity and integrity. As Palmer (1998) notes, 'Good teaching cannot be reduced to technique. Good teaching comes from the identity and the integrity of the teacher'. The emphasis implemented in the past few years on classroom technique, including the use of a board or PowerPoint, is important but not sufficient. Ultimately, the major issue is that the teacher must identify his/her strengths and his/her teaching style and preferences, both on the macro (e.g., seminar vs. lecture class) and micro levels (e.g., structured lesson vs. improvization). The teacher must ask himself/herself what are his/her strengths as a teacher? Is it being systematic point by point? Is it humor? Is it a one-on-one connection with students, as often happens in seminars? Buckingham and Clifton (2001) note,

'The real tragedy of life is not that each of us doesn't have enough strengths, it's that we fail to use the ones that we have'. In view of the unique and personal nature of the material taught in positive psychology courses, it is *important* that the teacher expresses his/her strengths, both for himself/herself and for the students' benefit.

Therefore, effective teaching emerges when there is passion, when it is most personal, when the teacher practices what he/she preaches, and when personal strengths are at play. Authenticity in teaching has been recognized as a significant concept with respect to learning and development in both teachers and students and has been found to be associated with encouraging a genuine dialog and reflections on ideas that matter, especially at the higher education level (Kreber, Klampfleitner, McCune, Bayne, & Knottenbelt, 2007). Another meaningful side of authenticity in teaching is the importance of exposing oneself, of sometimes climbing out of one's 'comfort zone' in front of a class. The more the teacher can bring of himself/herself to the classroom, the more effective the material transmitted will be.

'Modeling the way': In order to be an effective and influential teacher, he/she must serve as a role model, to show the way. Benjamin Franklin noted that 'Well done is better than well said', and Ralph Waldo Emerson remarked that 'What you do speaks so loudly that I cannot hear what you say'. The integration of the message with the messenger cannot be over-emphasized. A teacher makes an impact when he/she is authentic and not trying to live up to an image. This theme is especially evident in research on emotional and behavioral contagion (e.g., Barsade, 2002; Johnson, 2008). Furthermore, it has been found that mood contagion is one of the psychological mechanisms by which charismatic leaders influence followers (Bono & Ilies, 2006). A leader's mood can influence a group's mood, its affective tone and group processes (Sy, Côté, & Saavedra, 2005). The leader, or the teacher, creates the climate in a classroom, and therefore, if one wants to create motivation and passion, one must be motivated and passionate.

There is a story about Mahatma Gandhi that is told in class which exemplifies this theme. A woman in India came to Mahatma Gandhi and asked for his help with her child, who was eating too much sugar. The Mahatma asked the mother to come back with her child after a month. When they returned Gandhi said to the child 'Stop eating too much sugar!' to which the child agreed. The mother, curious and frankly baffled, asked Gandhi why he had asked them to return after a month, why could not he have just said that when they first came. Gandhi responded: 'A month ago I was eating too much sugar'. In other words, he first had to undergo the change in himself that he wanted to see in the child – to stop eating too much sugar, to set an example. Gandhi's saying 'Be the change you want to see in the world' reflects the essence of this story. A teacher who wants to influence and effect a change in the classroom and among students must begin with himself/herself by cultivating those characteristics he/she wants to see in the classroom and in the students. Research by McNeese-Smith (1997) shows that if leaders want to be effective, they must exemplify the behavior they want to see. If they want excellence, they must exemplify it. If they want an ethical organization, they must first be ethical themselves. Throughout the course, the instructor demonstrates the different ideas presented in class. For example, modeling the idea of enjoying the learning process rather than merely the final goal or emphasizing that as his students, he also experiences failures that are a natural part of being human, enabling students to identify with him and learn from his personal stories about their own lives.

This theme concurs with the importance of teaching and learning as an active process, using first-hand experiences and in-class activities, aiming to encourage students to connect with the material through application. In conclusion, leading by example, being a role model for students and an effective messenger for the material requires authenticity, knowing oneself, and exemplifying the behavior one wants to see in others. It must become personal to be effective, both for the teacher and for the students.

Methods used in the course

The following section explores the methods used in the course which were identified as effective teaching instruments both at Harvard and in Israel.

Use of media

The message, the material, is presented through the use of diverse and eclectic media to cater to multiple levels of intelligence and to different learning methods. Building on Gardner's (1983) work, it is important to address multiple intelligence levels of students as it allows them to both use their own strengths and enhance their ability to learn, thereby finding personal meaning in their studies, especially at the higher education level (e.g., Barrington, 2004). *Music* is a critical component of the course's format. Every class has a theme song (For instance, 'I am what I am' by Gloria Gaynor or 'I did it my way' by Frank Sinatra for a class on self-esteem; 'I hope you dance' by Lee Ann Womack or 'Make your own music' by the Mamas & Papas for a class on self-concordant goals; 'When you're smiling' by Louis Armstrong for a class on emotional contagion; 'Man in the mirror' by Michael Jackson for a class on change). There are a few reasons why it is beneficial to include music as part of the course, and why a class should start with a piece of music. Firstly, although not all kinds of music induce positive emotions (see Bushman & Huesmann, 2006 for review), our experience showed that selecting specific types of music played at adequate contexts throughout the course arouses positive emotions (Lenton & Martin, 1991) which, based on the 'broaden-and-build' theory (Fredrickson, 2001), can lead to creativity and more openness to the material. It can create a positive atmosphere in the classroom and improve the students' mood, making them ready to absorb information and knowledge. Secondly, in accordance with the work on priming effect (e.g., Bargh & Chartrand, 2000; Bargh, Chen, & Burrows, 1996), beginning a class with the use of certain words in a song about relationships, for instance, words about love or about togetherness, might arouse interest and generate certain emotions which can be associated with the topic of the material being taught in that specific class. Indeed, music and lyrics were found to have the potential of influencing human behavior (e.g., North & Hargreaves, 2008). For example, an exposure to prosocial songs was found to be associated with a significant increase in tipping behavior (Jacob, Guéguen, & Boulbry, 2010). Furthermore, single young women exposed to romantic songs complied with a dating solicitation more readily than women exposed to neutral songs (Guéguen, Jacob, & Lamy, 2010). The third reason for using music has to do with retention. It was evident, from numerous students' accounts following the course, that songs played in the class served as an auditory trigger for them, which made them think back to optimism, to flow, to change, so that the class and its contents stayed with them for much longer.

Another effective tool which engages the students through the induction of positive emotions and results in better retention is *humor*. Humor helps to relieve tension, allows sensitive topics to be discussed, and reduces social distance (Smith & Powell, 1988). Also, the use of humor with medium diversity throughout the course makes it possible to deal with the short attention span of the 'click generation' and keeps students alert and involved. It is important to note that the use of humor does not necessarily mean that a teacher who has trouble getting the students to laugh has to learn to use this powerful tool himself/herself. Humor can also be 'imported' using technology. For example, funny videos excerpts (from TV, movies, commercials, etc.) can thus be shown in class. As a rule of thumb, the course uses one or two humorous videos in every class.

Stories, quotes, and metaphors

To vividly exemplify the material taught, the course uses various forms of excerpts and stories extensively. People naturally think and define themselves through *stories* as a way to grasp the world and make sense of it (e.g., McAdams, 2001). The effectiveness of stories is rooted in the powerful way they represent and convey complex, multi-dimensional ideas, making the message better understood and remembered. As a collective art, stories make it possible to broaden understanding in meaningful and relevant ways and therefore can be used as a highly efficient instructional tool (Kaye & Jacobson, 1999). Furthermore, they are more convincing than statistics (e.g., Martin & Powers, 1983) and bear the potential of moving people much more than theories because they engage emotions (e.g., Denning, 2002), which in turn can lead to movement and an impetus to act.

Stories form an important part of every class when teaching positive psychology topics, regardless of whether they are personal stories or stories about other people. Each of the topics discussed in the course includes presenting a story as an introduction to research on the topic, followed by an application. In other words, the story 'sets the stage' for a study or a theory, which in turn leads to action – the implications of the ideas presented and how they can be implemented in 'real-life'. It is important to tell stories that will inspire the students, move them and enable them to better remember the material. Stories can also bring research to life. There are some experiments that are interesting stories by themselves – for example, the experiment of Pygmalion in the classroom (Rosenthal & Jacobson, 1968) that can be used to exemplify the importance of beliefs as self-fulfilling prophecies.

Personal stories or biographies bring out emotions because they humanize a subject, make something feel real rather than remain abstract. Marva Collins' story, for example, can illustrate the importance of role models, agency, and expectations for positive development, whereas Roger Bannister's four-minute-mile story may inspire a discussion on positive priming and self-efficacy theory (Bandura, 1997). It is easier to grasp and relate to a story about a person rather than to statistics and large numbers. As the Soviet dictator Joseph Stalin, who put this to bad use, said, 'One is a tragedy and millions are a statistic'. Stories make theories and numbers come alive. Another important form of communicating messages vividly is the use of *metaphors and quotes*. The power of metaphors and analogies has long been recognized by philosophers and poets (Weick, 2003). Historically, metaphors have been used in clinical psychology in order to help clients access intuitive and unconscious material (e.g., Jung, 1961), and are increasingly considered to be an important factor in promoting changes in a patient during psychotherapy (Martin, Cummings, & Hallberg, 1992). Research, especially in the field of leadership, shows that the most effective leaders, in politics or business, use rhetorical imagery such as metaphors (e.g., Hartog & Verburg, 1997; Milward, 2007). Metaphors appeal to the listener's diverse senses, engage emotions, imagination, creative thinking, and values, all of which act to maintain the vividness of the experience (Conger, 1989).

Throughout the course, quotes are repeated extensively as metaphors. For example, when the importance of resilience in face of adversity or failures is studied, Edison is quoted saying, 'I failed my way to success'. The same method is used when teaching the idea of the 'hedonic treadmill' which suggests that people adapt rapidly to positive changes in their surroundings and soon return to their baseline levels of happiness (e.g., Brickman, Coates, & Janoff-Bulman, 1978; Gilbert, Pinel, Wilson, Blumberg, & Wheatley, 1998; Kahneman, 1999). To highlight this idea that good and bad events temporarily affect happiness (Diener, Lucas, & Scollon, 2006), the message that is repeated over and over again is that 'Happiness depends more on our state of mind rather than on our status or the state of our bank account'. By the end of the semester students remember this message.

Making it personal

As stated above, the course deals first and foremost with issues that relate personally to the students' lives. Alongside with introspection, reflections, response papers, and application on the students' part, the personal nature of the material is also reflected onto the teacher. By sharing personal examples, telling personal stories, the teacher can create a deeper connection between himself/herself and students. Another important aspect of personalizing the material is the use of experiential demonstrations of the material throughout the course. This method is powerful because it allows the students to experience first-hand the benefits of the tool or practice that is being taught. For example, at the beginning of a class on mindfulness, the students are led through a few minutes of meditation. Subsequently, they are exposed to research on the benefits of meditation. At a class concerning the permission to be human, the students are instructed to visualize an experience from their past in which they gave themselves the permission to be human, and to reflect on their feelings following the experience. Afterwards, students are asked to imagine how they can bring more of these qualities and insights to their lives today.

The class, while drawing on personal anecdotes, using music, and other 'fun' means, is still rigorous and based on scientific evidence. It is important to keep in mind that most people have their personal views and opinions about happiness and are reluctant to let go of these even when they encounter conflicting empirical evidence. The class, therefore, whether through lectures, sections, and readings, emphasizes that what distinguishes positive psychology from the field of self-help is precisely the reliance on science. In other words, personal views and opinions can provide a starting point, the beginning of the inquiry process, however the gate keeper protecting the field must be rigorous research and evaluation.

Rituals

Lastly, since the course aims to bring about positive change, a transformation in the students' lives, it is important to be aware of a phenomenon known as 'the honeymoon effect' (e.g., Goleman, Boyatzis, & McKee, 2002). This occurs after the students have been inspired by a lecture; they become excited and want to make a difference, to make a change in their personal lives and environment. Very soon after the 'honeymoon effect' wears off, they go back to their base level of excitement. The issue is how to teach students to make a significant difference in their lives, a difference that can yield a lasting change that reaches beyond the 'honeymoon phase'. Here again, the key is combining both action and reflection. According to Locke and Latham (1984) and Baumeister, Bratslavsky, Muraven, and Tice (1998), the key to lasting change lies in distancing the students from the need for self-discipline or control, which is a limited resource, and instead create rituals. Students learn to set precise goals and ritualize activities in order to arrive at a routine. John Dryden, a British poet said, 'We first make our habits, and then our habits make us'. The key is to create positive rituals in the students' lives through their own choices and goals, whether it is a ritual of keeping a gratitude journal, a ritual of meditation, a ritual of exercising at particular times every week, or a ritual of spending time with family and friends.

Unique challenges and summary

This article has addressed various concerns regarding the construction and formation of a positive psychology course in higher education, using a popular course as a case study. The course under discussion consists of a combination of research, which looks at a phenomenon indirectly by studying people, and a search which looks at a phenomenon directly through introspection. Many of the students' evaluations remarked that the course had changed their lives for the better. In an attempt to unlock the course's 'success code', it can perhaps be suggested that several factors combined together to explain its popularity. The material's relevance and importance to the students' lives and well-being, facilitated by accessible and practical tools along with a supportive and holding environment, are of special importance considering the variety of stressors students face during college life, including academic pressure and multiple demands (e.g., Kadison & DiGeronimo, 2004). Striving for a happier and balanced life, not as one of the many goals to be obtained in the future, but as a legitimate and meaningful state to be in the present, may present a unique challenge, especially at a demanding and high-achieving university like Harvard. Recent growing concerns regarding mental health problems among university students, such as depression and anxiety (e.g., Eisenberg, Gollust, Golberstein, & Hefner, 2007), may clarify this urgent need to address issues, such as personal well-being and self-fulfillment.

By using the methods described above, the teacher was able to meet the challenges of teaching intimate issues in large, crowded classes. As mentioned previously, an important part of the course was based on writing a journal, as proposed by Pennebaker and Seagal (1999) and King (2001); this assignment facilitates the absorption of the materials in the students' lives, especially when there is a large crowd of students. Hence, regardless of class size, personally engaging students in the material through exercises and journal writing seems to contribute to their experience, growth, retention, and depth of understanding.

Another important method used was that of dividing the class into sections where groups of 20 students met with a teaching assistant (graduate students and professional group moderators) for one weekly hour to discuss the material taught in the course. These group sections formed an integral part of the class, enabling students to discuss and better understand ideas from lectures and readings as well as sharing experiences from the response papers. The sections also included exercises and activities in order to get the students to practice and apply key concepts from the course. The activities were chosen from varied lecture topics based on the criteria that they could be easily done by students over a week, appropriate for a class setting. These activities stretched the students to take some risks outside of their 'comfort zones' but were not too emotionally challenging or risky. Some activities took place outside the classroom setting, according to the topic's characteristics. For example, in a section concerning mindfulness, to give the students a more comprehensive experience of the concept taught, they were encouraged to go outside and find private reminders or signs for personal well-being by association and to share them with the group. The message was that lessons are all around us, hidden in a flower, person, etc., likewise a sign 'Park Here' can be used as a reminder to relax,

to be present; a stop sign, to slow down; a flower, to experience the beauty in the smallest things.

The use of dyadic interactions or working in small groups is an important tool in a large classroom, especially when personal and intimate issues are concerned. The joint work, both in group sections and in lectures, allowed sharing ideas, insights, and feelings with one another regarding the relevance of the material to their lives. For example, during a class on gratitude and learning to focus on the positive (being a 'benefit finder' rather than a 'fault finder'), each student turned to a classmate to share something that he/she was grateful for, as well as share different situations from their own lives using the 'benefit finder' point of view. Conversational learning enables integration of thinking and feeling, talking and listening, and recognizing individuality and relatedness (A.Y. Kolb & D.A. Kolb, 2005). From students' accounts and feedback, it seems evident that working in small-group sections, along with online communications (through emails and the course website) enabled them not only the opportunity for intensive application, but also to foster relationships building and positive social connection that may serve as a valuable support system and a contributor to the their well-being, especially as undergraduate students during their first years of higher education.

It is important to note that the exact same course was taught both at Harvard and in Israel, with the same success, both in terms of the numerous students enrolled (relatively to the department's size) and in students' responses and evaluations. In Israel, the course is taught using the same syllabus, slides, and exercises, both in English (for a foreign students program) and in Hebrew (for Israeli students). Its vast impact was manifested in the different programs the students in Israel independently initiated based on the course, aiming for contribution to their community. A few examples of these projects are programs for at-risk population in different cities, an intervention program in Sderot for children living under the fear of attacks, and a program for sick children in hospitals.

Furthermore, the same ideas were also taught in Asia, Africa, Australia, and Europe with very few modifications. The essential ideas, principles, and methods were the same across different cultures and countries. As stated, the material taught included issues that are relevant to people's lives in different cultures, emphasizing the study and exploration of the self, both theoretically based on research and experientially through exercises and application.

In other words, while cultural differences are important to understand and are certainly very real and relevant to the study of happiness in terms of emotion expressions (e.g., Kuppens, Realo, & Diener, 2008), orientations (individualism/

collectivism), or motivations (e.g., Oishi & Diener, 2001), similarities, regardless of whether they are superficial or profound, are more pronounced than differences. The 'big developmental theories' (such as those of Freud, Erikson, Piaget, etc.) are based upon their basic premise regarding universal human nature (e.g., Rutter & Rutter, 1992). Likewise, whereas different cultures can highlight different values or have different elements that they find meaningful, pleasurable, and engaging as major components defining one's happiness (Seligman, 2002), the essence is the same – people inherently want to be happy and strive to live a flourishing life. Uchida, Norasakkunkit, and Kitayama (2004) note that although happiness and well-being were found to be 'significantly grounded in socio-cultural modes and contexts, it certainly does not deny universal underpinnings of happiness and well-being' (p. 235). For example, Australians or Americans may experience more flow when engaging in individualistic activities, while in Kenya or in China, for instance, people may find more flow engaging in group or communal activities. Nevertheless, attaining happiness, in its different and broad manifestations, represents a core human, universal, goal that is not necessarily restricted to specific circumstances or events.

In sum, the topics contained in the field of positive psychology which address a person's pursuit of fulfillment and happiness, concerns that are inherent to human nature, have potential for personal growth as well as scholarly development. It is possible to bridge theory and practice and action and reflection by exploring the self as well as the material. The course discussed in this article puts a prominent emphasis on the personal–experiential aspect of learning, enabling transformation along with information, based on a premise that to study psychology and to forgo studying the self, is to forgo the most important source of truth available to us. It is, to our understanding, the key to learning not only positive psychology – but human psychology in general. Accordingly, it can be stated that in order to teach materials as unique as positive psychology effectively at the higher education level, one must address both the message and the messenger. It is our hope that the principles and methods presented in this article and acquired from the experience of the course will contribute to broadening the resources available for teaching in the developing field of positive psychology at the undergraduate level and beyond.

References

Arnett, J.J. (2000). Emerging adulthood: A theory of development from the late teens through the twenties. *American Psychologist, 55*, 469–480.

Bandura, A. (1997). *Self-efficacy: The exercise of control.* New York, NY: Freeman.

Bargh, J.A., & Chartrand, T.L. (2000). The mind in the middle: A practical guide to priming and automaticity research. In H.T. Reis & C.M. Judd (Eds.), *Handbook of research methods in social and personality psychology* (pp. 253–285). New York, NY: Cambridge University Press.

Bargh, J.A., Chen, M., & Burrows, L. (1996). Automaticity of social behavior: Direct effects of trait construct and stereotype activation in action. *Journal of Personality and Social Psychology, 71*, 230–244.

Barrington, E. (2004). Teaching to student diversity in higher education: How multiple intelligence theory can help. *Teaching in Higher Education, 9*, 421–434.

Barsade, S.G. (2002). The ripple effect: Emotional contagion and its influence on group behavior. *Administrative Science Quarterly, 47*, 644–675.

Baumeister, R.F., Bratslavsky, E., Muraven, M., & Tice, D.M. (1998). Ego depletion: Is the active self a limited resource? *Journal of Personality and Social Psychology, 74*, 1252–1265.

Baylis, N. (2004). Teaching positive psychology. In P.A. Linley & S. Joseph (Eds.), *Positive psychology in practice* (pp. 210–217). Hoboken, NJ: Wiley & Sons.

Bono, J.E., & Ilies, R. (2006). Charisma, positive emotions and mood contagion. *The Leadership Quarterly, 17*, 317–334.

Bransford, J.D., Brown, A.L., & Cocking, R.R. (2002). *How people learn: Brain, mind and experience and school.* Washington, DC: National Academy Press.

Brickman, P., Coates, D., & Janoff-Bulman, R. (1978). Lottery winners and accident victims: Is happiness relative?. *Journal of Personality and Social Psychology, 36*, 917–927.

Buckingham, M., & Clifton, D.O. (2001). *Now, discover your strengths.* New York, NY: Free Press.

Bushman, B.J., & Huesmann, L.R. (2006). Short-term and long-term effects of violent media on aggression in children and adults. *Archives of Pediatrics and Adolescent Medicine, 160*, 348–352.

Carr, A. (2003). *Positive psychology: The science of happiness and human strengths.* London: Brunner-Routledge.

Conger, J.A. (1989). *The charismatic leader: Behind the mystique of exceptional leadership.* San-Francisco, CA: Jossey-Bass.

Cooperrider, D.L., & Whitney, D. (2005). *Appreciative inquiry: A positive revolution in change.* San Francisco, CA: Berrett-Koehler Publishers.

Denning, S. (2002). The narrative lens: Storytelling in 21st century organizations. *Knowledge Directions, 3*, 92–101.

Diener, E., Lucas, R.E., & Scollon, C.N. (2006). Beyond the hedonic treadmill: Revising the adaptation theory of well-being. *American Psychologist, 61*, 305–314.

Eisenberg, D., Gollust, S.E., Golberstein, E., & Hefner, J.L. (2007). Prevalence and correlates of depression, anxiety, and suicidality among university students. *American Journal of Orthopsychiatry, 77*, 534–542.

Eyler, J. (2002). Reflection: linking service and learning – linking students to communities. *Journal of Social Issues, 58*, 517–534.

Falchikov, N. (2001). *Learning together: Peer tutoring in higher education.* London: Routledge-Falmer.

Fredrickson, B.L. (2001). The role of positive emotions in positive psychology: The broaden-and-build theory of positive emotions. *American Psychologist, 56*, 218–226.

Gardner, H. (1983). *Frames of mind: The theory of multiple intelligences.* New York, NY: Basic Books.

Gilbert, D.T., Pinel, E.C., Wilson, T.D., Blumberg, S.J., & Wheatley, T.P. (1998). Immune neglect: A source of durability bias in affective forecasting. *Journal of Personality and Social Psychology, 75,* 617–638.

Goleman, D., Boyatzis, R., & McKee, A. (2002). *Primal leadership: Realizing the power of emotional intelligence.* Boston, MA: Harvard Business School Press.

Guéguen, N., Jacob, C., & Lamy, L. (2010). 'Love is in the air': Effects of songs with romantic lyrics on compliance with a courtship request. *Psychology of Music, 38,* 303–307.

Hartog, D.N.D., & Verburg, R.M. (1997). Charisma and rhetoric: Communicative techniques of international business leaders. *The Leadership Quarterly, 8,* 355–391.

Jacob, C., Guéguen, N., & Boulbry, G. (2010). Effects of songs with prosocial lyrics on tipping behavior in a restaurant. *International Journal of Hospitality Management, 29,* 761–763.

Johnson, S.K. (2008). I second that emotion: Effects of emotional contagion and affect at work on leader and follower outcomes. *The Leadership Quarterly, 19*(1), 1–19.

Jung, C. (1961). *Memories, dreams, reflections.* New York, NY: Vintage Books.

Kadison, R., & DiGeronimo, T.F. (2004). *College of the overwhelmed: The campus mental health crisis and what to do about it.* San Francisco, CA: Jossey-Bass.

Kahneman, D. (1999). Objective happiness. In D. Kahneman, E. Diener, & N. Schwarz (Eds.), *Well-being: The foundations of hedonic psychology* (pp. 3–25). New York, NY: Russell Sage Foundation.

Kaye, B., & Jacobson, B. (1999). True tales and tall tales. *Training and Development, 53,* 44–52.

Keeton, M.T., Sheckley, B.G., & Griggs, J.K. (2002). *Efficiency and effectiveness in higher education.* Dubuque, IA: Kendall/Hunt Publishing Company.

Keyes, C.L.M., & Haidt, J. (Eds.). (2003). *Flourishing: Positive psychology and the life well-lived.* Washington, DC: American Psychological Association.

King, L.A. (2001). The health benefits of writing about life goals. *Personality and Social Psychology Bulletin, 27,* 798–807.

Kolb, A.Y., & Kolb, D.A. (2005). Learning styles and learning spaces: Enhancing experiential learning in higher education. *Academy of Management Learning and Education, 4,* 193–212.

Kreber, C., Klampfleitner, M., McCune, V., Bayne, S., & Knottenbelt, M. (2007). What do you mean by "Authentic"? A comparative review of the literature on conceptions of authenticity in teaching. *Adult Education Quarterly, 58,* 22–43.

Kuppens, P., Realo, A., & Diener, E. (2008). The role of positive and negative emotions in life satisfaction judgment across nations. *Journal of Personality and Social Psychology, 95,* 66–75.

Lenton, S.R., & Martin, P.R. (1991)The contribution of music vs instructions in the musical mood induction procedure*Behavioral Research Therapy 29,* 623–625.

Linley, P.A., Joseph, S., Harrington, S., & Wood, A.M. (2006). Positive psychology: Past, present and (possible) future. *The Journal of Positive Psychology, 1,* 3–16.

Locke, E.A., & Latham, G.P. (1984). *Goal setting: A motivational technique that works.* Englewood Cliffs, NJ: Prentice-Hall.

Lyubomirsky, S., Sousa, L., & Dickerhoof, R. (2006). The costs and benefits of writing, talking, and thinking about life's triumphs and defeats. *Journal of Personality and Social Psychology, 90,* 692–708.

Martin, J., Cummings, A.L., & Hallberg, E.T. (1992). Therapists' intentional use of metaphor: Memorability, clinical impact, and possible epistemic/motivational functions. *Journal of Consulting and Clinical Psychology, 60,* 143–145.

Martin, J., & Powers, M. (1983). Truth or corporate propaganda: The value of a good war story. In L. Pondy, P. Frost, G. Morgan, & T.C. Dandridge (Eds.), *Organizational symbolism* (pp. 93–107). Greenwich, CT: JAI Press.

McAdams, D.P. (2001). The psychology of life stories. *Review of General Psychology, 5,* 100–122.

McKillop, C. (2005). *Storytelling grows up: Using storytelling as a reflective tool in higher education.* Paper presented at the Scottish Educational Research Association conference (SERA 2005), November 24–26, Perth, Scotland.

McNeese-Smith, D. (1997). The influence of manager behavior on nurses' job satisfaction, productivity, and commitment. *Journal of Nursing Administration, 27,* 47–55.

Milward, R.E. (2007). Leaders understand the power of words. *Journal of Leadership Studies, 1,* 81–83.

North, A.C., & Hargreaves, D.J. (2008). *The social and applied psychology of music.* Oxford: Oxford University Press.

Oishi, S., & Diener, E. (2001). Goals, culture, and subjective well-being. *Personality and Social Psychology Bulletin, 27,* 1674–1682.

Palmer, P.J. (1998). *The courage to teach.* San Francisco, CA: Jossey-Bass.

Pennebaker, J.W., & Seagal, J.D. (1999). Forming a story: The health benefits of narrative. *Journal of Clinical Psychology, 55,* 1243–1254.

Rosenthal, R., & Jacobson, L. (1968). *Pygmalion in the classroom: Teacher expectation and pupils' intellectual development.* New York, NY: Holt, Rinehart & Winston.

Rutter, M., & Rutter, M. (1992). *Developing minds.* London: Penguin Books.

Seligman, M.E.P. (2002). *Authentic happiness.* New York, NY: Free Press.

Seligman, M.E.P., Steen, T.A., Park, N., & Peterson, C. (2005). Positive psychology progress: Empirical validation of Interventions. *American Psychologist, 60,* 410–421.

Smith, C.M., & Powell, L. (1988). The use of disparaging humor by group leaders. *The Southern Speech Communication Journal, 53,* 279–292.

Sy, T., Côté, S., & Saavedra, R. (2005). The contagious leader: Impact of the leader's mood on the mood of group members, group affective tone, and group processes. *Journal of Applied Psychology, 90,* 295–305.

Uchida, Y., Norasakkunkit, V., & Kitayama, S. (2004). Cultural construction of happiness: Theory and empirical evidence. *Journal of Happiness Studies, 5,* 223–239.

Weick, C.W. (2003). Out of context: Using metaphor to encourage creative thinking in strategic management courses. *Journal of Management Education, 27,* 323–343.

An experiential approach to teaching positive psychology to undergraduates

Robert Biswas-Diener[a] and Lindsey Patterson[b]

[a]Positive Acorn and Portland State University, Portland, Oregon, USA; [b]Department of Psychology, Portland State University, Portland, Oregon, USA

Positive psychology is not only a science, but an applied science as well. As such, the undergraduate classroom can act as a laboratory in which students can personally experience the interventions associated with this field. In this article, we argue that an experiential approach to teaching positive psychology is, potentially, the most impactful form of instruction for this subject. We provide examples of how to increase experiential learning including syllabus development, creating practical assignments, and using course relevant technology.

Teaching positive psychology to undergraduates

Positive psychology is a topic of increasing interest. The enthusiasm for this subject can also be seen in the proliferation of undergraduate university courses on positive psychology. To date, most positive psychology courses offered at the undergraduate level are the creations of their respective instructors. Surprisingly, there have been few platforms that support professional discussion about the best methods for teaching positive psychology. In this article, we outline important issues relevant to the teaching of positive psychology at the undergraduate level including: experiential teaching, the strategic use of assignments, and the use of technology to augment teaching.

What makes good teaching? A case for experiential teaching

Kolb and Kolb (2005) developed the highly utilized model of education called the experiential learning cycle which views learning as a holistic, transactional process that includes continual re-learning and conflict resolution between different ways to see the world. Through the learning cycle, social knowledge is translated into personal knowledge. In their model of education, experience plays a key role in understanding the subject matter. As students learn about a particular topic, they compare information presented to them to concrete experience. This experience initiates a process of reflective observation, reconciling the differences between the information and the experience. Following reflection, students create their own hypotheses about

the way in which the information can be applied. Finally, students take these hypotheses to the test, actively evaluating the applicability and truth to the subject matter. The cycle continues with re-evaluation based again on concrete experiences. In this way, knowledge is created by the learner through continual interactions between experience, reflection, and action. Experiential learning can result in a kind of information that can be more easily remembered and utilized by the learner because it is now in the form of personal knowledge or information that has already been experienced, understood, and applied by the learner.

The experiential learning cycle described by Kolb and Kolb (2005), as well as its variations, is highly relevant to positive psychology. Unlike more specialized branches of science, such as the study of molds or research on the properties of electrons, positive psychology deals with everyday human concerns – such as hope and happiness – that affect everyone. This means that students universally have real-world experience with the topics common to positive psychology courses, and therefore have an observable and experiential personal framework with which to understand the information presented in class. Further, much of positive psychology concerns emotion, especially the experience of positive emotion. This means that one of the topics of learning in positive psychology courses can also be one of the vehicles of learning, given an experiential approach to teaching that harnesses the emotional experience of students.

Research on information processing suggests that moods and emotions play an important role in learning.

For instance, it has been found that negative moods can negatively impact an individual's attention span, schematic coding of information, acquisition of information, short- and long-term memory recall, and response to stimuli (Isen, 1987; Hartlage, Alloy, Vázquez, & Dykman, 1993; Leight & Ellis, 1981; Pekrun, 1992). On the other hand, positive affect has been found to influence cognitive organization by aiding problem-solving and decision-making processes (Isen, 1984, 1999; Isen, Daubman, & Nowicki, 1987). Moreover, studies on 'state-dependent learning' suggest that mood at the time of learning, mood at the time of recall, and information content should be congruent for optimal information retrieval (Bower, Monteiro, & Gilligan, 1978; Pekrun, 1992). Although researchers have arrived at several important conclusions about the way in which mood impacts information processing for students, there is only limited research on emotional state learning in relation to higher education, specifically, and this is dominated primarily by studies on test anxiety (Pekrun, 2007). Beyond the topic of test anxiety, Pekrun, Goetz, Titz, & Perry (2002) and Pekrun (2007) have found that emotions (i.e., achievement emotions and social emotions) are an important element in the learning process and abundant within universities. In the few studies on emotional state learning in university settings, it has been reported that positive process emotions (e.g., enjoyment), prospective emotions (e.g., hope), and retrospective emotions (e.g., pride) are positively related to motivation to study, effective study strategy (i.e., elaboration), and self-regulated learning and negatively related to irrelevant thinking (Pekrun et al., 2002). On the other hand, negative process (e.g., boredom), prospective (e.g., anxiety), and retrospective (e.g., anger) emotions are negatively associated with motivation to study, effective study strategy, and self-regulated learning and positively associated with irrelevant thinking (Pekrun et al., 2002). Taken together, the studies on emotional states and information processing suggest that instructors of positive psychology courses should consider the student experience of the course – notably their emotional experience – as well as basic course content.

The experiential positive psychology classroom

Shifting emphasis from course content to the learning environment (e.g., the relationship between the instructor and the students, the physical classroom) is a radical departure from the content driven approach that describes most education. We believe this is particularly relevant as positive psychology is not only a science but an applied science. As such, the goal of instruction cannot responsibly be solely the transference of knowledge about scientific research but must also necessarily include the presentation of practical tools that can be applied to work, relationships, and other 'real world' situations. Connecting the topics of positive psychology to the students' personal and work lives is, we argue, the most impactful way to present this information. In this section, we will discuss several aspects of typical undergraduate courses such as classroom discussion and the role of teaching assistants, and we will make recommendations for experiential activities.

The course syllabus

Instructors of undergraduate courses will be familiar with the notion that students are interested in receiving a clear course syllabus, often before the first day of class. Course syllabi help students determine which classes they will be most interested in, articulate expectations for behavior and provide an outline of grading policies. Interestingly, course syllabi are almost always created by the course instructors with little input from students. A range of research suggests that freedom to choose and personal control are associated with happiness at the national level (Helliwell, Barrington-Leigh, Harris, & Huang, 2010), at the organizational level (Fenton, 2010; Warr, 1999) and that autonomy is a basic human motivation (Deci & Ryan, 2000). It is surprising, then, that many instructors do not use the syllabus and basic course design as an opportunity to give students control and autonomy and thereby showcase this aspect of positive psychology. To this end, we have been inspired by 'open space technology' (OST; Owen, 2008), a method by which facilitators (such as course instructors) allow stakeholders (such as students) to take responsibility for their own learning and behavior by 'co-creating' the environment in which work happens. The process begins by having students sit in a circle – where possible – and discuss their reasons for taking the course and their educational hopes for the course. They, rather than the instructor, are then immediately held personally accountable for these educational outcomes. A student who is interested in a topic that might not be normally presented – how positive psychology is used in prisons, for instance – would be held responsible for researching positive psychology programs in prisons and sharing this information with the class in the form of discussion, a presentation and/or a paper. For OST to work, instructors must be psychologically flexible to accommodate probable changes to course content based on student interests and investment.

OST approaches can work on aspects of the syllabus as fundamental as grading policy. For example, in a recent positive psychology course, we allowed students to create their own criteria for grading. We set basic parameters, such as 'grading options must include at least one objective (e.g., multiple choice test or pass/no pass homework assignment) and one subjective (e.g., classroom participation) activity to form the basis of your grade'. From this starting point, the students had autonomy to discuss and vote on grading strategies that they felt best addressed their academic performance and unique learning styles. Interestingly, this simple activity had a powerful effect on the students. First, many students reported that they were immediately invested in the course because they felt a sense of ownership of the class and that it was a 'good match' for them. Students commented on 'feeling in control' and 'being listened to' even during the first class meeting. Second, this approach served to shift the focus away from students as individual learners and toward interacting with their peers as a learning community. Several students commented that working together to co-create the course set the psychological stage for a greater appreciation of their peers. This autonomy-support approach does not sacrifice the authority of the instructor as he or she still has ultimate power to set policy parameters and facilitate the OST process.

Classroom participation

Classroom discussion is a ubiquitous element of undergraduate education. Classroom discussions are frequently seen as an opportunity for students to employ and demonstrate critical thinking skills. We argue that classroom discussions are also opportunities for employing positive psychology skills. For example, instead of asking questions that are 'critical', students might be coached to ask questions that are 'curious'. It has been our experience that instructing students to attend to their own subjective curiosity and use this to guide questions can lead to more positive, engaging and friendly discussions, and these interactions can be spotlighted *in vivo* and tied directly to research on the benefits of curiosity. Indeed, curiosity has been found to be correlated with happiness, engagement, and a sense of meaning (Peterson & Seligman, 2004). In addition, classroom discussion can also be an opportunity for students to express social support for one another. For instance, students can share small, personally relevant goals as part of discussion on topics such as success, motivation, or optimism and give each other support relevant to progressing on these goals. One consequence of expressed social support in the classroom setting is the creation of an atmosphere of collective, rather than individual learning. This is consistent with a larger trend in positive psychology toward happiness and flourishing as being social, rather than individual concerns (see Biswas-Diener, 2011). We have noticed that when students develop a shared identity as a class, rather than as individual learners, there is an increase in the sharing of notes with students who have been absent,

an increase in helping peers access books and other resources, and an increase in out-of-class contact. Positive classroom discussion can lead to an upward spiral in which positive emotion leads to an increase in positive emotion (Fredrickson, 2003). This can be seen in the instance of spontaneous compliments and other forms of celebration in the classroom. In a typical example of this, one student in our positive psychology course brought ice-cream for the 100 students to celebrate the last day of class, and gave away a year's worth of ice cream to one student chosen at random! Another class spontaneously chose to pool financial resources and donated money to a charitable cause. Members of yet another class – students who did not previously know one another – volunteered and went hiking together on weekends. Positive psychology instructors can encourage positive classroom discussion by emphasizing curiosity, rewarding pro-social behavior and scheduling time for public celebrations. Another place where positive student interactions can take place is in on-line classroom forums. In our courses, we have taken steps to foster positive self-disclosure by prompting commentary on discussion groups. In one instance, for example, we posted a query asking students to – optionally – briefly describe a time 'when you were at your best'. This question coincided with a unit on character strengths and the students had participated in a two-person version of this activity in class. The relative social distance provided by an on-line post offered an additional opportunity to students who were initially reluctant to share their own strengths. By making such participation, optional instructors can avoid discriminating against those who might be less computer literate and allowing those students who are most engaged in the course to participate further.

Experiential assignments

Since it has been made clear that experiential teaching and positive psychology are compatible, it is appropriate that class assignments reflect this approach. To reiterate, the purpose of learning, and thus assignments, is to translate subject matter (i.e., social knowledge) into relatable, practical, and experientially supported personal knowledge. This knowledge should foster the learner's personal growth through the experiential learning cycle as well as the learner's intellectual growth by way of learning the material in a manner that is understood best by the student (i.e., experience). Furthermore, the most effective assignments, instigating both personal and intellectual development, require both reflection and action. Take for example, the way we introduce the topic of happiness: we offer students 1 h (of a 2-h class period) to 'engage in whatever legal activity you believe will make you a small amount happier in one hour'. In the past, students have used the hour to exercise, walk in the park, go bowling, drink beer, telephone friends, complete homework, take a nap, and a variety of other activities. Returning to the classroom, the students then have a personal experience of a happiness increasing strategy. The resulting discussion can be mined to introduce topics that will be covered later in the class including affective forecasting errors (Gilbert, Pinel, Wilson, Blumberg, & Wheatley, 1998), the independence of positive and negative affects (Schimmack, 2008), and happiness interventions (Lyubomirsky, Sheldon, & Schkade, 2005).

As a second example, we assign students to 'select an achievable, personally valued and measurable goal that can be completed by the end of the academic term'. In the past, students have chosen to pay down credit card bills, increase their physical exercise regimes, volunteer at charities, and clean their apartments, among other goals. These goals represent growth opportunities that can also be used to make class content personally relevant. When studying motivation, for example, the students can write reflective homework assignments or engage in discussion on whether their personal goal is framed as 'approach or avoidant' (Sheldon, 2001), and can reframe their goals accordingly. Similarly, when studying optimism, students can discuss how optimistic they are about the successful achievement of their goal and relate this to concepts such as personal control (Snyder, 2002) and effort and goal progress (Sheldon, 2001). The emphasis is not on the success or failure of the goal, but on the evolution of the goal as students learn more about relevant positive psychology topics. In fact, this is a perfect place to illustrate the benefits of learning versus performance goals (Grant & Gelety, 2009)!

Conclusion

We argue that, as an applied science, positive psychology is best taught with attention to scientific research as well as practical uses of the content. Because positive psychology concerns topics such as hope and happiness that constitute everyday experiences, courses on positive psychology are well-poised to use experiential learning. Research and experience suggest that experiential activities engage students more actively than traditional methods. We believe that the goal of instruction in such courses is not only to transfer intellectual knowledge but infect students with a passion for the topic so that they continue to engage in self-directed learning after the conclusion of the course. This is especially appropriate as this is in keeping with the underlying philosophy of positive psychology itself. Experiential teaching methods and the use of OST often require additional investment of time and other resources,

and therefore might not be equally attractive to all instructors. In our experience, however, they are attractive to the students who are the very *raison d'etre* of positive psychology courses.

References

Biswas-Diener, R. (2011). *Positive psychology as social change*. Dordrecht, The Netherlands: Springer Academic Press.

Bower, G.H., Monteiro, K.P., & Gilligan, S.G. (1978). Emotional mood as a context for learning and recall. *Journal of Verbal Learning and Verbal Behavior, 17*, 573–585.

Deci, E.L., & Ryan, R.M. (2000). The "what" and "why" of goal pursuits: Human needs and the self-determination of behavior. *Psychological Inquiry, 11*, 227–268.

Fenton, T. (2010). Organizational democracy as a force for social change. In R. Biswas-Diener (Ed.), *Positive psychology as social change* (pp. 175–189). Dordrecht, The Netherlands: Springer Academic Press.

Fredrickson, B. (2003). Positive emotions and upward spirals in organizational settings. In K. Cameron, J. Dutton, & R. Quinn (Eds.), *Positive organizational scholarship: Foundations of a new discipline* (pp. 163–175). San Francisco, CA: Berrett-Koehler.

Gilbert, D.T., Pinel, E.C., Wilson, T.D., Blumberg, S.J., & Wheatley, T.P. (1998). Immune neglect: A source of durability bias in affective forecasting. *Journal of Personality and Social Psychology, 75*, 617–638.

Grant, H., & Gelety, L. (2009). Goal content theories: Why differences in what we are striving for matter. In G.B. Moskowitz & H. Grant (Eds.), *The psychology of goals* (pp. 77–97). New York, NY: The Guilford Press.

Hartlage, S., Alloy, L.B., Vázquez, C., & Dykman, B. (1993). Automatic and effortful processing in depression. *Psychological Bulletin, 113*, 247–278.

Helliwell, J., Barrington-Leigh, C., Harris, A., & Huang, H. (2010). International evidence on the social context of well-being. In E. Diener, J. Helliwell, & D. Kahneman (Eds.), *International differences in well-being* (pp. 291–327). Oxford: Oxford University Press.

Isen, A.M. (1984). The influence of positive affect on decision making and cognitive organization. *Advances in Consumer Research, 11*, 534–537.

Isen, A.M. (1987). Positive affect, cognitive processes, and social behavior. In L. Berkowitz (Ed.), *Advances in experimental social psychology* (Vol. 20, pp. 203–253). San Diego, CA: Academic Press.

Isen, A.M. (1999). On the relationship between affect and creative problem solving. In S. Russ (Ed.), *Affect, creative experience, and psychological adjustment* (pp. 3–17). Philadelphia, PA: Taylor & Francis.

Isen, A.M., Daubman, K.A., & Nowicki, G.P. (1987). Positive affect facilitates creative problem solving. *Journal of Personality and Social Psychology, 52*, 1122–1131.

Kolb, A.Y., & Kolb, D.A. (2005). Learning styles and learning spaces: Enhancing experiential learning in high education. *Academy of Management Learning and Education, 4*, 193–212.

Leight, K.A., & Ellis, H. (1981). Emotional mood states, strategies, and state-dependency in memory. *Journal of Verbal Learning and Verbal Behavior, 20*, 251–265.

Lyubomirsky, S., Sheldon, K., & Schkade, D. (2005). Pursuing happiness: The architecture of sustainable change. *Review of General Psychology, 9*, 111–131.

Owen, H. (2008). *Open space technology: A user's guide* (3rd ed.). San Francisco, CA: Barrett-Koehler.

Pekrun, R. (1992). The impact of emotions on learning and achievement: Towards a theory of cognitive/motivational mediators. *Applied Psychology: An International Review, 41*, 359–376.

Pekrun, R. (2007). Emotions in students' scholastic development. In R.P. Perry & J.C. Smarts (Eds.), *The scholarship of teaching and learning in higher education: An evidence-based perspective* (pp. 553–610). New York, NY: Springer.

Pekrun, R., Goetz, T., Titz, W., & Perry, R.P. (2002). Academic emotions in students' self-regulated learning and achievement: A program of qualitative and quantitative research. *Educational Psychologist, 37*, 91–105.

Peterson, C., & Seligman, M.E.P. (2004). Strengths of character and well-being. *Journal of Social and Clinical psychology, 23*, 603–619.

Schimmack, U. (2008). The structure of subjective well-being. In M. Eid & R. Larsen (Eds.), *The science of subjective well-being* (pp. 97–123). New York, NY: The Guilford Press.

Sheldon, K. (2001). The self-concordant model of healthy goal striving: When personal goals correctly represent the person. In P. Schmuck & K. Sheldon (Eds.), *Life goals and well-being: Towards a positive psychology of human striving* (pp. 18–36). Seattle, WA: Hogrefe & Huber.

Snyder, C.R. (2002). Hope theory: Rainbows of the mind. *Psychological Inquiry, 13*, 249–275.

Warr, P. (1999). Well-being and the workplace. In D. Kahneman, E. Diener, & N. Schwartz (Eds.), *Well-being: The foundations of hedonic psychology* (pp. 392–412). New York, NY: Russell Sage Foundation.

Illustrating positive psychology concepts through service learning: Penn teaches resilience

Amy Kranzler[ab], Acacia C. Parks[bc] and Jane Gillham[d]

[a]Department of Psychology, Rutgers University, New Brunswick, NJ, USA; [b]Department of Psychology, University of Pennsylvania, Philadelphia, PA, USA; [c]Department of Psychology, Hiram College, Hiram, OH, USA; [d]Department of Psychology, Swarthmore College, Swarthmore, PA, USA

We describe an undergraduate service-learning research course in which undergraduates are trained to disseminate an intervention designed to promote resilience and well-being in middle-school youth. The course provides undergraduates with an opportunity for active and collaborative learning in psychology and serves as a new model for the wide-scale dissemination of evidence-based prevention programs through supervised undergraduates. We provide insights into the strengths and weaknesses of the course, along with some thoughts about ways that readers might implement something similar at their own institutions, using the Penn Resiliency Program or other related interventions.

In the spring of 2009, we offered an innovative *service-based* research experience course for the first time at the University of Pennsylvania, redesigning the department's standard undergraduate psychology course to include hands-on, real-world experience. In this course, titled 'Penn Teaches Resilience,' undergraduate students learned about the theoretical bases of both cognitive-behavioral and positive psychology-based interventions, and then received training to administer a manualized cognitive-behavioral intervention, *The Penn Resiliency Program* (PRP; Gillham, Reivich, & Jaycox, 1990), to middle-school youth attending an after-school program in Philadelphia. As part of the course, students also collected and analyzed feedback data.

The goals of this article are to (1) provide an overview of our rationale both for service learning in general and for resilience as an ideal topic for a service-learning course in positive psychology, (2) describe the course for readers in sufficient detail that they might model a similar course at their own institution, and (3) provide some insights based on our experiences teaching this course at two institutions, including suggestions for how it might be improved.

Why service learning?

Service-based learning has been described as a 'course-based, credit-bearing educational experience that allows students to (a) participate in an organized service activity that meets identified community needs and (b) reflect on the service activity in such a way as to gain further understanding of course content, a broader appreciation of the discipline, and an enhanced sense of civic responsibility' (Bringle & Hatcher, 1995).

Research on service-learning courses suggests that the integration of learning and service can have many beneficial effects on students. For example, a review of service-learning courses suggests that these courses can facilitate personal growth such as the development of a sense of personal efficacy, personal identity and moral growth, as well as interpersonal growth such as the development of communication skills, leadership, and the ability to work well with others (Eyler, Giles, Stenson, & Gray, 2001). Reviews of these courses also document several benefits to students' learning and engagement in school, such as increased complexity of understanding, critical thinking, cognitive development and satisfaction with their school (Eyler et al., 2001). In addition, service-learning courses provide students with meaningful opportunities to help others and can strengthen the connections between academic institutions and the surrounding community (Eyler et al., 2001). For these reasons, faculty and administrators are often eager to develop and offer service-learning courses.

There has been a movement toward the development of increased service-learning and practicum courses in many undergraduate psychology curricula (Bringle & Duffy, 1998; Vandercreek & Fleischer, 1984). Across many universities, courses have used service learning to teach a wide range of topics within psychology such as child psychopathology (Glenwick & Chabot, 1991), developmental psychology (McCluskey-Fawcett & Green, 1992), and abnormal psychology (Scrogin & Rickard, 1987). Service-based courses offered within the psychology department help ground psychological theory in the reality of contemporary society, and engage students in the application and illustration of psychological concepts through active and collaborative learning (Bringle & Duffy, 1998).

Furthermore, evaluations of existing service-based psychology courses suggest that undergraduates benefit from hands-on experience teaching psychological interventions. At UCLA, an established service-learning course (The Developmental Disabilities Immersion Program) offers students an opportunity to study developmental disabilities by combining traditional classroom teaching with service to individuals with disabilities (Fluharty & Kassaie, 1998). Evaluations of this program, which has been in existence for over 20 years, suggest that it increased students' self-confidence, sense of achievement, and personal insight, and often had a significant effect on their attitude toward community involvement (Fluharty & Kassaie, 1998).

While service learning shows promise for a variety of courses in psychology, it is a pedagogical approach that fits particularly well with the framework of positive psychology. Hands-on experience can provide opportunities for growth by exposing students to new experiences and pushing students beyond the comfort zone of the academic classroom. In so doing, service learning provides opportunities for students to develop, discover, and apply skills and strengths that may not be called upon in typically classroom-based work. Because service-learning projects typically require a team effort, service learning also can help to promote interpersonal skills and positive relationships among students, between students and faculty, and between students and faculty and their community partners. Finally, service learning provides opportunities for meaning through connections and contributions to others.

Overview of a service-learning course on resilience

This course was taught at the University of Pennsylvania for two years as an advanced course in psychology that served to fulfill the major's research requirement. It had three prerequisites: introductory psychology, abnormal psychology, and one semester of statistics. Because the course was, first and foremost, a research experience course, undergraduates were trained to teach the program as well as to evaluate its effectiveness. The course contained 18 students in the first year and 11 students in the second year.

Course preparation

Service-learning courses typically require extensive preparation and lead time, as well as ongoing logistical support. Given the logistical demands of setting up and running a service-learning course, we recommend hiring a teaching assistant, if possible, to serve as a liaison to the site and assist with logistics. During the course of the semester, there were often ongoing logistics that required continued collaboration with the site, such as addressing scheduling conflicts or reporting behavioral problems that arose. A teaching assistant is invaluable for negotiating these issues.

It is helpful if logistics are arranged before the start of the semester; so that undergraduates can receive training and immediately begin running the intervention. The first step in establishing this course was contacting and collaborating with local communities. This course was run in collaboration with a local after-school program serving middle-school youth in a poor urban community in West Philadelphia. We arranged with the after-school program coordinators and the school social worker for undergraduates to work with youth at the after-school program. The school's social worker was instrumental in the initial establishment of this course, expressing support and helping create a working alliance with the after-school program coordinators. The social worker was extremely receptive to the program, expressing concern about the inadequacy of mental health resources available to students and his hope that a prevention program might help target risk factors before problems arise. Dissemination of interventions to youth can also be done in collaboration with schools, community centers, or clinics. However, we highly recommend working within an existing infrastructure, such as an after-school program, as doing so can provide a pre-existing group of participants who are available at the same time every week. Other logistics to be considered include transportation for undergraduates to service sites or supervised transportation for youth to your academic institution. While it can be more logistically challenging to invite youth to a university campus, in our experience, this added an element of excitement for the youth and served as an added incentive to join the program.

Once we established a partnership with a site, the next step was recruitment. This can be challenging given the number of activities that youth are involved with after school; so, it was important to collaborate with each site to determine the best method of informing parents and youth. We found it beneficial to hold an informational meeting with parents in which the goals, structure and content of the intervention were described. Many parents voiced questions and concerns about the nature of the program, which we were able to address in the information session. We found that these sessions helped spark parental interest and increased the likelihood of parents encouraging their children to participate. Information sessions can also be held for the youth themselves, in which the intervention can be described and framed to them in a way that is fun and relevant.

While the task of making these arrangements may seem daunting at first, once made, community ties can often be maintained from year to year, requiring far less preparatory work. In addition, working closely with the community in the creation of the course can be a rewarding process in its own right, providing a better understanding of the needs and nuances of the local community.

Training

At the beginning of the semester, undergraduates received 6 h of training in the philosophy and rationale of the intervention. Training began with the reading of primary sources on the design and efficacy of the PRP (see Gillham, Brunwasser, & Freres, 2008 for a review). We then provided an overview of the intervention itself. The activities in PRP fall into two broad categories. The *cognitive skills* consist of techniques like thought disputing and cognitive reappraisal; for example, the kids learn about different common thinking errors and learn to notice when they are making these errors themselves so that they can challenge them. The *behavioral skills* consist of skills for social problem-solving, building assertiveness, and coping with stress. These activities are outlined in greater depth by Gillham et al. (2008).

PRP has a structured curriculum, including a group leader's manual and workbooks for students. The curriculum includes detailed lesson plans that outline the activities, discussion questions and main points of each unit. The curriculum also includes an example script, to serve as a model for running groups. Students are encouraged to use the script to become deeply familiar with the lesson plans and to then develop their own style and voice in leading the lessons.

Undergraduates received weekly training before each session from the course instructor, in which they reviewed and practiced leading the manualized lesson they would be teaching that week. They then broke into smaller groups of two co-leaders to role-play sections of the lesson. During these weekly supervision meetings, undergraduates also voiced difficulties and challenges they faced in the previous session and brainstormed with their classmates and the course instructor about how to best handle them. In addition, undergraduates participated in the planning of the following week's session by helping design additional interactive activities and games to engage the youth. In this sense, the input of the undergraduates, many of whom had previous experience working with youth, was extremely helpful to the program's success.

Intervention implementation

The undergraduates taught the program to 19 middle-school youth at a school near the University's campus. The program was taught as part of an existing after-school program for community youth. Sessions were held once a week for a total of eight 90-min sessions, amounting to a total of 216 h of service provided to the community through this course. The teaching assistant attended the group lessons and helped to supervise the intervention. The social worker who coordinated the after-school program also provided support by occasionally joining sessions and helping address behavioral issues that arose.

Each lesson began with a short game or activity that was prepared by the undergraduates and conducted with the entire group. The students then broke into their designated small groups, with two undergraduates and two youth working together in each group. Each group engaged in discussions and activities based on the weekly PRP lesson. These groups of four were small enough for youth to feel comfortable sharing, but large enough to maintain a flow of conversation. Children received a snack during their group meeting. While all groups met at the same time and in the same room, each group spread out and found its own space within the room to allow for privacy and group cohesion.

Structured reflection

Structured opportunities for reflection are a central component of service-learning courses, and so it is important to create opportunities for both ongoing and retrospective self-reflection (Bringle & Hatcher, 1995; Eyler et al., 2001). Undergraduates were asked to keep an ongoing journal of their experiences throughout the course, which they used to inform discussions in weekly supervision meetings. They also used their journal entries to add a personal reflection component to their final paper; in this written report, undergraduates worked to integrate and compare their own experiences with the data collected by the class.

Program evaluation

In order to evaluate the success of the program, at the end of the last session, students distributed feedback forms to youth, asking them to rate their satisfaction with the program and the extent to which they learned different skills. Youth completed these forms anonymously. The undergraduates then collected and analyzed these data, and then wrote up their findings, along with a literature review on the rationale and efficacy of PRP, in an APA-format paper at the end of the semester. Each undergraduate developed their own research questions and used the data to answer them (e.g., '*Is there a correlation between attendance and program satisfaction?*' or '*Does gender predict which skills youth learned the most?*'). The research paper component was required in order for the course to be consistent with the department's 'Research Experience' course model.

Problems encountered

One challenge that often arises when working in collaboration with after-school programs is attendance. Many children attended the program inconsistently, which made it difficult for them to establish relationships with their mentors and to complete the resilience curriculum. In addition, some undergraduates expressed that they felt uncomfortable and anxious at the start of the program as they were pushed to step out of their comfort zone. While some had had previous experience with youth, many were nervous about the prospect of running an intervention. As such, it is extremely important to provide adequate support and guidance to undergraduates and to create a space for them to voice concerns and reflect about their experiences. Another challenge in this type of course is that when working in real-world settings, many factors are outside of one's control and it is not uncommon for setbacks and programming changes to occur that might disrupt a planned schedule for the intervention. However, despite these challenges, the benefits of this university–community partnership are numerous for both the youth and undergraduates involved.

We also had some issues around our decision to follow the 'Research Experience' course model. Because students did get hands-on experience with a research-based intervention and learned much about the logistics of conducting and evaluating a psychological intervention, the decision to include a research paper requirement seemed appropriate at the time that we created the course. However, in practice, we found that the research paper was not feasible for two reasons. First, the students were far less prepared for this assignment than we had anticipated; they struggled with every aspect of the paper, from writing the literature review to entering, analyzing, interpreting, and reporting data. We simply did not budget (and, in fact, could not have budgeted) sufficient time to walk students through the process. Second, the time that we *did* budget was significantly compromised by logistical setbacks such as recruiting kids and obtaining their consent, transportation to and from the after-school program, and weather issues. It is our impression, having now taught several iterations of this course at multiple placement sites, that such delays and setbacks are both inevitable and unpredictable. Thus, we have concluded that this course may be more appropriate as an elective or 'special topics' course rather than a 'research experience' course. This is not to say that grounding in the research is not valuable – we considered it, and still consider it, a central aspect of our training. However, we believe that the inclusion of both structured reflection and a research paper resulted in neither assignment receiving adequate attention.

An alternative model

It may be helpful to instructors hoping to offer an intervention-based service-learning course to hear briefly about an alternative model for offering such a course, outside of the 'research experience' paradigm used at the University of Pennsylvania. In spring 2009, a similar course ran through Swarthmore College, but in the form of a practicum course open to advanced undergraduates (juniors and seniors) who were majoring in psychology and/or educational studies.

As at Penn, students learned about the theoretical and empirical background of the intervention and practiced the intervention lessons during class meetings. Students also ran an after-school program for middle-school students in the community. At Swarthmore, the program was advertised to parents through flyers distributed at area schools, but the groups were conducted on campus at Swarthmore College rather than through an after-school program in the community. Youth walked or took the bus to the college after school. They walked home or were picked up by parents following each lesson. Groups met once a week for eight lessons. Youth were divided into two groups based on grade level (sixth grade versus seventh and eighth grade). Three undergraduate students led each group of five to eight students. The program was based largely on PRP, but included additional lessons designed to help students identify and use their character strengths.

In the past two years, this course has expanded. Students who are currently enrolled in the course deliver a resilience and strengths-based intervention (based largely on PRP) as a weekly after-school program in three schools in the Philadelphia/ Swarthmore area. In addition to examining feedback and feasibility data, we are gathering data that will allow us to examine the effects of this service-learning course on adolescents' social and emotional well-being.

Future directions

This model of a service-based research experience course can be replicated at any university. To create one's own intervention-based service-learning course, the authors recommend the following steps: choose an effective intervention to disseminate, and an appropriate population to whom the undergraduates will teach the intervention. It is also important to choose an intervention that is appropriate for undergraduates to implement, namely an intervention that has structured materials and is preventive, focusing on teaching skills for promoting positive experiences or coping with everyday problems, rather than addressing clinical levels of symptoms that might require advanced clinical training to address.

Establish a positive relationship with the school or community in which you will work. It is important to note that it requires ongoing effort to maintain this relationship, such as staying in constant contact, remaining flexible to the needs of the community, and communicating with the program or site liaison. It can also be beneficial to work through existing organizations seeking to improve community partnerships. For example, this course was established through the help of the Netter Center for Community Partnerships. Organizations like the Netter Center now exist on many campuses and can assist in the creation and maintenance of community partnerships and can also be possible sources of funding.

Next, ensure that the undergraduates receive adequate training in the background and theory of the intervention. This includes providing reading and classroom discussions that address the underlying theory, history, and critical components of the intervention. Finally, create a structure for the continued supervision of undergraduates, and a forum for group reflection. Reflection can take place in the form of weekly journal entries or group discussions and should push students to consider what they have gained and what they have struggled with throughout the program, as well as how their experiences extend, clarify, or challenge what they have learned through their coursework.

If replicated on a large scale, this model of service-learning has the potential to engage undergraduate psychology students in active and collaborative learning, while simultaneously enlisting them to help address the growing mental health needs of today's youth. We concur with Elias and Gambone (1998, pp. 159–160) that 'service-learning programs meet the complementary needs of both the underserved and the undergraduate, and we encourage all universities to continue to develop and support such programs'.

References

Bringle, R.G., & Duffy, D.K. (1998). *With service in mind: Concept and models for service-learning in psychology.* Washington, DC: American Association for Higher Education.

Bringle, R., & Hatcher, J. (1995). A service learning curriculum for faculty. *Michigan Journal of Community Service Learning, 2*, 112–122.

Brunwasser, S.M., Gillham, J.E., & Kim, E.S. (2009). A meta-analytic review of the Penn Resiliency Program's effect on depressive symptoms. *American Psychological Association, 77*, 1042–1054.

Elias, M., & Gambone, G. (1998). Bringing undergraduate service-learning into a high-risk, urban environment. In R.G. Bringle & D. Donna (Eds.), *With service in mind: Concepts and models for service-learning in psychology* (pp. 151–160). Washington, DC: American Association for Higher Education.

Eyler, J.S., Giles, D.E., Stenson, C.M., & Gray, C.J. (2001). At a glance: What we know about the effects of service-learning on college students, faculty, institutions and communities. Retrieved from http://servicelearning.org/filemanager/download/aag.pdf

Fluharty, A.L., & Kassaie, P. (1998). Reflections on an established service-learning program: The developmental disabilities program at UCLA. In R.G. Bringle & D. Donna (Eds.), *With service in mind: Concepts and models for service-learning in psychology* (pp. 178–189). Washington, DC: American Association for Higher Education.

Gillham, J.E., Brunwasser, S.M., & Freres, D.R. (2008). In Abela J.R.Z., Hankin B.L. (Eds.), *Preventing depression in early adolescence: The Penn resiliency program.* New York, NY: Guilford Press.

Gillham, J.E., Reivich, K., & Jaycox, I.H. (1990). *The Penn Resiliency Program.* Unpublished manual, University of Pennsylvania, Philadelphia.

Glenwick, D.S., & Chabot, D.R. (1991). The undergraduate clinical child psychology course: Bringing students to the real world and the real world to students. *Teaching of Psychology, 18*, 21–24.

McCluskey-Fawcett, K., & Green, P. (1992). Using community service to teach developmental psychology. *Teaching of Psychology, 19*, 150–152.

Scrogin, F., & Rickard, H.C. (1987). A volunteer program for abnormal psychology students: Eighteen years and still going strong. *Teaching of Psychology, 14*, 95–97.

Vandercreek, L., & Fleischer, M. (1984). The role of practicum in the undergraduate psychology curriculum. *Teaching of Psychology, 11*, 9–14.

Teaching positive psychology using team-based learning

Marie D. Thomas[a] and Barbara J. McPherson[b]

[a]Department of Psychology, California State University San Marcos, San Marcos, CA, USA; [b]Department of Psychology, MiraCosta College, Oceanside, CA, USA

This article describes a class in positive psychology taught using an innovative pedagogy, team-based learning (TBL). The course employed the use of permanent teams, processes that encourage students to come to class prepared, and interesting activities designed to promote active learning, develop team cohesion, and encourage the application of positive psychology principles to everyday life. The use of TBL fostered students' responsibility for their own learning as well as for their team. Delivering positive psychology course content through a TBL class format allowed students the opportunity to consider and develop their own strengths and to practice many of positive psychology values including openness, cooperation, kindness, and trust.

In this article, we describe our experiences teaching an undergraduate positive psychology class using an innovative pedagogy, team-based learning (TBL; Michaelsen, Knight, & Fink, 2004). Snyder and Lopez (2007, p. 3) define positive psychology as '...the scientific and applied approach to uncovering people's strengths and promoting their positive functioning'. We (Marie as the course instructor, Barbara as the teaching assistant) structured our positive psychology syllabus around the six strengths and virtues identified by Peterson and Seligman (2004): Wisdom/Knowledge, Courage, Love/Humanity, Justice, Temperance, and Spirituality/Transcendence. In developing the class, we wanted to create an environment that would reflect the components of what Snyder and Lopez (2007) call 'positive schooling' – a classroom that demonstrates and encourages care, trust, respect for diversity, goals, plans, motivation, hope, and concern for society. Implementing TBL, a technique that uses permanent teams to organize learning activities, assignments, and assessments, helped us achieve our goal of positive schooling. Each carefully constructed and goal-directed TBL class session promoted active group participation and student responsibility for learning. In addition, by implementing the TBL team structure, positive psychology values such as openness, cooperation, and kindness were reinforced; this, in turn, motivated students to share and apply course content in and outside the classroom. Because students were evaluated on a combination of individual and team performance, it was crucial that we help students learn to trust and care for their team members. In order to share this successful way of teaching positive psychology, we will discuss how TBL works, how we integrated the elements of TBL with the subject matter, how the subject matter changed traditional TBL, and students' reactions to the course content and its structure.

What is TBL?

The idea for TBL was developed by Larry Michaelsen in the late 1970s as an attempt to provide students in a large lecture class with a small class experience (Michaelsen, 2004a) by promoting course-long student interaction within teams of about five to seven students. Since that time, TBL has been used in a wide variety of disciplines and higher education settings (Michaelsen & Fink, 2008). Resources available to faculty who are interested in developing TBL courses include a TBL website (http://www.teambasedlearning.org/) and listserv (TEAMLEARNING-L@LIST.OLT.UBC.CA).

TBL uses strategically constructed permanent teams to help students progress in their learning from basic content knowledge to the application of that knowledge. For each major unit of course material, students study independently and come to class prepared to take a short individual quiz on the assigned content. This individual quiz is followed by the team taking the same quiz, with team members needing to come to consensus on their answers. Immediate feedback is provided for team quiz performance. The quiz is followed by a short lecture that is very specific, often addressing problems in understanding that were uncovered through quiz performance. The majority of learning in class takes place through carefully constructed class activities and assignments that encourage students to apply, synthesize, and evaluate their content knowledge.

Teaching a positive psychology class using TBL

From the description above, four important elements of TBL can be abstracted: carefully constructed permanent teams, accountability, feedback, and assignments. Each of these elements contributed to the positive schooling environment we sought to create in our course.

Carefully constructed permanent teams

The first element of TBL is carefully constructed teams that remain together throughout the term. Typically in TBL, teams are purposefully created to spread assets (e.g., performance in previous course work) and liabilities (e.g., no or poor preparation, language barriers), as well as to avoid pre-existing, cohesive subgroups (Michaelsen, 2004b). To enhance the positive psychology theme, we chose a different strategy for team member selection. On the first day of class, we handed out a list of strengths and virtues as classified by Peterson and Seligman (2004): Wisdom/Knowledge, Courage, Love/Humanity, Justice, Temperance, and Spirituality/Transcendence. Students were asked to rank these characteristics from 1 (highest) to 6 (lowest) in terms of which they thought they were highest in, or which of the characteristics most appealed to them. We organized students into teams by highest or second highest ranked strength (i.e., putting students with similar strengths/virtues in the same team). While diversity, at least in terms of strengths and virtues, was reduced within teams, we believed that students would experience diversity across teams when they interacted during class activities. We also hoped that having a strength/virtue preference in common would help team members bond more quickly; in most of the teams, our assumption proved to be correct, although in no case were the team assignments perfect. It would have been wiser to use a validated assessment tool and to take additional variables into consideration to make decisions about team assignments. Nonetheless, cohesion was evident in all the teams and resources seemed to be distributed equitably.

Accountability

A second essential element of TBL is accountability. Students are held accountable, not only for individual preparation and learning, but also for their team participation (Sweet & Pelton-Sweet, 2008) through the Readiness Assurance Process (RAP) and through peer evaluations. The RAP is designed to increase students' motivation, goals, and planning with regard to their study habits. At the beginning of most class sessions (the course met once a week), students took the individual Readiness Assurance Test (RAT), which was a short quiz (10–15 multiple-choice items) on the assigned reading material. When the individual student answer sheets were turned in, the RAT was immediately taken again by the entire team. The RAT component of each student's final grade consisted of a combination of his or her mean individual score and the average team score (with the individual average having greater weight than the team average). Not surprisingly, team RAT grades were almost always better than individual RAT grades and, therefore, the team scores served to raise the RAT component of the final grade. We observed that as team members became confident they could rely on each other to come to class prepared, team cohesion increased.

Few students who engaged in social loafing were held accountable by end-of-semester peer evaluations that affected their final grades (see Michaelsen & Fink, 2004, for information on conducting peer evaluations). A mid-semester formative evaluation served the purpose of letting students know what their teammates thought of their contributions thus far. This mid-term peer evaluation often serves as a wake-up call for social loafers as well as for students who have not made enough of an effort to integrate themselves into their team. For the two students in our positive psychology class who were surprised by the low ratings they received from their team members, this provided a chance to open up a discussion about their team's group dynamics, as well as what needed to change for them to be perceived as fully functioning members. This early feedback resulted in an opportunity for team relationships to deepen through the offering of constructive feedback.

It is very important to note that the RAP had an effect on the course beyond increased student accountability. Because students were more likely to come to class prepared, we were freed from the need to lecture about the assigned material. Instead, we spent class time on interesting activities and on deeper discussion and real-world application of the research literature. In addition, we were able to invite guest speakers because we did not have a set amount of material that we felt obligated to cover each week. For example, the head of campus Career Services, who was trained in the use of StrengthsQuest (www.strengthsquest.com), discussed the instrument and student results in one class. A visiting scholar discussed her dissertation work on forgiveness. Finally, a psychologist on the staff of Counseling and Psychological Services spent a full class discussing mindfulness, presenting exercises and having the students sit for a period of meditation.

Frequent and immediate feedback

Another key aspect of TBL that is closely linked to student motivation is frequent immediate student feedback. This element is seen most clearly in the RAP. Students used an answer form that is formatted like a scantron sheet and works like a scratch-off lottery ticket (IF*AT form, http://www.epsteineducation.com). The correct answers to the multiple-choice items were keyed to the particular IF*AT form used for that quiz. Teams received immediate feedback on their quiz performance as they scratched off their chosen answer to each question; if they were correct, they uncovered a star (this also provided students with feedback on their individual performance). Especially at the beginning of the semester, there was much excitement each time a team scratched off their choice and found a star. Teams were told not to scratch a choice until they reached consensus on an answer, so discussions were often lively as team members made their case for a particular choice. The immediate feedback had an interesting side effect. A few wrong answers insisted upon by more dominant team members encouraged them to sit back and listen to their colleagues. This fostered team trust and the positive psychology values of openness and prudence.

Team activities

In a typical TBL class, creating effective assignments and activities is the most difficult and time-consuming part of TBL implementation (see Michaelsen & Knight, 2004 for a discussion and tips on how to create effective assignments). Fortunately, the positive psychology literature is filled with empirically supported interventions that can easily be taught to students. Additional sources for activities are books written by positive psychologists for the popular press (e.g., Lyubomirsky, 2007; Seligman, 2004). Throughout the semester, the activities were selected not only to cover the theory and scope of positive psychology but also to convey the values of positive psychology such as openness, cooperation and kindness.

We believe that the TBL method enhanced the use of these positive psychology activities in three ways. First, since we spent little time lecturing, the class was a true active learning environment; sessions consisted primarily of students working in their teams to apply content knowledge. Second, the team structure and activities provided reinforcement for the activities that students conducted individually between class sessions. Third, teams provided a built-in support system for the

personal change that we encouraged through many of the assigned activities.

Assignments and activities were developed to promote both deep learning and team cohesion. According to Michaelsen and Sweet (2008), TBL activities should reflect the four Ss: (1) Significant problem – to illustrate a concept's relevance and capture student attention; (2) Same problem – all teams should work on the same problem to promote within and between team discussion; (3) Specific choice – teams should have to make a choice among clear alternatives; and (4) Simultaneous report – teams should report their choice at the same time to avoid early responses influencing later ones. In our course, we often had teams work on the same problem, (e.g., signature strengths). However, many other activities did not lend themselves to specific choices which, in turn, made it difficult to have teams respond simultaneously (our small class size meant that each team had a chance to report); therefore, our activity selection was the biggest departure from traditional TBL.

As an example, we describe parts of two class sessions (each session was 3 h long) devoted to the study of wisdom and knowledge. These classes were structured around the five facets of wisdom (open-mindedness, perspective, love of learning, creativity, curiosity) described by Peterson and Seligman (2004). Both sessions began with an individual and team RAT (which took a total of about 20 min). During the first session, Marie briefly discussed the facets of open-mindedness, perspective, and love of learning. Students then watched a video clip from an episode of the TV show 'House' and discussed in their teams which facets of wisdom were illustrated. Teams simultaneously reported by holding up giant Post-Its with their answers. Another activity for this session used the Berlin wisdom paradigm; students had read the Baltes and Smith (2008) article as part of their preparation for class. Each team was presented with one of two problems ('You are advising a 15-year-old girl who wants to get married right away'; or, 'You are advising a dual-career couple who have to weigh the gains and losses involved if one partner accepts a job offer in a different state'). Students were first asked to formulate an individual solution, paying attention to the processes they used to come up with an answer. Then they discussed solutions with their team and tried to arrive at a consensus solution that reflected a high level of wisdom. Finally, teams presented their problem and solution to the class, and we had a general discussion about what are characteristics of advice that show a high level of wisdom.

During the week between the two classes, students chose one of two activities for their journal: 'Interview someone you think is wise and ask that person for a definition of wisdom. Write about your interview, what the interviewee said, and what you think about the answer(s)'; or, 'Think of the wisest person you know and try to live one day as if you were that person'. The Wisdom and Knowledge team helped us prepare an activity based on an experience one member had gone through at a workshop (all teams worked with us to develop at least one activity for the class that presented their theme). The class activity was for each student to develop a personal goal for one of the wisdom facets based on what he/she had learned through the journal activity that week. The goal had to be specific, reachable (not a fantasy goal), have a time limit, and quantifiable (i.e., the goal can be broken down into smaller steps to measure progress). After students developed their goal, they shared it with their teammates, seeking feedback on whether the goal was within guidelines. Over the rest of the semester, team members were to check in with each other to monitor the progress of the goal.

While the activities we used were not unique, we believe that the experience of going through them was enhanced within the TBL framework. Personal change is difficult under the best circumstances. The teams provided a consistent source of social support for change. We are convinced that, because students were accustomed to being vulnerable to their teammates, they also were more open to sharing what they learned with family and friends. Journal entries and the final papers supported this conclusion.

Student reactions to the course

Student reactions to the course were overwhelmingly positive. While our positive psychology course is a small sample, the reactions are consistent with those Marie obtained from other, larger TBL classes. Comments relating directly to aspects of TBL include: 'Group work effectively aided in understanding of course material'. 'We had *choices* as students and the class wasn't just about grades and tests!' 'I loved the journal assignments, group activities, and team tests!'

The final student evaluations for this course were some of the highest Marie has received in her 30+ years of teaching. All item ratings were between 4.75 and 5 (out of 5), and all item scores exceeded department and college averages. Much of this positive reaction came, of course, from the subject matter itself; more than one student told us that, given how much of the course could be applied to everyday life, the course should be a university requirement. The percentage of students who were very interested in the subject matter went from 56.3% at the beginning of the course to 80% at end, and 93% reported that their participation in all aspects of the learning process was very (53.3%) or moderately (40%) active. In the evaluation comments, students mentioned specific aspects of the class that they found especially valuable. 'The various

activities were *much* better than a pure lecture course.' 'This class was so interesting – I loved being a part of it because it was different than any class I have ever taken. Fun to be at class and participate.'

Conclusions

Before ending, we need to bring up two issues that new TBL instructors will possibly face. First, given that team performance is almost always better than individual performance, students' grades are raised by their team participation. This may lead to grade inflation. We have not satisfactorily solved this problem, but Michaelsen (2004a) has some suggestions.

Second, the major complaint from students in previous classes that Marie had converted to TBL was that the RATs were administered *before* rather than *after* we discussed the material. Since RATs are designed to encourage student preparation for team assignments and activities, there is no question of changing this format. The key is to prepare students adequately for the use of TBL. We spent a substantial portion of the first class describing the TBL process, its purpose and benefits. We also gave a quiz on the syllabus that students first took as individuals, and then in groups to demonstrate how this portion of the RAT works. We found that the extra time taken at the beginning of the semester eliminated complaints later on.

In conclusion, the subject matter in a positive psychology class is so engaging and relevant that it would be difficult to go wrong how ever the class is taught. That being said, we believe that using TBL adds another element to the subject by encouraging students to be active participants in the learning process, by supporting students' individual strengths and, through team activities, by promoting such values as responsibility to others, cooperation, openness, and kindness.

Acknowledgments

Special thanks to Elisa Grant-Vallone and Kim Pulvers for their careful reading of this manuscript and their very helpful comments and suggestions.

References

Baltes, P.B., & Smith, J. (2008). The fascination of wisdom: Its nature, ontogeny, and function. *Perspectives on Psychological Science, 3*, 56–64.

Lyubormirsky, S. (2007). *The how of happiness: A scientific approach to getting the life you want.* New York, NY: Penguin Press.

Michaelsen, L.K. (2004a). Team-based learning in large classes. In L.K. Michaelsen, A.B. Knight, & L.D. Fink (Eds.), *Team-based learning: A transformative use of small groups in college teaching* (pp. 153–167). Sterling, VA: Stylus.

Michaelsen, L.K. (2004b). Frequently asked questions about team-based learning. In L.K. Michaelsen, A.B. Knight, & L.D. Fink (Eds.), *Team-based learning: A transformative use of small groups in college teaching* (pp. 209–227). Sterling, VA: Stylus.

Michaelsen, L.K., & Fink, L.D. (2004). Calculating peer evaluation scores. In L.K. Michaelsen, A.B. Knight, & L.D. Fink (Eds.), *Team-based learning: A transformative use of small groups in college teaching* (pp. 229–239). Sterling, VA: Stylus.

Michaelsen, L.K., & Fink, L.D. (2008). Preface. In L.K. Michaelsen, M. Sweet, & D.X. Parmelee (Eds.), *Team-based learning: Small group learning's next big step* (pp. 1–5). San Francisco, CA: Jossey-Bass.

Michaelsen, L.K., & Knight, A.B. (2004). Creating effective assignments: A key component of team-based learning. In L.K. Michaelsen, A.B. Knight, & L.D. Fink (Eds.),

Team-based learning: A transformative use of small groups in college teaching (pp. 51–72). Sterling, VA: Stylus.

Michaelsen, L.K., Knight, A.B., & Fink, L.D. (Eds.) (2004). *Team-based learning: A transformative use of small groups in college teaching.* Sterling, VA: Stylus.

Michaelsen, L.K., & Sweet, M. (2008). The essential elements of team-based learning. In L.K. Michaelsen, M. Sweet, & D.X. Parmelee (Eds.), *Team-based learning: Small group learning's next big step* (pp. 7–27). San Francisco, CA: Jossey-Bass.

Peterson, C., & Seligman, M.E.P. (2004). *Character strengths and virtues: A handbook and classification.* Washington, DC: American Psychological Association.

Seligman, M.E.P. (2004). *Authentic happiness: Using the new positive psychology to realize your potential for lasting fulfillment.* New York, NY: Free Press.

Snyder, C.R., & Lopez, S.J. (2007). *Positive Psychology: The scientific and practical explorations of human strengths.* Thousand Oaks, CA: Sage.

Sweet, M., & Pelton-Sweet, L.M. (2008). The social foundations of team-based learning: Students accountable to students. In L.K. Michaelsen, M. Sweet, & D.X. Parmelee (Eds.), *Team-based learning: Small group learning's next big step* (pp. 29–40). San Francisco, CA: Jossey-Bass.

Teaching tools for positive psychology: A comparison of available textbooks

Grant J. Rich

Department of Social Sciences, University of Alaska Southeast, Juneau 99801, AK, USA

This article analyzes and compares available textbooks in positive psychology. In addition to describing six major standard textbooks, supplemental materials are also discussed, including special issues of professional journals devoted to the topic, specialized sole-authored and edited books on core subtopics in positive psychology, and strengths-focused books from related fields, such as anthropology, business, social work, history, and philosophy. Available supplements for existing textbooks, such as test banks and Powerpoint presentations, are also discussed.

Introduction

Positive psychology grew from a 'gleam in the eyes of three people in the Yucatán during the first week in January 1998 to a scientific movement', wrote past president of the American Psychological Association, Martin E.P. Seligman (2002, p. 265). With fellow Akumal sojourners, including senior scholars such as Mihaly Csikszentmihalyi and Ray Fowler, Seligman has helped build the movement from this foundation. Indicative of the field's success are the appearance of the present journal – the *Journal of Positive Psychology*, research funding and national and international professional conferences specific to positive psychology, numerous encyclopedias (e.g., Lopez, 2009) and handbooks (e.g., Lopez & Snyder, 2009) on the subject, a veritable cottage industry of popular books tailored to the general reader on related topics (e.g., Weiner, 2008), and so on.

With the excitement surrounding the emerging field, came the desire among university professors to share this knowledge with students in seminars specifically devoted to positive psychology. Lacking course materials such as textbooks on positive psychology, early courses on the topic typically relied upon utilizing special issues or sections of academic journals devoted to the topic (e.g., Rich, 2001; Seligman & Csikszentmihalyi, 2000; Sheldon & King, 2001) or selected relevant journal articles. Other options included adoption of texts by psychologists 'doing positive psychology' before the term became widely used by the present movement in the late 1990s. For instance, *Flow* by Csikszentmihalyi (1990), *Learned Optimism* by Seligman (1991), or *Health and Optimism* by Peterson and Bossio (1991), all represented work of leading positive-psychologists-to-be that could form a component of a broader survey course in positive psychology (Rich, 2002). By 2002, *Authentic Happiness* by Martin E.P. Seligman was published. Subtitled 'Using the New Positive Psychology to Realize Your Potential for Lasting Fulfillment,' this well-written book targeted the general reader, included numerous high quality self-assessment activities, sold like a best-selling pop psychology book, yet was firmly grounded in psychological science. It made a helpful and convenient substitute for a yet to be written, dedicated academic positive psychology textbook.

Finally, in 2004, the first positive psychology textbooks were published. Carr (2004) of University College Dublin published *Positive Psychology* and the late Bolt (2004) of Calvin College published *Pursuing Human Strengths: A Positive Psychology Guide*. Other textbooks soon followed: Compton (2005) offered *Introduction to Positive Psychology* and Peterson (2006) wrote *A Primer in Positive Psychology*. The year 2007 saw the publication of the first edition of *Positive Psychology* by Snyder and Lopez (2007) and *Positive Psychology*, published in 2009, by Baumgardner and Crothers (2009), both of the University of Wisconsin-Eau Claire round out the list of available positive psychology texts. Thus, in less than a decade since Martin Seligman and other leaders met in Akumal, half a dozen positive psychology textbooks have become available (Table 1). While the market size is clearly smaller than that of Introduction to Psychology courses, or service courses such as

Table 1. Comparison of available positive psychology textbooks.

Title	Author	Year	Number of pages	Number of chapters	Supplements	Planned revision?	Test bank	Instructor Powerpoint
Positive Psychology	Baumgardner and Crothers	2009	338	12	Instructor's manual w/exercises, discussion questions, and multiple choice questions	Not yet	Y	Y
Pursuing Human Strengths: A Positive Psychology Guide	Bolt	2004	216	9	None, but chapters include many exercises and self-assessments	Author passed away in 2009; publisher may plan revised edition with another author	N	N
Positive Psychology	Carr	2004	388	9	None, but chapters include self-assessments and chapter ends include personal development and research questions as well as resource lists	Revised 2nd edition for 2011; currently in press	N	N
Introduction to Positive Psychology	Compton	2005	276	12	None, but chapter ends include resource lists and personal exploration activities	2nd edition in progress for 2012 (w/Edward Hoffman)	N	N
A Primer in Positive Psychology	Peterson	2006	386	12	None, but chapter ends include exercises and resource lists	Not yet	N	N
Positive Psychology (2nd edition)	Snyder, Lopez, and Pedrotti	2011	588	18	Instructor's website and chapters include personal mini-experiments and life enhancement strategies	2011 is most recent edition	Y	Y

Lifespan Development, psychologists teaching positive psychology should be pleased that they now have a range of quality texts from which to select. This article aims to offer a comparison of these textbooks, as well as their supplements, and other texts which may be helpful for those engaged in the teaching of positive psychology.

A comparison of core positive psychology textbooks

Perhaps the first question a prospective instructor of a positive psychology seminar has concerning textbooks is 'are they all the same?'. The quick answer to that is 'yes and no'. The six positive psychology books currently available that aim at serving as a core classroom textbook each cover a number of topics relevant to the field, yet the textbooks vary significantly in length and depth and in the specific content areas covered. In addition, only two of the six textbooks currently have supplements, such as instructor Powerpoint presentations and test banks, available. In brief, it is not that one book excels and the others fail, it is that each book has a set of strengths that make it more appropriate for some settings than others.

Briefer textbooks well-suited to serve as a supplement

Bolt's (2004) *Pursuing Human Strengths: A Positive Psychology Guide* and Compton's (2005) *Introduction to Positive Psychology* are the briefest texts available, at 216 and 276 pages, respectively. Bolt's book included the following nine chapters: love, empathy, self-control, wisdom, commitment, happiness, self-respect, hope, and friendship. The chapters presented are well-written surveys of the expected literature. The notable absence of chapters related to positive institutions, one pillar of positive psychology, can be remedied with extra readings as desired. Compton's book has 12 chapters on the following topics: introduction; emotions and motivation; subjective well-being; leisure, optimal and peak experiences; wellness, health psychology and positive coping; excellence, aesthetics, creativity, and genius; positive mental health; interventions for enhanced well-being; religion, spirituality, and well-being; work, community, culture, and well-being; and a look toward the future of positive psychology. Both books seem somewhat short to serve as the sole text at most colleges and universities, and the brevity means that certain topics were excluded. For instance, both the Bolt text and the Compton text are missing chapter length treatments of character strengths and virtues, resilience, culture, and goals (for further comparison of textbook content, see Table 2). Most instructors will wish to supplement these texts with further books or journal articles, unless

student preparation levels or an unusual term length indicate otherwise. Notably, Bolt's text was originally envisioned to be utilized itself as a supplement for other psychology courses, in particular, as a supplemental reading for introduction to psychology courses. It could serve ably in that role, and the book includes numerous activities, exercises, and self-assessments that could aid in encouraging student engagement in large introductory psychology courses and in correcting for the historical negative focus of psychology. Sadly, Martin Bolt passed away in 2009 and the future of the textbook is unclear at present, although it is possible that a new author may revise and update this textbook at some time in the future. William Compton is currently at work on a revised edition of his 2005 textbook and has added co-author Edward Hoffman of Yeshiva University in New York City. Hoffman brings a background in clinical psychology, especially humanistic psychology, as he is an editor for the *Journal of Humanistic Psychology* and author of a biography of Maslow (Hoffman, 1999). This edition is scheduled for publication in early 2012. While neither of these textbooks currently has supplements available, such as a test bank or instructor Powerpoint presentations, both textbooks do offer numerous exercises, personal exploration activities, and self-assessments, many of which seem promising for actual classroom use.

In-depth textbooks

Peterson's (2006) *A Primer in Positive Psychology* and Baumgardner and Crothers's (2009) *Positive Psychology* seem closer to what many instructors are accustomed to in terms of classroom textbooks. At 386 and 338 pages, respectively, these two textbooks are significantly longer than the Bolt and Compton offerings, yet still run shorter than the 650 to 750 or so pages common among introduction to psychology textbooks. Thus, once again, instructors may need to search for supplemental readings, such as journal articles, edited books, or special topics books. An early proponent of positive psychology, Peterson is well-positioned to make an important contribution with his textbook, and indeed his well-written accessible book accurately describes positive psychological research (including much of his own seminal work, e.g., Peterson & Seligman, 2004) at a level that many teachers of psychology will find is truly helpful for students entering the field. The Peterson textbook includes the following 12 chapters: What is positive psychology?; learning about positive psychology: not a spectator sport; pleasure and positive experience; happiness; positive thinking; character strengths; values; interests, abilities, and accomplishments; wellness; positive interpersonal relationships; enabling

Table 2. Comparison of the chapter content of available positive psychology textbooks.

Chapter Content	Positive Psychology — Baumgardner and Crothers (2009)	Pursuing Human Strengths — Bolt (2004)	Positive Psychology — Carr (2004)	Introduction to Positive Psychology — Compton (2005)	A Primer in Positive Psychology — Peterson (2006)	Positive Psychology (2nd Edition) — Snyder et al. (2011)
Introduction	Y	Y	N	Y	Y	Y
Happiness	Y	Y	Y	Y (ch. 3)	Y	Y (ch. 6)
Self-control	Y	Y	N	N (but see pp. 48–49; 121)	N	N
Relationships	Y	Y (ch. 1; ch. 9)	Y	Y	Y (ch. 10)	Y (ch. 12)
Positive emotions/traits	Y	Y (ch. 2 empathy)	Y (also ch. 2, ch. 4, and ch. 7)	Y (ch. 2; ch. 8)	Y (ch. 3 pleasure/positive experience)	Y (ch. 6 and others)
Character strengths/virtues	Y	N	N (but see pp. 51–3, 73–74, 182–184)	N (but see pp. 172–173; 181)	Y	Y (ch. 3)
Resilience	Y	N	N (but see pp. 188–189; 270–271; 300)	N (but see pp. 151–153; 187–188)	N (but index cites relevant pages throughout text)	N (but see ch. 5, esp. pp. 91–100)
Hope/optimism	N (but see pp. 193–204)	Y (ch. 8)	Y	Y (ch. 6)	Y (ch. 5 positive thinking)	Y (ch. 8)
Culture	N (but see ch. 6 money, happiness, and culture)	N	N	N	N (but index cites term numerous times)	Y (ch. 2 and ch. 4)
Wisdom	N (but see pp. 213–220)	Y (ch. 4)	Y (ch. 5)	N (but see pp. 155–158)	N	Y (ch. 9 wisdom and courage)
Goals	Y	N (but see ch. 5)	N (but see pp. 314–315)	N	N (but index cites term numerous times)	N (but see pp. 396–397)
Conclusion	Y	N	N	Y	Y	Y

institutions; and the future of positive psychology. Each chapter ends with numerous student exercises and resource lists including books, articles, web sites, films, and even songs that relate to each chapter. Some professors may wish to utilize these lists to enhance their seminars with discussion starters such as playing brief film clips or songs from these lists at the beginnings of class. There is ample humor in the book as well. A major strength of the text is that its author, as a major player in the field, has insured that important positive psychology topics that have been ignored or neglected by some other authors are included here. Such topics include positive institutions and human accomplishments, such as creativity.

The Baumgardner and Crothers book covers some expected ground, but also some relatively unique topics for a positive psychology textbook. This content may encourage some professors to select this particular text and discourage others. The 12 chapters include: what is positive psychology?; the meaning and measure of happiness, positive emotions and well-being; resilience; happiness and the facts of life; money, happiness, and culture; personal goals; self-regulation and self-control; positive traits; virtue and strengths of character; close relationships and well-being; and a summary chapter, life above zero. The inclusion of chapters on personal goals and on self-regulation and self-control is unique among the positive psychology textbooks. One strength of the Baumgardner and Crothers textbook is the availability of an instructor's manual with exercises, discussion questions, and multiple choice questions. In addition to the test bank, there is also a Powerpoint presentation set available for instructors.

The two most recently published positive psychology texts are also the most extensive. Snyder et al.'s (2011) *Positive Psychology* runs to 588 pages, while the revised edition of Alan Carr's *Positive Psychology* (the first edition ran to 388 pages) is currently in press and scheduled for 2011 publication. Both of these textbooks seem in general to be written at a somewhat higher level than the other four books, in terms of scientific and academic rigor and demands on the reader. Carr, the director of the doctoral training program in clinical psychology at University College Dublin, is the only positive psychology textbook author writing in English who resides outside the US. Perhaps his unique position explains the frequent citation of scholars both within and beyond the US. As psychology becomes increasingly internationalized, Carr's inclusion of scholarship from across the globe is a special strength. The nine chapters of his book include chapters on happiness; flow; hope and optimism; emotional intelligence; giftedness, creativity, and wisdom; positive traits and motives; the positive self; positive relationships; and positive change. Like a number of positive psychology textbooks, there is not a stand-alone chapter on topics relating to positive

institutions (such as schools and workplaces), although some of the literature surveyed obviously touches on these issues. There are no supplements for the Carr textbook (such as a test bank or instructor Powerpoints), but chapters include self-assessments, personal development and research questions, and resource lists, including (in separate lists) academic and self-help readings, as well as references for measures for use in research. Such resources are bound to be helpful for students considering term papers or even beginning research projects.

The Snyder et al. (2011) textbook *Positive Psychology* is unique in that it is the first positive psychology textbook to become available in a revised edition. Since the writing of the first edition, published in 2007, C.R. Snyder has passed away and a new co-author, Jennifer Pedrotti (see her article in this special issue) of California Polytechnic State University has been added. The coverage of this nearly 600-page textbook is obviously more detailed and extensive than many of the other positive psychology textbooks. For instance, this textbook runs nearly three times the length of the Bolt text. The 18 chapters include: an introductory chapter; Eastern and Western perspectives; classification and measures of strengths and positive outcomes; developing strengths and living well in a cultural context; living well at every stage of life; positive affect, positive emotions, happiness, and well-being; emotion-focused coping, emotional intelligence, socioemotional selectivity theory; self-efficacy, optimism, and hop' mindfulness, flow, and spirituality; empathy, altruism, gratitude, and forgiveness; attachment, love, and relationships; balanced conceptualizations of mental health and behavior; interceding to prevent the bad and enhance the good; positive schooling; good work; building better communities; and a concluding summary chapter. One of the real strengths of this textbook, beyond its ample proportions are its coverage of a number of neglected fields of positive psychology. Instructors wishing chapter length treatments of positive institutions such as schools and work would be strongly encouraged to review this book. Another major strength of this textbook is that it stands virtually alone in terms of its cross-cultural and cross-national coverage. Several entire thought provoking chapters focus specifically on this critical dimension. Students will be appropriately challenged to consider what assumptions about well-being, happiness, and other states and traits positive psychologists make when they fail to consider the issues across the globe. The revised edition of the textbook expanded and improved what was already a considerable strength in this regard.

The Snyder, Lopez, and Pedrotti book comes with an instructor's website and chapters include ample personal mini-experiments, integrated case studies, and life enhancement strategies. Ample graphics and photos, as well as text boxes which offer interesting sidebars greatly enhance the readability of the text. In addition, the textbook supplements include instructor Powerpoints and a high quality test bank.

As a final note, international readers may be interested to learn that a number of the core positive psychology textbooks discussed in this section have been published in languages other than English. Peterson's (2006) book is available in Japanese, Korean, and Chinese. The Baumgardner and Crothers textbook (2009) has been published in Korean. Carr's (2004) book is now available in Polish, German, Chinese, and Spanish.

In sum, positive psychology instructors should be excited that, only a decade after its founding, there are now six solid core positive psychology textbooks from which to choose. Each of these textbooks has its own strengths, though in general one could argue that virtually all of the books could provide more coverage about positive institutions (such as families, schools, work, and religion), about cognitive strengths (such as creativity), and especially about cross-cultural and cross-national factors. One choice for instructors who wish to enhance the cross-cultural component of their positive psychology seminar may be to add *Culture and Well-Being*, Diener (2009), an affordable collection of mostly previously published articles on the topic, by Diener and colleagues. Suitable for advanced undergraduates and graduate students, the collection could also serve the added purpose of exposing students to original research. Another notable fact about the current crop of positive psychology core textbooks is that only two of the six books come with formal supplements, such as instructor Powerpoints and test banks, a potentially significant factor for some professors considering an unfamiliar or new course preparation.

Supplemental readings

Special issues of journals

Some instructors may choose to expand their positive psychology seminar readings through the use of special journal issues devoted to the topic. Depending upon the preparation level of the students, such an arrangement may work well, as a number of the special issues tend to focus on conceptual and theoretical reviews and literature surveys, rather than single experiments or research requiring knowledge of advanced statistics or methods. Among these special issues are *American Psychologist, 55*(1) (2000), *American Psychologist, 56*(3) (2001), *Journal of Humanistic Psychology, 41*(1) (2001), *Journal of Youth and Adolescence, 32*(1) (2003), *Review of General Psychology, 9*(2) (2005), and *Theory & Psychology, 18*(5) (2008). Often these individual back issues are available from publishers at reduced cost and

may be purchased individually or in classroom size volumes.

Activities: film resource

One exciting option for a supplement to a positive psychology textbook is *Positive Psychology at the Movies: Using Films to Build Virtues and Character Strengths* (Wedding & Niemiec, 2008). Here, the authors lead the readers through the six virtues and 24 strengths identified by positive psychology leaders Seligman, Peterson, and colleagues, describing one relevant key film in detail, and summarizing many other worthy films. For instance, Paul Rusesabagina in the film *Hotel Rwanda* is described as an exemplar of courage (p. 58), while *Gandhi* is discussed as an exemplar of leadership (p. 152). Notably, the authors describe numerous international films appropriate for each book section. The authors include helpful sidebars describing practical applications, such as relating the films to events in one's own life. A number of helpful appendices allow readers to delve more deeply into cinema, with ample suggestions in list form of films that may serve as exemplars of character strengths. Another appendix lists stimulating questions for classroom, therapy, and movie group discussions. Professors who teach positive psychology will much appreciate appendix C which lists a number of brief film clips (including the times and scene descriptions) appropriate for classroom use. The book may also be used as a core text for a course specifically focusing upon positive psychology and film. Indeed, the authors include a sample syllabus of just such a course. At any rate, all prospective instructors of positive psychology will want to be familiar with this book.

Conclusion

Just over a decade ago, positive psychology was formally founded. Since that time, the field has grown dramatically, with its own journal, conferences, and funding. Instructors quickly became interested in sharing this emerging and rapidly expanding field with their students. Initially, professors were forced to assemble seminars in *ad hoc* haphazard fashion, with materials from a range of sources. Now, as positive psychology enters its second decade, the field has matured. With six core positive psychology textbooks to choose from, several of which are in revised editions, and a veritable plethora of supplemental special journal issues and related books, the question is not, 'when will a positive psychology textbook become available?', but 'do I have to pick just one?'.

References

Baumgardner, S.R., & Crothers, M.K. (2009). *Positive psychology*. Upper Saddle River, NJ: Prentice Hall.

Bolt, M. (2004). *Pursuing human strengths: A positive psychology guide*. New York, NY: Worth.

Carr, A. (2004). *Positive psychology: The science of happiness and human strengths*. New York, NY: Routledge.

Compton, W.C. (2005). *Introduction to positive psychology*. Belmont, CA: Thomson Wadsworth.

Csikszentmihalyi, M. (1990). *Flow: The psychology of optimal experience*. New York, NY: Harper & Row.

Diener, E. (2009). *Culture and well-being: The collected works of Ed Diener*. New York, NY: Springer.

Hoffman, E. (1999). *The right to be human: A biography of Abraham Maslow*. Boston, MA: McGraw Hill.

Lopez, S.J. (Ed.). (2009). *The encyclopedia of positive psychology*. Malden, MA: Wiley-Blackwell.

Lopez, S.J., & Snyder, C.R. (Eds.). (2009). *Oxford handbook of positive psychology* (2nd ed.). New York, NY: Oxford University Press.

Peterson, C. (2006). *A primer in positive psychology*. New York, NY: Oxford University Press.

Peterson, C., & Bossio, L.M. (1991). *Health and optimism*. New York, NY: Free Press.

Peterson, C., & Seligman, M. (2004). *Character strengths and virtues: A handbook and classification*. New York, NY: Oxford University Press.

Rich, G. (Ed.). (2001). Positive psychology [Special issue]. *Journal of Humanistic Psychology, 41*, 4–153.

Rich, G. (2002). *Positive psychology*. Poster session presented at the National Institute on the Teaching of Psychology (NITOP), St. Petersburg Beach, FL.

Seligman, M.E.P. (1991). *Learned optimism*. New York, NY: Alfred A. Knopf.

Seligman, M.E.P. (2002). *Authentic happiness*. New York, NY: Free Press.

Seligman, M.E.P., & Csikszentmihalyi, M. (2000). Positive psychology: An introduction. *American Psychologist, 55*, 5–14.

Sheldon, K.M., & King, L. (2001). Why positive psychology is necessary. *American Psychologist, 56*, 216–217.

Snyder, C.R., & Lopez, S.J. (2007). *Positive psychology: The scientific and practical exploration of human strengths*. Thousand Oaks, CA: Sage.

Snyder, C.R., Lopez, S.J., & Pedrotti, J.T. (2011). *Positive psychology: The scientific and practical explorations of human strengths*. Thousand Oaks, CA: Sage.

Wedding, D., & Niemiec, R.M. (2008). *Positive psychology at the movies: Using films to build virtues and character strengths*. Cambridge, MA: Hogrefe.

Weiner, E. (2008). *The geography of bliss*. New York, NY: Hachette Book Group.

Insight or data: Using non-scientific sources to teach positive psychology

Eranda Jayawickreme[ab] and Marie J.C. Forgeard[a]

[a]Department of Psychology, University of Pennsylvania, Philadelphia, PA, USA; [b]Department of Psychology, Wake Forest University, Winston-Salem, NC, USA

Teaching positive psychology is a fascinating experience, in part because many of the issues it addresses are fundamental questions about living. One advantage of taking an interdisciplinary approach is that instructors can help students balance the valuable insights gained from the non-empirical literature on well-being with those gained from science. Positive psychology is distinctive, however, because its findings result from empirical investigation. Any inclusion of non-scientific sources should thus be accompanied with the caveat that claims about happiness need to be backed up with evidence. We discuss how positive psychology instructors can incorporate non-empirical material (from philosophy, the self-help literature, and religious) in their classes, while encouraging their students to think critically about them.

The question of what makes for a happy, fulfilling life has occupied laypeople, thinkers, philosophers, religious scholars, and politicians since the beginning of recorded history (McMahon, 2006). In the context of this long intellectual history, positive psychology is a relative newcomer. Moreover, the contemporary study of happiness and well-being is not limited to empirical research, but also includes important conceptual developments in economics (e.g., Sen, 2009), philosophy (e.g., Tiberius, 2008), human development (e.g., Nussbaum, 2000), and other disciplines in the social sciences and humanities. Political philosophers and human development researchers have, for example, proposed various accounts of the good life over the last 60 years (Ranis, Stewart, & Samman, 2006). Including non-scientific sources thus acknowledges that there is much about the nature of well-being that can be understood by going beyond the realm of positive psychology.

We believe that taking an interdisciplinary approach to teaching positive psychology carries many advantages. For one, the study of well-being and happiness has a long multidisciplinary history (Forgeard, Jayawickreme, Kern, & Seligman, 2011; Kesebir & Diener, 2008), and any successful class on positive psychology should, at the very least, acknowledge this heritage. Additionally, given the salience of 'the pursuit of happiness' in American culture, connecting the science of happiness to real-world discussions about the nature of happiness in the popular media (e.g., self-help books and magazines) highlights the relevance of positive psychology to important aspects of students' daily lives. Finally, such an approach underlines the fact that positive psychology provides the scientific tools to better identify truths about what well-being is and how it can be increased.

The challenge: Privileging the science

What distinguishes positive psychology from other disciplines investigating well-being is its focus on science and empirically derived insights. Positive psychology has repeatedly highlighted its commitment to the scientific method (Peterson, 2006). In their flagship article, Seligman and Csikszentmihalyi (2000) specifically distinguish positive psychology from the older humanistic psychology tradition and from the self-help movement, which both lacked a cumulative empirical base: '[P]ositive psychology does not rely on wishful thinking, faith, self-deception, fads, or hand-waving; it tries to adapt what is best in the scientific method to the unique problems that human behavior presents to those who wish to understand it in all its complexity'.

Two recent popular books, *The How of Happiness* (Lyubomirsky, 2007), and *Positivity* (Fredrickson, 2009), constitute excellent examples of positive psychology's commitment to privileging empirically derived insights into the nature of well-being.

Both texts – which we have used in our positive psychology classes – highlight the scientific nature of their recommendations. Lyubomirsky (2007, pp. 3–4) explicitly states this commitment:

> First, the star of *The How of Happiness* is science, and the happiness-increasing strategies that I and other social psychologists have developed are its key supporting players. My story is that of a research scientist, not a clinician, life coach or self-help guru... *The How of Happiness* is different from many self-help books inasmuch as it represents a distillation of what researchers of the science of happiness, including myself, have uncovered in their empirical investigations. Every suggestion that I offer is supported by scientific research; if evidence is mixed or lacking on a particular subject, I plainly say so.

Is it possible to incorporate non-empirical sources without diluting this message? In the remainder of this article, we discuss a number of ways in which we have found non-scientific readings useful and instructive in the positive psychology classes that we have taught as instructors or teaching assistants. Next, we briefly overview the different empirical materials that can be employed, and provide some anecdotal evidence for the utility of these sources from student evaluations of an undergraduate class and from discussion sections we taught. We end with a cautionary note about the limitations of combining empirical and non-empirical materials.

Uses of non-empirical materials in the classroom

Some researchers within positive psychology have advocated an interdisciplinary approach to teaching well-being. For example, interdisciplinarity is a central premise of *The Happiness Hypothesis* (Haidt, 2006). This text is an excellent introduction to the science of happiness,[1] yet Haidt structures the book around 10 'Great Ideas,' which, while having some empirical support, have their origins in philosophical and religious traditions. One promising approach to introducing the field of positive psychology therefore involves placing this discipline in the broader context of a search for well-being that has probably continued for as long as human civilization. The *Happiness Hypothesis* model presents one such method for introducing the science of well-being to undergraduate students.

In our experience, incorporating non-empirical materials into positive psychology curricula provides at least three main benefits. First, non-empirical sources give instructors the opportunity to set up the intellectual foundations of the discipline of positive psychology and place the discipline in a broader historical context. Second, non-empirical sources can introduce students to ideas that lend themselves to empirical exploration in a way that may reinforce and/

or deepen their understanding of the topic at hand. Finally, non-empirical sources can be used to explore the applicability of empirical findings to the real world.

Setting up the intellectual foundations of the discipline

Incorporating a discussion of historical trends of well-being plays an important role in highlighting the relationship between positive psychology and the broader intellectual history of well-being. Explaining the history of important ideas in psychology is an important task for instructors (Gleitman, 1984), and this is especially true for positive psychology given the long-standing intellectual history of happiness and well-being. For example, discussing the evolution of conceptions of happiness from Aristotle's notion of eudaimonia, to Epictetus' argument that happiness lies in distinguishing between changeable and non-changeable aspects of one's life, through to the privileging of pleasure by utilitarian philosophers such as Bentham, can help students better appreciate the preponderance of different well-being constructs in positive psychology – for example, distinguishing between the subjective well-being and the more eudaimonic psychological well-being approaches (Ryan & Deci, 2001). Students will better understand the mission of positive psychology if they are aware of the intellectual traditions that inspired it, including long-standing debates about the very nature of central concepts such as happiness or virtue. Including philosophical discussions of different types of well-being constructs can therefore serve a useful role in motivating students to think critically about the intellectual history of happiness, including positive psychology's contribution to this history (e.g. Haybron, 2008; Jayawickreme & Pawelski, in press; McMahon, 2006; Sen, 1992).

Presenting interesting ideas that lend themselves to scientific exploration

Non-empirical materials can serve an important pedagogical function by introducing students to interesting questions that have the potential to be empirically investigated. For example, techniques proposed in self-help books – such as the best-seller *Don't Sweat the Small Stuff – and It's All Small Stuff* (Carlson, 1996), which provides 100 meditations and interventions for increasing meaning in life by countering daily stressors – can serve as the basis for a discussion of the utility of such intervention techniques for promoting well-being. While many of the assertions in such books lack empirical support, some do tie in well with contemporary questions in the field. Such material can also help instructors highlight the superiority of empirical investigation. For example, one can begin a discussion of the benefits of optimism by posing some of the criticisms levied against having a rose-tinted outlook on life. One student, for instance, made the following comment on the challenges of cultivating acceptance of past negative events while remaining optimistic about the future:

> Many authors have argued that we should want to conform our desires to the events in life, rather than try to conform events to our desires. The idea that we should accept the fact that we cannot change our past and the present moment is something that I can easily relate to. And I totally agree that we shouldn't dwell on the past as it cannot be changed! One way to be satisfied with your life is just to accept what we have. But it is easier said than done. I think sometimes it is not that easy to just accept your life as it is. People always try to change things and it might be hard for them to make this distinction between future and present moments that cannot be changed.

In addition to introducing students to ideas that can be empirically studied, non-empirical sources of information can make the material 'come alive' for students, and allow them to actively participate in constructing the knowledge that is being imparted to them. The topic of savoring – the act of paying attention to and fully appreciating present positive experiences (Bryant & Veroff, 2007) – provides a useful example of the different manners in which a concept can be taught to students, including ways in which non-scientific sources can be used to promote active learning (Bonwell & Eison, 1991).

There are at least three ways in which students can come to understand what savoring entails, including what it 'feels' like. The first way is for them to learn the definitions that their instructors have provided, or to read scientific descriptions such as the ones provided in academic articles or books. While this approach may be satisfactory for many students, it is possible that other students in the class may learn better when they are asked to actively construct definitions and descriptions for themselves. A second way is to ask students to engage in experiential learning, by having them complete a savoring exercise and develop strategies to enhance their experience. In a small discussion section conducted by the second author, students brought in something for everyone to savor, including food, smells, music, and brief movie clips. In addition to this in-class savoring exercise, students had also been asked to practice savoring during the week leading up to the discussion group. Aside from being an extremely enjoyable discussion section, students commented that completing the exercise had provided them with insights that went beyond what they had read in their textbooks, and suggested new empirical questions they would like to see answered. One student explained:

> I took away a lot of interesting insight from this exercise. First, savoring can be difficult if one is hungry, thirsty, or does not enjoy the object to be savored. Second, I discovered that there may be individual differences when it comes to savoring. Some people may be more disposed to savor certain things over others (e.g., I can savor music more easily than I can savor food).

In addition to personal experiential evidence, students may also benefit from reading literary descriptions of positive psychology constructs. Literary materials may also help students gain a deeper understanding of what is meant in scientific descriptions. For savoring, the second author likes to use short stories by French writer Delerm (1999, p. 52) in his collection *We Could Almost Eat Outside: An Appreciation of Life's Small Pleasures*. Among other little pleasures, Delerm describes the feeling of walking through a garden in August:

> Summertime, early afternoon in the middle of August, and you're walking through a garden somewhere in Aquitaine. Not a breeze for miles around. Even the light seems to have fallen asleep over there by the tomatoes: a single spot illuminates the redness of each fruit. They're stained with little specks of soil from the last time it rained. You feel a sudden urge to rinse them in cold water and eat them while their flesh is still warm. Time seems to stand still as you register the subtle color variations. Some of the tomatoes are pale green, hinting at deeper hues in their hearts, and others are almost acidic orange.

Highlighting the practical applicability of positive psychology

One of the exciting developments of positive psychology in recent times has been the potential for the practical application of well-being findings. For example, there has been increasing interest in the relevance of well-being research for public policy (Diener, Lucas, Schimmack, & Helliwell, 2009; Forgeard et al., 2011). Another important area of relevance for positive psychology is the workplace. For example, in *Delivering Happiness*, Hsieh (2010) lays out the corporate philosophy of the online retail company Zappos, which is mostly derived from theoretical work in positive psychology. In our experience, such applied topics are ideal material for the final weeks of a course, when the focus shifts from basic research to its practical applicability. The first author assigned chapters from *Delivering Happiness* for his lecture on positive psychology in the workplace, which elicited the following response from a student:

> I thought this chapter was an excellent reading to wrap up the last week's discussion board. Throughout the semester, I have found the topic of Positive Psychology to be full of useful information and ideas. It has provided me with various strategies for seeking out and maintaining my own happiness. This is obviously a worthwhile goal. However, I have worried that trying to build a life around happiness is unwise, as other facets may be neglected... [T]he ideas laid out by

Hsieh are obviously closely related to Seligman's ideas about a happy life. While Hsieh refers to Pleasure, Passion, and Higher Purpose, Seligman talks about the Pleasurable Life, the Engaged Life, and the Meaningful Life. While the terminology differs very slightly, the ideas are almost identical. However, I think Hsieh succeeds in incorporating these theories into a model that we can all relate to these days: industry.

These readings can also motivate students to think critically about the possible limits of the application of positive psychology. The following student for example wondered whether happiness could truly replace profits as the 'bottom line' in business:

> I highly doubt Hsieh would have been made CEO of Zappos had he not considered the company's profits first. Further, I'm sure he would not be concerning himself with happiness to this degree if the profits were not already secure.

Including such material – if used carefully – can help foster critical thinking by making students think about the implications of positive psychology research, and the manner in which it can contribute in meaningful ways to making life better (Zimbardo, 2004).

Types of relevant non-scientific materials

As we have discussed, non-scientific resources can play an important pedagogical role in the dissemination of positive psychology research. We briefly discuss different types of material that instructors can utilize in their positive psychology classes.

Philosophy

There is a very rich literature on happiness and well-being in the philosophy literature, and we have utilized a number of resources in the positive psychology classes we have instructed (e.g., Irvine, 2009; Nussbaum, 2000; Sen, 2009; Sumner, 1999). For example, the first author recently taught a senior undergraduate seminar on well-being and public policy, in which he examined the potential of happiness and well-being research to inform public policy. While he focused on contrasting standard economic indicators such as GNP with alternate approaches from positive psychology, students also read the work of important thinkers who have written extensively about this issue. The work of Sen (1992, 1999), for instance, lends itself to interesting conversations about ways in which policy-makers may want to improve the well-being of their citizens. Sen's work constitutes a good example of the 'objective-list' account of well-being, which stipulates that individuals can achieve well-being if they have access to particular objective circumstances. This account departs from the subjective approach, which equates well-being with feeling good

and being satisfied with one's own life (Layard, 2005). However, Sen did not spell out exactly *which* functionings should be pursued and valued, thus allowing different cultures and individuals to determine this themselves. His approach stands in contrast with Nussbaum's (2000) specific list of capabilities, which can also serve as a good basis for a class discussion.

In addition, a commendable interdisciplinary endeavor to link current research in positive psychology with important philosophical questions has helped maintain a sustained dialog between philosophy and psychology (e.g., Jayawickreme & Pawelski, in press; Jayawickreme, Pawelski, & Seligman 2008; Kesebir & Diener, 2008; Kristjánsson, 2010; Nussbaum, 2007; Seligman, 2002, 2011; Tiberius, 2008). Over-utilizing philosophical texts can however potentially confuse students early on in the course. We therefore recommend picking select texts that tie in specifically with current conceptual or empirically questions in positive psychology (see our earlier point on demarcating the intellectual history of ideas in the field). To find such texts, we recommend Cahn and Vitrano's (2007) *Happiness: Classic and contemporary readings in philosophy*. This volume provides an excellent selection of philosophical perspectives on happiness. In particular, the 'Contemporary Theories' section includes readings that can be used to highlight debates surrounding the nature of happiness. This section, for example, reviews the work of Davis (1981) on happiness as pleasure, Tatarkiewicz (1966) on happiness as satisfaction, Kraut (1979) on happiness as Aristotelian eudaimonia, and Annas (1998) on happiness as virtue.

Literature

Literary texts can play an important instructive role in teaching positive psychology. In particular, such material can provide vivid examples of positive psychology concepts, such as character, gratitude, happiness, resilience and post-traumatic growth. One example of a relevant literary text is *Letter to My Daughters* (Angelou, 2008), which includes illuminating essays on character and philanthropy. In one assigned section – 'Porgy and Bess' – the author recounts when she was instructed to 'write (her) blessings' (Angelou, 2008, p. 66). Another example is *Wild Poets of Ecstasy* (Moores, 2011), which collects together poetry across many cultures and time periods highlighting human behavior at its best. Such material can be especially helpful in the early stages of a course, especially when used as motivation for assignments, as noted earlier with the example of savoring. Persian poet Rumi (2000), for example, provides great material to discuss positive subjective experiences, such as love or beauty, as conveyed in the following poem:

> With the Beloved's water of life, no illness remains

In the Beloved's rose garden of union, no thorn
remains.

They say there is a window from one heart to another
How can there be a window where no wall remains?

Literary texts can also be used to illustrate some of
the basic tenets of positive psychology, by providing
concrete examples for students to ponder. For
example, the mental state of Meursault, Camus'
(1946) main protagonist in the famous novel *The
Stranger*, provides an interesting illustration of the
necessity to conceive happiness as more than the mere
absence of misery. While Meursault does not appear to
suffer from great unhappiness or depression, his
inability to find meaning in life or to establish
satisfying relationships with others clearly lead him
to live in a 'limbo-like psychological condition'
(Bozorgnia, 2009, p. 27).

Self-help books

One should be especially careful in using self-help texts
in positive psychology given the preponderance of such
books, which are in many cases are based on highly
questionable beliefs. One egregious example of such a
text is *The Secret* (Byrne, 2006), which promotes
magical thinking as providing the key to happiness.
Moreover, it is important that students are instructed
clearly that positive psychology's unique contribution
to the understanding of happiness and well-being lies
comes from its focus on empirical findings and its
commitment to the scientific method (as noted earlier).
Some self-help texts can, however, be useful in helping
students understand some of the core ideas behind
positive psychology interventions. For example, *Don't
Sweat the Small Stuff – and It's All Small Stuff*
(Carlson, 1996) clearly presents a series of positive
interventions, some of which have already been
subjected to empirical examination. The first author
has successfully used some of these interventions as
homework assignments, while being careful to highlight the empirical research behind positive interventions (e.g., Fredrickson, 2009; Lyubomirsky, 2007;
Schueller, 2010, 2011; Seligman, Steen, Park, &
Peterson, 2005).

Business- and policy-related material

As noted earlier, motivational books (Hsieh, 2009) that
highlight the applicability of positive psychology can
help make students think more critically about
applications of positive psychology research. Students
also find these materials exciting, as they showcase the
cutting-edge possibilities of the field. The literature on
well-being and public policy (Diener et al., 2009) offers
a similarly exciting synthesis that can serve as a
springboard for discussion on how the 'true' wealth
of nations should be assessed (Diener & Seligman,

2004). To illustrate the challenges raised by measuring
well-being for public policy, we recommend the Gallup
World Poll videos available on YouTube. In our
experience, students have found these classes to be
among the most enjoyable of the course.

Films

Using feature films as part of a class project is an
excellent method of showcasing some of the main
themes of a positive psychology class. This medium can
be especially useful for helping students think about
the relevance of positive psychology research in their
own lives. There are many resources available to assist
instructors in picking relevant films, and we direct
readers to Niemiec and Wedding's (2008) excellent
*Positive Psychology at The Movies: Using Films to
Build Virtues and Character Strengths*. One film that
the first author found to be especially useful in
teaching positive psychology was the film *Amélie*
(Deschamps, Ossard, & Jeunet, 2001), which Jon
Haidt has also used successfully in his class on
'Flourishing' at the University of Virginia. The film
focuses on the ways in which the title character
manages to overcome a lonely and traumatic childhood by savoring the simple pleasures of daily life.
Amélie's character however undergoes a personal
transformation after hearing of the death of Diana
the Princess of Wales, and discovering an old box of
childhood memorabilia (left there by a previous tenant)
in the wall of her apartment. These experiences trigger
a peak experience within Amélie, turning her into a
Good Samaritan focused on anonymously performing
good deeds for others. The first author found this film
to be a perfect springboard for discussion of many
topics, such as altruism, love, happiness, savoring, and
especially the emotion of moral elevation as felt by
both the audience and the title character.[2] Consider the
scene in which the narrator of the movie describes
Amélie's peak experience:

Amélie has a strange feeling of absolute harmony. It's
a perfect moment. Soft light. A scent in the air, the
quiet murmur of the city. She breathes deeply. Life is
simple and clear. A surge of love, an urge to help
mankind comes over her.

The film is also relevant to discussions of growth
following adversity, as Amélie later overcomes her
shyness and initial disappointments to find true love.
Such films have the potential to drive home the real-life
lessons of positive psychology. Additionally, students
love movie nights!

Conclusion: Promises and pitfalls

We believe that incorporating non-scientific materials
into positive psychology classes provides many

benefits. However, we caution that the success in using such material depends on the instructor's skill in highlighting both the insights and limits of such material. We illustrate this challenge with another student's comment:

> [T]he non-scientific readings did help me with my understanding of positive psychology because they were in easier language....It made the subject material more benign ... and therefore was faster for me to digest. I plan on doing some of the exercises suggested by the non-scientific readings as they seem to be holding a lot of promise. They are also in line with a lot of spiritual traditions and time-tested family wisdom.

While readings helped this student gain interest in positive psychology and connect it to his own life, his feedback was concerning as it did not identify the necessity to supplement such readings with careful scientific reasoning and consideration of the empirical evidence. Instead, the student emphasized that he appreciated materials because they were easy to understand, and because they confirmed previously held beliefs. This view is in line with the common belief that positive psychology is 'just stuff my mother already knows', an unfortunate misconception in light of the counterintuitive and surprising scientific findings the discipline has brought to light (e.g., Forgeard, 2011).

We have thankfully received this type of response infrequently in our classes, yet it highlights a challenge perhaps unique to the teaching of positive psychology. Many insights about the roots and ends of happiness are intuitively appealing, yet empirical research has proven many of these insights to be inaccurate. When incorporating non-scientific material into positive psychology classes, we need to be mindful of the potency of such material, select wisely, and – hardest of all – teach well.

Notes

1. The first author has used this text in all his Positive Psychology classes, in part because of the very positive response from students.
2. Many thanks to Jon Haidt for providing the first author notes on *Amélie* from his Flourishing class, from which the ideas in this paragraph are adapted, as well as for his permission to use these materials in this article.

References

Angelou, M. (2008). *Letter to my daughter*. New York, NY: Random House.

Annas, J. (1998). Virtue and eudaimonism. *Social Philosophy and Policy, 15*, 37–55.

Bonwell, C., & Eison, J. (1991). *Active learning: Creating excitement in the classroom*. Washington, DC: Eric Clearinghouse on Higher Education, George Washington University.

Bozorgnia, B. (2009). *All imaginable splendors: Positive psychology and literary criticism* (Unpublished master's thesis). University of Pennsylvania, Philadelphia, PA.

Bryant, F., & Veroff, J. (2007). *Savoring: A new model of positive experience*. Mahwah, NJ: Erlbaum.

Byrne, R. (2006). *The secret*. New York, NY: Atria.

Cahn, S.M., & Vitrano, C. (2007). *Happiness: Classic and contemporary readings in philosophy*. New York, NY: Oxford University Press.

Camus, A. (1946). *The stranger*. New York, NY: Knopf.

Carlson, R. (1996). *Don't sweat the small stuff – and it's all small stuff*. New York, NY: Hyperion.

Davis, W. (1981). Pleasure and happiness. *Philosophical Studies, 39*, 305–317.

Delerm, P. (1999). *We could almost eat outside: An appreciation of life's small pleasures*. New York, NY: Picador.

Deschamps, J.-M., Ossard, C. (Producers), & Jeunet, J.-P. (Director). (2001). *Amélie* [Motion Picture]. France: UGC (France) & Miramax Zoe (USA).

Diener, E., Lucas, R., Schimmack, U., & Helliwell, J. (2009). *Well-being for public policy*. New York, NY: Oxford University Press.

Diener, E., & Seligman, M. (2004). Beyond money: Toward an economy of well-being. *Psychological Science in the Public Interest, 5*, 1–31.

Forgeard, M.J.C. (2011). Happy people thrive on adversity: Pre-existing mood moderates the effect of emotion inductions on creative thinking. *Personality and Individual Differences, 51*, 904–909.

Forgeard, M.J.C., Jayawickreme, E., Kern, M.L., & Seligman, M.E.P. (2011). Doing the right thing: Measuring well-being for public policy. *International Journal of Wellbeing, 1*, 79–106.

Fredrickson, B. (2009). *Positivity*. New York, NY: Crown.

Gleitman, H. (1984). Introducing psychology. *American Psychologist, 39*, 421–427.

Haidt, J. (2006). *The happiness hypothesis*. New York, NY: Basic Books.

Haybron, D.M. (2008). *The pursuit of unhappiness: The elusive psychology of well-being*. New York, NY: Oxford University Press.

Hsieh, T. (2010). *Delivering happiness*. New York, NY: Hachette.

Irvine, W. (2009). *A guide to the good life: The ancient art of stoic joy*. New York, NY: Oxford University Press.

Jayawickreme, E., & Pawelski, J. (in press). Positivity and the capabilities approach. *Philosophical Psychology*.

Jayawickreme, E., Pawelski, J., & Seligman, M.E.P. (2008). Happiness: Positive psychology and Nussbaum's capabilities approach. In R. Auxier (Ed.), *Library of living philosophers: The philosophy of Martha Nussbaum*. Chicago, IL: Open Court.

Kesebir, P., & Diener, E. (2008). In pursuit of happiness: Empirical answers to philosophical questions. *Perspectives on Psychological Science, 3*, 117–125.

Kraut, R. (1979). Two conceptions of happiness. *The Philosophical Review, 88*, 167–197.

Kristjánsson, K. (2010). Positive psychology, happiness, and virtue: The troublesome conceptual issues. *Review of General Psychology, 14*, 296–310.

Layard, R. (2005). *Happiness: Lessons from a new science.* London: Penguin Books.

Lyubomirsky, S. (2007). *The how of happiness.* New York, NY: The Penguin Press.

McMahon, D. (2006). *Happiness: A history.* New York, NY: Grove/Atlantic.

Moores, D.J. (Ed.). (2011). *Wild poets of ecstasy: An anthology of ecstatic verse.* Nevada City, CA: Blue Dolphin.

Niemiec, R.M., & Wedding, D. (2008). *Positive psychology at the movies: Using films to build virtues and character strengths.* Cambridge, MA: Hogrefe.

Nussbaum, M. (2000). *Women and human development.* New York, NY: Cambridge University Press.

Nussbaum, M. (2007). Who is the happy warrior? Philosophy poses questions to psychology. *The Journal of Legal Studies, 37,* S81–S113.

Peterson, C. (2006). *A primer in positive psychology.* New York, NY: Oxford University Press.

Ranis, G., Stewart, F., & Samman, E. (2006). Human development: Beyond the Human Development Index. *Journal of Human Development, 7,* 323–358.

Rumi (2000). *Rumi – thief of sleep: 180 quatrains from the Persian.* (S. Shiva, Trans.). Prescott, AZ: Hohm Press.

Ryan, R.M., & Deci, E.L. (2001). On happiness and human potentials: A review of research on hedonic and eudaimonic well-being. *Annual Review of Psychology, 52,* 141–166.

Schueller, S.M. (2010). Preferences for positive psychology exercises. *Journal of Positive Psychology, 5,* 192–203.

Schueller, S.M. (2011). To each his own well-being boosting intervention: Using preference to guide selection. *Journal of Positive Psychology, 6,* 300–313.

Seligman, M.E.P. (2002). *Authentic happiness.* New York, NY: Free Press.

Seligman, M.E.P. (2011). *Flourish.* New York, NY: Free Press.

Seligman, M.E.P., & Csikszentmihalyi, M. (2000). Positive psychology: An introduction. *American Psychologist, 55,* 5–14.

Seligman, M.E.P., Steen, T., Park, N., & Peterson, C. (2005). Positive psychology progress: Empirical validation of interventions. *American Psychologist, 60,* 410–421.

Sen, A.K. (1992). *Inequality reexamined.* Oxford: Clarendon Press.

Sen, A.K. (1999). *Development as freedom.* New York, NY: Anchor Books.

Sen, A.K. (2009). *The idea of justice.* Cambridge, MA: Belknap Press.

Sumner, L. (1999). *Welfare, happiness, and ethics.* New York, NY: Oxford University Press.

Tatarkiewicz, W. (1966). Happiness and time. *Philosophy and Phenomenological Research, 27,* 1–10.

Tiberius, V. (2008). *The reflective life.* New York, NY: Oxford University Press.

Zimbardo, P. (2004). Does psychology make a significant difference in our lives? *American Psychologist, 59,* 339–351.

Broadening perspectives: Strategies to infuse multiculturalism into a positive psychology course

Jennifer Teramoto Pedrotti

Department of Psychology and Child Development, California Polytechnic State University, San Luis Obispo, CA 93407, USA

As educators in any area of psychology, one has a responsibility to address issues of multicultural competence and to provide inclusive education for students from all walks of life. The specific discipline of positive psychology is aptly poised to use multiculturally competent teaching to undo some of the past pathologizing of individuals from traditionally marginalized groups. To this end, it is imperative that positive psychology courses operate from a framework that incorporates cultural context as a key feature in understanding the value, manifestation, and functioning of both strengths and weaknesses. Following a brief history of the integration of multiculturalism within the field of positive psychology, benefits are discussed with regard to infusing cultural context into a positive psychology course, and specific strategies for accomplishing this goal are offered.

As multiculturally competent educators, we must understand the necessity of infusing outlooks that incorporate individuals from different cultures into all of our classes. As Guideline 3 of the American Psychological Association's (APA, 2003, p. 10) Guidelines on Multicultural Education, Training, Research, Practice, and Organizational Change states: 'As educators, psychologists are encouraged to employ the constructs of multiculturalism and diversity in psychological education'. This, of course, also applies to courses in the areas of positive psychology as well.

Similarly to the way in which positive psychology and its goals of discussing strengths and assets in individuals and their environments have been neglected until more recent times (Seligman & Csikszentmihalyi, 2000), there has also been a lack of attention given to issues of culture and diversity in general (Sue & Sue, 2008). This lack of information, in both the realm of strengths and that of diversity, has provided us as psychologists with an incomplete understanding of how *humans* function. Indeed, we have only been discussing how *some humans* function, and only in *certain* ways (i.e., with regard to weakness and deficit; Pedrotti & Edwards, 2009). For historically marginalized groups, this lack of attention given to strengths is particularly damaging as these individuals are often victims of 'double jeopardy' in that they are pathologized, in general, because of strict adherence to the medical model in our field and are then pathologized again in comparison to the 'White standard' by

ethnocentric theories that leave no room for diverse descriptions of 'normal' behavior (Pedrotti & Edwards; Sue & Sue, 2003). Thus, it becomes imperative to include multicultural topics and discussion of context into any discussion of strengths and assets. Positive psychology may be an area that could be particularly beneficial to traditionally marginalized groups (e.g., people of color, LGBTI individuals, individuals from lower social classes; Pedrotti, Edwards, & Lopez, 2009).

In this article, a brief history of the inclusion of multiculturalism in the field of positive psychology will be given, as well as an introduction to the benefits of infusing culture in a positive psychology course. Following this, strategies will be given to assist positive psychology educators in developing class content that comes from a multicultural viewpoint.

Culture-free or culturally imbedded: A debate about relevance of culture

Within the field of positive psychology, there has been divergent thought about the inclusion of culture in interpreting and viewing strengths. Those on the 'culture-free' side of the debate hold that universal strengths exist and that the science used to measure them is robust enough to avoid error in this area (Peterson & Seligman, 2004). These scholars make the point that our empirical investigations are inherently objective, and thus research conducted on strengths can 'transcend particular cultures and politics and approach universality' (Seligman & Csikszentmihalyi, 2000, p. 5). Researchers in these areas have conducted multiple cross-cultural studies (i.e., those comparing various countries) and state that certain strengths or virtues can be found in all cultures (Myers, 1993; Peterson & Seligman, 2004). On this side of the debate, proponents state that happiness, for example, is something that all cultural groups value.

Those on the 'culturally imbedded' side of the debate assert that while all cultures do have strengths, they may be manifested differently in different groups (Pedrotti & Edwards, 2009; Snyder, Lopez, & Pedrotti, 2010). Courage, in the United States' majority culture, may be manifested as standing up for oneself or making one's viewpoint known despite its unpopularity. In other cultures, particularly those such as Eastern cultures who value conformity and harmony, courage may be manifested as enduring for the group, despite personal discomfort or dissent with a particular viewpoint. This is one example of the diverse ways that strengths using the same name (i.e., both of the above displays might be called courageous) may be operationalized and experienced differently. In addition, proponents of the culturally imbedded viewpoint state that though different strengths may be present in diverse cultures, the level of value placed on these strengths may differ substantially. While the strength of happiness is given a key role and value in the life of those in the United States and even incorporated in government documents such as the Constitution, personal happiness may not be given top priority in other cultural groups who believe that group happiness should be valued as more important despite the lack of personal satisfaction that these actions might bring (Snyder et al., 2010).

APA (2003) has emphasized the importance of viewing all topics from within a cultural context and as such many positive psychologists have decided to take the culturally imbedded approach of studying and teaching about these important topics (Pedrotti et al., 2009). While it is of course true that all cultures (and individuals within them) do possess strengths, it seems clear that these strengths may be manifested, operationalized, and ranked differently with regard to importance within different groups (Snyder et al., 2010). In talking about strengths in a 'culture-free' sense, we risk missing strengths that are conceptualized in cultures other than those to which we belong and/or unfairly pathologizing these individuals (Pedrotti et al., 2009). According to researchers, working within this approach, one must examine three areas: (a) how the strength became valued by the group; (b) how the strength is currently functioning positively; and (c) how the strength became important or valuable in the lives of the individuals (Christopher, 2005; Snyder et al., 2010). One might achieve this first step

(identifying how the strength becomes valued) by looking to cultural norms and aims. Often a strength gains status as such if it moves a society toward a desired goal. As an example, the construct of harmony is something that helps collectivist groups to achieve the communalism that they desire as a group in their society (Snyder et al., 2010). How the strength is functioning currently in a positive way can be gleaned through careful observation of such a community. Finally, the question of how the strength becomes valued by the individuals within a group must be assessed. This may occur over time as one develops value in being a member of that particular group. The group may transmit this information to the individual in various ways, but one simple vehicle is through the stories they tell. For example, in many Western fairy tales characters who are depicted as heroes have certain traits (e.g., bravery, solitary independence and strength, trickery and cleverness, etc.), while those in Eastern fairy tales may emphasize heroes with more collectivist values (e.g., working together, asking for help from wise elders, not being greedy, etc.; Snyder et al., 2010). Social interaction may become dependent on exhibiting certain traits that are thought to be desirable and in this way these strengths become important to the individual who would like to succeed within their particular culture. In working to answer these questions, one has a better understanding of how the strength manifests and operates within one's particular cultural context.

In addition, as educators, we are expected to translate and clarify research in such a way that our students, who may be of varying levels developmentally, can understand the conclusions put forth by researchers in the field. At a basic level, this may mean training our students to understand what 'significance' versus 'non-significance' means and how to read the appropriate statistics to understand these distinctions. Other examples might include being able to understand a correlation as a simple relationship as opposed to a causal one. When our students are able to interpret these various pieces of research, they are better able to judge the validity of such research as well.

As teachers of positive psychology who are also looking to incorporate a multicultural focus into our lectures and activities, a different, and more in-depth, reading of research is often required. Though researchers sometimes state emphatically that this is 'normal' or that this 'good result' has been found 'across cultures', we must recognize that distinctions such as 'normal', 'good', 'healthy', or 'appropriate' are all couched within cultural context (Hays, 2008). We must, therefore, teach our students to read 'between the lines' in all research; for example, looking to see if representative samples were used in the research, if definitions of constructs were conceptualized in one culture but are being used in another, if hypotheses made and confirmed are from a certain cultural worldview that may not be relevant to all groups. In this way, we can teach our students to read results with a critical eye before making decisions about the utility of such research for different groups.

Strategies for incorporating multiculturalism in positive psychology courses

The task of integrating any new component to a course is often viewed as a daunting one, but the resistance to the addition of multicultural topics is unfortunately a common occurrence (Gurung, 2009). Gurung (2009, p. 16) cites many examples of excuses including statements such as 'There's no time to cover diversity' or 'It does not fit my course'), however, a very common source of resistance is a source of confusion on how to best go about the integration of this topic. To facilitate this, a list of recommended readings for popular topics in positive psychology is presented in Table 1, and five strategies for instructors of positive psychology courses who wish to become more multiculturally competent in their teaching are presented below.

Emphasizing culture from the beginning of the course

As with any course, it is often the task of the instructor to introduce the class topic on the first day of class, and hence this is the best time to introduce the concept of culture as an integral part of talking about human strengths. When multiculturalism is discussed at the end of a course as a 'special topic', as it is in many textbooks, the student is robbed of the opportunity to apply what they learn about this important topic (Pedrotti, 2007). In addition, relegating this topic to a special lecture or even a separate course runs the risk of unintentionally marginalizing the topic as something that is 'extra' and thus not salient to the main discussion (Gurung, 2009). In addition, by presenting material regarding cultural context on the first day of class, the stage is easily set for referring back to these concepts throughout the course.

In talking about culture the first day, one might present the different sides, as listed previously, regarding 'culture-free' and 'culturally imbedded' viewpoints within the field. A discussion of the APA's (2003) view on inclusion of culture within teaching, research, and practice might also be prompted. Examples of various ways in which ignoring cultural context can be dangerous and damaging to traditionally marginalized populations may also be given.

One example I often give in my courses to explain the importance of paying attention to context discusses viewing behavior outside of its context. In this example, I talk about a fictional client who claims to hear a voice from inside that directs him in his life

during times of hardship. This entity is important to him, and thus he makes time for worship of this entity, including a weekly visit to a special building, which he claims is sacred. This individual believes that as part of a ritual conducted inside of this building, he is actually ingesting blood and body of this entity and feels that it speaks to him in various ways that help him in times of trouble. Without context, one might suggest varying diagnoses, including schizophrenia (ideas of reference, auditory hallucinations, etc.), however, when one is told that the context is a Catholic church, and that this is an individual who finds particular strength in spirituality and religion, this behavior is normalized as a practice that many millions of individuals in our world participate in each week. This type of example can then set the stage toward discussing other ways in which context is important in viewing psychological strength and/or weakness.

Explaining culture as a multifaceted concept

Many have advocated that the term 'culture' does not incorporate just one particular facet. Though we commonly think of the facets of race and ethnicity when the word 'culture' is mentioned (and it must be noted that these are very salient facets of culture in our society), other personal identifications such as gender, socioeconomic status or social class, sexual orientation, and others are also cultural facets that may be more or less salient for different individuals. Hays (2008) has developed a framework known as the ADDRESSING model in which each of the letters of the word 'addressing' stand for a particular facet (Figure 1). In this model, Hays delineates Age (specifically with regard to generation), Disability (developmental), Disability (acquired), Religion, Ethnicity (and/or race), Sexual orientation, Socioeconomic status (or social class), Indigenous heritage, Nation of origin, and Gender as different facets which may each influence development and identity in the life of the individual. Individuals may hold certain facets as more salient than others, and it is here that the dynamic process of cultural identity formation lies (Hays 2008). Strengths are often derived from these personal affiliations. For example, one individual may find strength in her caring nature, which she sees as coming from her gender identity as a woman. Another may feel that his strength of courage in standing up for himself even in the face of threat comes from his national identity as an American. These strengths may be seen in coming through various hardships as well. For example, a student in a lower socioeconomic status group may feel that experiencing a lack of resources has forced him to become more creative in getting his needs met (Edwards & Pedrotti, 2004; Pedrotti & Edwards, 2009).

Table 1. Reference articles for positive psychology in multicultural contexts.

General resources

Aronson, J., & Rogers, L. (2008). Overcoming stereotype threat. In S.J. Lopez (Ed.), *Positive psychology: Exploring the best in people: Vol. 3. Growing in the face of adversity* (pp. 109–121). Westport, CT: Greenwood Publishing Group.

Christopher, J.C., & Hickinbottom, S. (2008). Positive psychology, ethnocentrism, and the disguised ideology of individualism. *Theory and Psychology, 18*, 563–589. doi: 10.1177/0959354308093396.

Hays, P.A. (2008). *Addressing cultural competencies in practice* (2nd ed.). *Assessment, diagnosis, and therapy*. Washington DC: American Psychological Association.

Miranda, J., Bernal, G., Lau, A., Kohn, L., Hwang, W.C., & LaFromboise, T. (2005). State of the science on psychosocial interventions for ethnic minorities. *Annual Review of Clinical Psychology, 1*, 113–142.

Pedrotti, J.T., & Edwards, L.M. (2009). The intersection of positive psychology and multiculturalism in counseling. In J.G. Ponterotto, J.M. Casas, L.A. Suzuki, & C.M. Alexander (Eds.), *Handbook of multicultural counseling* (3rd ed.) (pp. 165–174). Thousand Oaks, CA: Sage.

Pedrotti, J.T., Edwards, L.M., & Lopez, S.J. (2009). Positive psychology within a cultural context. In S.J. Lopez & C.R. Snyder (Eds.), *Oxford handbook of positive psychology* (pp. 49–57). New York: Oxford University Press.

Ponterotto, J., Costa-Wofford, C., Brobst, K., Spelliscy, D., Kacanski, J., Scheinholtz, J., & Martines, D. (2007). Multicultural personality dispositions and psychological well-being. *The Journal of Social Psychology, 147*, 119.

Snyder, C.R., Lopez, S.J., & Pedrotti, J.T. (2010). *Positive psychology: The scientific and practical explorations of human strengths* (2nd ed.). Thousand Oaks, CA: Sage.[a]

van der Zee, K.I., & van Oudenhoven, J.R. (2001). The Multicultural Personality Questionnaire: A multidimensional instrument of multicultural effectiveness. *European Journal of Personality, 35*, 278–288.

Specific constructs

Emotional intelligence

Sharma, S., Biswal, R., Deller, J., & Mandal, M.K. (2009). Emotional intelligence: Factorial structure and construct validity across cultures. *International Journal of Cross Cultural Management, 9*, 217–236.

Empathy

Wang, Y., Davidson, M.M., Yakushko, O.F., Savoy, H.B., Tan, J.A., & Bleier, J.K. (2003). The scale of ethnocultural empathy: Development, validation, and reliability. *Journal of Counseling Psychology, 50*, 221–234.

Flow

Asakawa, K. (2004). Flow experience and autotelic personality in Japanese college students: How do they experience challenges in daily life? *Journal of Happiness Studies, 5*, 123–154.

Moneta, G.B. (2004a). The flow experience across cultures. *Journal of Happiness Studies, 5*, 115–121.

Forgiveness

Paz, R., Neto, F., & Mullet, E. (2008). Forgiveness: A China-Western Europe comparison. *The Journal of Psychology, 142*, 147–157.

Hope

Chang, E.C., & Banks, K.H. (2007). The color and texture of hope: Some preliminary findings and implications for hope theory and counseling among diverse racial/ethnic groups. *Cultural Diversity and Ethnic Minority Psychology, 13*, 94–103. doi: 10.1037/1099-9809.13.2.94.

Love

Landis, D., & O'Shea, W.A., III. (2000). Cross-cultural aspects of passionate love: An individual differences analysis. *Journal of Cross-Cultural Psychology, 31*, 752. doi: 10.1177/0022022100031006005.

Optimism

Chang, E.C. (2001). Cultural influences on optimism and pessimism: Differences in Western and Eastern construals of the self. In E.C. Chang (Ed.), *Optimism & pessimism: Implications for theory, research, and practice* (pp. 257–280). Washington, DC: American Psychological Association.

Positive affect

Ong, A.D., & Edwards, L.M. (2008). Positive affect and adjustment to perceived racism. *Journal of Social and Clinical Psychology, 27*, 105–126.

Resilience

Belgrave, F.Z., Chase-Vaughn, G., Gray, F., Addison, J.D., & Cherry, V.R. (2000). The effectiveness of a culture and gender-specific intervention for increasing resiliency among African American preadolescent females. *Journal of Black Psychology, 26*, 133–147.

Self-efficacy

Wu, C. (2009). Factor analysis of the general self-efficacy scale and its relationship with individualism/collectivism among twenty-five countries: Application of multilevel confirmatory factor analysis. *Personality and Individual Differences, 46*, 699–703. doi: 10.1016/j.paid.2009.01.025.

(continued)

Table 1. Continued.

Well-being

Ahuvia, A. (2001). Well-being in cultures of choice: A cross-cultural perspective. *American Psychologist, 56*, 77–78.

Diener, E. (2000). Subjective well-being: The science of happiness and a proposal for a national index. *American Psychologist, 55*, 34–43.

Icard, L. (1996). Assessing the psychosocial well-being of African American gays: A multidimensional perspective. In J.F. Longres (Ed.), *Men of color: A context for service to homosexually active men* (pp. 25–49). New York: Haworth Press.

Utsey, S., Hook, J., Fischer, N., & Belvet, B. (2008). Cultural orientation, ego resilience, and optimism as predictors of subjective well-being in African Americans. *The Journal of Positive Psychology, 3*, 202–210. doi: 10.1080/17439760801999610.

Wisdom

Ardelt, M. (2009). How similar are wise men and women? A comparison across two age cohorts. *Research in Human Development, 6*, 9–26.

Takahashi, M. (2000). Toward a culturally inclusive understanding of wisdom: Historical roots in the east and west. *International Journal of Aging and Human Development, 51*, 217–230.

Note: [a]This is the only undergraduate textbook that offers a cultural perspective imbedded within each chapter.

Age

Disability (Acquired)

Disability (Developmental)

Religion

Ethnicity

Sexual orientation

Socioeconomic status

Indigenous heritage

Nation of origin

Gender

Figure 1. Hays' (2008) ADDRESSING framework.

Each of these facets may also give us a different lens through which to look when deciding what is or is not a strength. An individual from a higher social class status, for example, may view the construct of hope as a boundless determination as a strength and a desirable trait that would help one to self-actualize and achieve full potential. An individual from a lower socio-economic class, however, might not view the boundless nature of this idea as a particularly beneficial one, as there may be financial obstacles that could summarily prevent an individual from this social class toward achievement of a goal (e.g., attending an expensive and prestigious college regardless of grade point average; Pedrotti, in press). In this sense, continued use of this strength in a boundless sense might bring frustration and disappointment when certain rather immutable obstacles are encountered.

In my course, I present this model to the students, and then ask them to complete an activity that I call the Cultural Strengths Exercise (Pedrotti, 2007). Each student looks through the ADDRESSING framework (Hays, 2008) and chooses three facets with which they identify strongly (students are told ahead of time that we will next discuss these facets and may thus edit themselves by making sure to choose facets about which they feel comfortable discussing). Once identifying these, they then are directed to think of what strengths they personally derive from these particular cultural facets. In general class discussion following this personal search, students comment on strengths derived from all facets. For example, a student may feel that because his/her nation of origin is the United States, his/her value of freedom and fairness helps him/her to be just and fair to others in various situations. Others may cite a collectivist background as the source from which they learned to be altruistic and to put others first. This activity allows students to see the diversity among them and to see the importance their own culture has played in deriving and identifying their personal strengths (Pedrotti, 2007).

Challenging students to spot and remedy views that adhere to only one worldview

The discussion of the importance of culture in talking about strengths on the first day of class also allows students to process research findings and theories from a culturally competent viewpoint. Research varies in its attentiveness to cultural issues, and thus students can be challenged to read positive psychological research critically for ethnocentrism, sexism, heterosexism, and other areas that may make it less applicable and/or damaging to certain groups. There are three areas regarding equivalence of constructs between cultures that may assist in appropriate translations of these works when looking at any type of research: conceptual equivalence, linguistic equivalence, and metric equivalence (Mio, Barker, & Tumambing, 2009). *Conceptual equivalence* calls for us to take into consideration whether a particular construct means the same thing in different cultural groups. For example, do individuals from one background use the same definition when speaking about a construct like hope, life satisfaction, or courage. *Linguistic equivalence* and *metric equivalence* refer, respectively, to the ability of a particular measure to be used across cultures due to language differences (e.g., measures must be translated and back-translated appropriately so as to have the same meaning in both languages), and different orientations to scale distinctions regarding how likely different cultures are to endorse specific ends of a continuum (e.g., risk-adverse cultures may never use a 1 or a 10 on a 1–10 scale due to this orientation; Pedrotti & Edwards, 2009). With regard to linguistic equivalence, appropriate wording can make all the difference in making sure that valid and reliable results are achieved through the use of measures across linguistically different populations. In Snyder et al.'s (1991) Adult Hope Scale, for example, the first item reads 'I can think of many ways to get out of a jam'. In translating this measure into any other language, one would want to make sure that the idiom 'get out of a jam' was translated appropriately as this may not be understandable in other languages. In thinking about metric equivalence, if an individual from a risk-adverse culture treats a '9' on a scale of 1–10 as the highest that she or he can comfortably choose due to cultural norms, this means that overall scores cannot be reasonably compared with an individual who is not risk-adverse. These areas must be taken into consideration when discussing positive psychological research that has been conducted from both culturally imbedded and culture-free perspectives to make sure that the interpretation of results is reflective of what the data are actually able to show. As researchers each come from within their own cultural contexts, these types of equivalence may be neglected during research design, and hence certain findings are masked or unable to be determined (Mio et al., 2009). To ignore them in reporting their results, however, is to risk further pathologizing traditionally marginalized groups by setting up the familiar deficit model.

Once the ideas of conceptual, linguistic, and measurement equivalence are presented, students can then decide about the appropriate utility of the findings. Considering questions about existing research such as 'Was an appropriate norming sample used in modifying this measure?' or 'Was the operationalization of the strength construct tested out in different groups before assuming that it is the same across groups?' This type of exercise can not only help students in the area of positive psychology, but can also encourage them to be more aware of their consumption and production of research within a multicultural framework. I often start with a discussion of Freud's original samples in developing his theory and ask students to consider the lack of heterogeneity in this group (e.g., small sample size, all women, all affluent, all Viennese) and then ask them what biases might come into play in observing such a small number of individuals and then creating a theory around them. This is a good starting place as I then explain that while this does not mean that we should ignore Freud's obvious contributions to the field, we should read carefully to make sure that these ideas would hold true for all groups; it is likely they would not. The other examples of famous theories can be presented in this way as an activity and students can work together in groups to evaluate their multicultural competence in today's society.

Inclusion of diverse perspectives in research and theory

Presenting research from a variety of diverse perspectives is another way in which a multicultural focus can be brought to the positive psychology classroom. Although there is still a dearth of research about multicultural topics within this part of the field, many studies have been conducted on strength-based topics with diverse cultures. Chang's (2001) research on optimism in Chinese American and White American students and the differences found between pessimism, optimism, and correlations with depression and problem-solving found in the different groups presents students with an understanding of the importance in looking past preliminary research results. Chang found here that while levels of pessimism were found to be higher in the Chinese American students, there were no significant differences in the levels of depression.

In delving further into these findings, Chang found that while pessimism correlated negatively with problem-solving in the White American sample, it correlated positively with problem-solving in the Chinese American sample. Research such as Chang's is helpful in showing that cultural context may provide a different value for a construct like optimism and in promoting the understanding that culture is thus an important consideration in this research.

Discussing culturally relevant strengths inside and outside the classroom

Finally, educators in positive psychology can put forth the idea that one might try 'borrowing' strengths that seem to fit inherently within a particular cultural group or facet may be another way of developing personal strengths. Perhaps, a student admires some of the tenets of collectivism, for instance, and sees the ideas of working for the group above the individual as valuable in his or her own life. This student could be encouraged to investigate cultures that live within this framework to help him/her better understand on how to use this selflessness in his/her own life as a strength. As an activity for class, students could be encouraged to seek out individuals who differ from them on some cultural aspect and to interview this individual about the potential benefits this person might enjoy as a 'practicing member' of that cultural group. As an example, a student from a majority background could choose an interviewee from a traditionally marginalized group to see how that individual or group has used a difficult situation and somehow derived a strength from that. For example, one might value the strength of courage and persistence as developed by being subjected to racism, prejudice, or other discriminatory practices (Sue & Sue, 2008). Though these types of injustices may not be experienced by a particular student, perhaps there is a way to relate these struggles to something with which an individual has had difficulty in the past. In trying to determine how this strength prevailed despite obvious obstacles, a student may be able to 'borrow' this technique of cultivating courage in her or his own life. These types of experiences of noting a strength, borrowing it, and then cultivating it in one's own life might assist students in being able to understand that all cultural groups have strengths and that all can contribute to a discussion of 'the good life'.

Finally, in looking at the strengths of various cultures, we can begin to undo the demoralization that has occurred because of pathologizing of non-majority groups that has occurred throughout the field of psychology over the course of our discipline (Constantine & Sue, 2006; Sue & Sue, 2008). Instead of viewing Asian Americans in a negative light due to

their 'excessive pessimism', one might gain a better understanding via research such as Chang's (2001) of how something that seems like a weakness may function as a strength within a different cultural context. Viewing other cultures in less negative lights may have an effect on decreasing discrimination and stereotyping of groups which have been typically subjected to this.

Conclusion

In summary, taking a multiculturally competent approach in positive psychology courses allows us to be more inclusive of students from all walks of life and to broaden our understanding of strengths across cultures as well. As academics from any area of study within the field of psychology, we recognize that striving to become multiculturally competent through our teaching practices and curricula is essential to the growth of the field and toward making efforts to repair past damage that has been done to traditionally marginalized groups. Positive psychology is a particularly beneficial area in which to achieve these goals because of its strength-based approach to all populations.

References

American Psychological Association (2003). Guidelines on multicultural education, training, research, practice, and organizational change for psychologists. *American Psychologist, 58*, 377–402.

Chang, E.C. (2001). Cultural influences on optimism and pessimism: Differences in Western and Eastern construals of the self. In E.C. Chang (Ed.), *Optimism & pessimism: Implications for theory, research, and practice* (pp. 257–280). Washington, DC: American Psychological Association.

Christopher, J.C. (2005). Situating positive psychology. *Naming and nurturing: The e-newsletter of the Positive Psychology Section of the American Psychological Association's Counseling Psychology Division, 17*, 3–4.

Constantine, M.G., & Sue, D.W. (2006). Factors contributing to optimal human functioning of people of color in the United States. *The Counseling Psychologist, 34*, 228–244.

Edwards, L.M., & Pedrotti, J.T. (2004). Utilizing the strengths of our cultures: Therapy with Biracial women and girls. *Women and Therapy, 27*, 33–43.

Gurung, R.A.R. (2009). Got culture? In R.A.R. Gurung & L.R. Prieto (Eds.), *Getting culture: Incorporating diversity across the curriculum* (pp. 11–22). Sterling, VA: Stylus.

Hays, P.A. (2008). *Addressing cultural competencies in practice: Assessment, diagnosis, and therapy* (2nd ed.). Washington, DC: American Psychological Association.

Mio, J.S., Barker, L.A., & Tumambing, J. (2009). *Multicultural psychology: Understanding our diverse communities*. New York, NY: McGraw-Hill.

Myers, D. (1993). *The pursuit of happiness*. New York, NY: Avon Books.

Pedrotti, J.T. (2007, October). *Strategies for infusing multiculturalism into a positive psychology course*. Presentation given at the annual Global Well-Being Forum, Washington, DC.

Pedrotti, J.T. (in press). Positive psychology, social class, and counseling. In W.M. Liu (Ed.), *Handbook of social class*. New York, NY: Oxford University Press.

Pedrotti, J.T., & Edwards, L.M. (2009). The intersection of positive psychology and multiculturalism in counseling. In J.G. Ponterotto, J.M. Casas, L.A. Suzuki, & C.M. Alexander (Eds.), *Handbook of multicultural counseling* (3rd ed., pp. 165–174). Thousand Oaks, CA: Sage.

Pedrotti, J.T., Edwards, L.M., & Lopez, S.J. (2009). Positive psychology within a cultural context. In S.J. Lopez & C.R. Snyder (Eds.), *Oxford handbook of positive psychology* (pp. 49–57). New York, NY: Oxford University Press.

Peterson, C., & Seligman, M.E.P. (2004). *Character strengths and virtues: A handbook and classification*. Washington, DC: American Psychological Association.

Seligman, M.E.P., & Csikszentmihalyi, M. (2000). Positive psychology: An introduction. *American Psychologist, 55*, 5–14.

Snyder, C.R., Harris, C., Anderson, J.R., Holleran, S.A., Irving, L.M., Sigmon, S.T., . . . , Wu, W.Y. (1991). The will and the ways: Development and validation of an individual-differences measure of hope. *Journal of Personality and Social Psychology, 60*, 570–585.

Snyder, C.R., Lopez, S.J., & Pedrotti, J.T. (2010). *Positive psychology: The scientific and practical explorations of human strengths*. Thousand Oaks, CA: Sage.

Sue, D.W., & Sue, D. (2003). *Counseling the culturally diverse: Theory and practice* (4th ed.). New York, NY: Wiley.

Sue, D.W., & Sue, D. (2008). *Counseling the culturally diverse: Theory and practice* (5th ed.). New York, NY: Wiley.

Writing critically about personal growth: A 'writing in the disciplines' course on happiness

Acacia C. Parks[a] and Valerie Ross[b]

[a]*Department of Psychology, Hiram College, PO Box 67, Hiram, OH 44234*
[b]*University of Pennsylvania*

Many colleges and universities in the United States require incoming freshmen to take coursework in writing. While some schools offer these courses through English Departments (i.e. "English 101"), a growing number of institutions are moving towards a Writing In the Disciplines (WID) approach, wherein writing instructors come from departments all across the university (McLeod & Soven, 2006; O'Neill, 2002; Russell, 2002; Wilner, 2005). Every course in a WID curriculum has the common goal of teaching students to write; the instructor's area of interest provides discipline-based context.

The University of Pennsylvania's Critical Writing program (of which the second author is the director) is an example of such a program. Instructors – who represent a broad range of disciplines from across the university – share the same writing curriculum, but also have the freedom to select a topic within their discipline. The topic serves as the basis of assigned readings and in-class discussions, which provide students with ideas about which to write. While all of Penn's writing courses are on topics deliberately crafted to be interesting and engaging for students, often the most successful WID courses make their content personally relevant as well as appealing.

In both semesters of the 2008-2009 academic year, the first author offered a freshman writing seminar at Penn on "Happiness." Students were charged with writing critically about the topic of happiness. Their arguments and explanations were based on readings from a variety of disciplines, popular media coverage of happiness, and their own lives, including hands-on experiences using a research-based self-help book (*The How of Happiness* by Sonja Lyubomirsky; Lyubomirsky, 2008). We discovered that, while any engaging topic advances the goal of teaching students to write, the topic of happiness proved beneficial in ways that transcend customary pedagogy. We believe that a sustained exploration of happiness is an ideal way to introduce students to college-level writing and to life as an adult.

Research in positive psychology provides compelling evidence that happiness is personally important to people (e.g. Goldberg et al., 2009), suggesting that students will be drawn to a course on the topic. This interest, itself a positive emotion, inspires the approach and exploration of novel information and experiences (see the "Broaden and Build" model, e.g. Fredrickson, 2009). Given that student engagement leads to better learning outcomes (Carini, Kuh & Klein, 2006), this course topic may actually teach students more about writing than they might learn from a course topic to which they are less attracted.

Furthermore, a body of research over the past decade has articulated methods by which individual can successfully pursue happiness (see Parks & Biswas-Diener, 2013); by walking students through a personal exploration of these methods, instructors may be able to help students become happier themselves. Happier students are a goal of any institution, as happiness in early adulthood predicts a broad range of positive life outcomes, from better social relationships to higher resilience against stress and improved career attainment (Lyubomirsky, King & Diener, 2005).

Below, we provide an outline of our writing seminar on happiness with the hope that instructors at other institutions may be able to make use of the course in part or whole as a model for their own. We begin by describing Penn's general approach to teaching writing, which is important because not all institutions using WID freshman seminars provide a specific curriculum for teaching writing. The absence of a shared writing curriculum leaves instructors to design by themselves not only an entire curriculum for writing but also to integrate this with their topic and discipline. Uncertainty about how to teach writing can be a formidable barrier to success, especially for those who might be teaching a writing course for the first time. After describing the curriculum, we will turn to an exploration of the happiness-related content that we integrated with it. Lastly, we speculate on the extent to which the course was a success, and provide some general concluding remarks about the utility of happiness as a vehicle for orienting freshmen to their new lives in college.

Penn's critical writing program

The Critical Writing Program (CWP) was created in 2003 as part of Penn's Center for Programs in Contemporary Writing. CWP is an independent WID program that features a shared curriculum developed in large part by the contributions and demands of those who have taught in the program since its founding. The writing faculty are a mix of standing faculty, senior fellows and full-time lecturers, and graduate students on fellowship, drawn from a wide range of disciplines. In the early years of the program, they appreciated the customary form of orientation—bulk packs of articles on writing pedagogy, presentations by experienced teachers about successful assignments they had used in the class, discussions and analyses of student writing—but also found it too abstract and theoretical to be of much help in designing and teaching an effective writing seminar in their particular disciplines. Thus, beginning in 2004, various members of the writing faculty and administration set out to create a curriculum that would be useful, effective, and reasonably accessible to those who wished to teach a writing seminar in their discipline. This has proven to be a work in progress; each year, we add, rearrange, and refine the curriculum to reflect what we have learned from each other, what our students have learned from us, and what we aim to teach them. For example, we discovered in the early years a significant curricular bias toward the rhetoric and writing of literary studies, which differs significantly from that used by, say, philosophy or psychology; along with locating such differences, we continue to identify areas of common ground that serve as the basis of our writing curriculum.

This shared curriculum has proven to be beneficial in ways we had not anticipated. This chapter, for example, points to one of the advantages: it allows us to discover and share knowledge about writing from each of our disciplines, as well as share what seems to be working, or not, in our classes. Our communal approach has replaced the more conventional "center" model in which writing knowledge emanates from one discipline, English, which then must be adapted by hook or crook to another's discipline. In turn, this communal model has allowed us to use the collective intelligence and experience of our faculty to refine and adapt various components of the curriculum, to share experiences, classroom exercises, texts, and now even group grading, an outgrowth of our turn to portfolio assessment a few years ago. In short, the shared curriculum became a healthy antidote for the isolation and "shot in the dark" approach attendant upon teaching in most disciplines but especially true of writing. Our collaborative enterprise also insures that our students, who are required to take the course in order to graduate, are given a more consistent pedagogical and assessment experience, and they are taught by faculty who have been sensitized to the differences, as well as shared ground, of academic writing in a given discipline. Among other things, this helps faculty counsel students on how to approach writing and how to transfer the knowledge they are gaining in their writing courses to other writing experiences across and beyond the university.

Our curriculum is outcomes-based, student-centered, and collaborative. The writing assignments are mostly brief, incremental and structured in tandem with an ongoing and increasing immersion in the course's specific topic. In order to pass Penn's writing requirement, students must be able to: 1) identify and implement the basics of the rhetoric of reasoning, 2) research and produce works of simple and complex synthesis, and 3) demonstrate competence in terms of logical and semantic coherence, grammar, and mechanics. In the end, they must produce a portfolio that demonstrates their ability to write an effective cover letter, timed essay, and substantial research essay. They must also be able to speak knowledgeably about these not only in terms of the topic but also as writers—for example, why they arranged the reasoning as they did, why they chose to counter-argue their opening reason, why they introduced or closed the piece as they did.

In terms of the content of curriculum, our premise is that despite such matters as discipline-by-discipline differences in epistemology, the status of different types of evidence, the handling of citations, diction, and sentence complexity, the writing done by members of academic disciplines in the U.S. shares a great deal of common ground (for an excellent overview of academic writing, see MacDonald, 2010). These include:

- Writing as the operation used to demonstrate and authorize the production of knowledge
- The rhetoric of reason used as the means by which that knowledge is demonstrated and legitimated in writing (i.e. Nelson, 1990)
- Synthesis and acknowledgment of prior work on the topic, along with explicit citation of that work
- Focus on presenting an idea, followed by its logically persuasive demonstration – the order and form of which varies
- Clarity, precision, and concision of expression

By organizing our curriculum around these active concepts, we are able to prepare undergraduate students for the extraordinary demands made upon them: Some may face writing assignments from faculty in four or five very different disciplines in the course of one semester. By helping them to understand what doesn't travel from one discipline to the next (e.g., citation practices, sentence styles, types of evidence), while teaching them how to evaluate and emulate the generic features and logical architecture of scholarly work, these students not only advance their skills as writers, but also gain a metacognitive awareness that helps them negotiate the often unstated disciplinary expectations of the writing assignments they are given.

In turn, our instructors themselves gain a metacognitive understanding of the generic features and specific rhetorical demands of their disciplines and the extent to which these intersect or differ from others. This heightened awareness leads them to adjust their expectations and writing assignments for their undergraduate and graduate students, and teaches them how to provide discipline-specific writing instruction in their own courses in the disciplines.

While Penn's writing curriculum is refined each year, key features remain the same. These features – which include 1) gaining proficiency as a reader and writer with the rhetoric of reasoning and thus with a range of reasoning strategies, 2) building an identity and habits of a writer, 3) writing with the purpose of communicating with an audience, 4) testing the extent to which their writing, and that of their colleagues', successfully communicates their ideas and 5) revising to achieve the desired outcome – are outlined below.

First, students learn to identify and practice reasoning strategies, writing methodically, with a plan for exactly what they hope to communicate to their audience and how they hope to communicate it. The approach we use, described below, has its roots in the collaborative method pioneered by Kenneth Bruffee in his seminal book, *A Short Course on Writing* (Bruffee, 1972). Students are given strategies for inventing propositions, and are advised that

this very term "proposition" may be called a thesis, hypothesis, claim, argument, project, statement, etc., across the disciplines. They are taught that a proposition is a conclusion, that to arrive at a meaningful one requires a great deal of research and prewriting. This is a major change from their high school instruction, where students often begin with a proposition and simply pile up information to support it, rather than arriving at it through ongoing discussions, research, and testing. Students develop their propositions over the course of the semester through short exercises, outlining, and feedback from their colleagues and instructors. They spend time on four basic strategies of the rhetoric of reasoning ("rhetorical strategies"; See Table 1), while at the same time immersing themselves in the topic readings and discussions. Thus they become more proficient in both, and the papers they write and exchange grow in sophistication and transform into building blocks, or chunks, of the longer essays they will write for the course.

Second, students work to build some fundamental practices that bolster their identity as a writer: someone who writes often and without great fanfare. This is essential because undergraduates typically begin their college experience with the sense that writing is a big production – something that can only be done in certain times and places,

Table 1. Ways of supporting a proposition (based on Bruffee, 1972)

Strategy	Description
Two Reasons	Supply two strong reasons in favor of the proposition. State each reason in turn, spending at least a paragraph developing each as fully as possible. Key Concept: Reasons provide a solid ground for convincing others. Skills Needed: Understanding the difference between reasons and examples; making the transition from associative writing based on "topic sentences."
Nestorian Order	Supply three or more reasons, ordering the reasons in the most compelling way possible: save the best reason for last, starting with the second best reason, and giving all the remaining reasons in the middle. Key Concept: Some reasons are better than others, and the order in which you present then affects the reader's reception of them Skills Needed: Differentiating between reasons that are great, good, and just ok; introduction to the dynamics of arrangement
Counter-Argument: Refutation & Concession	Describe a counter-argument to your proposition. Then systematically refute it in whole or part. Key Concept: Academic arguments are always tested. An argument must be able to hold up in full or part to a counter-argument. In turn, the concerns of opposing views should be addressed. Skills Needed: Understanding opposing viewpoints well enough to represent them accurately and acknowledge, when appropriate, what remains persuasive about them. Refuting compellingly without alienating the reader. Demonstrating that you have considered all aspects of your proposition and reasons for supporting it.
Longer Papers	Employ the basic reasoning strategies, along with other strategies that you have observed or invented, to advance your proposition. If you are writing an essay to justify a particular position, be sure to demonstrate through counterargument that you have tested it. If you are writing an explanatory essay, be sure that what you are explaining is organized according to the dynamics of the explanation and the order that meets your reader's needs. In all cases, be certain that your proposition is worth advancing to your readers. Key Concept: Different propositions will require different approaches to best explain or justify them. The basic strategies of legitimation (logical coherence) will need to be employed in some fashion to accomplish your objectives. Skills Needed: Strong understanding of the strategies of reasoning so that these can be effectively deployed by the writer.

in a state of profound inspiration; and that a good writer is one whose prose comes out perfectly the first time. A core aspect of Penn's writing seminar is frequent short pieces of writing rather than the "boa constrictor" model of writing a few longer papers. For example, for the first half of the course, a daily blog is required in which students must write at least five lines that are shared by all students in the class.[1] These blog posts need not be course-relevant; they are open-topic. By requiring students to make room for writing nearly every day of the semester, perfectionism – waiting for inspiration, waiting to deliver the perfect thought and its error-free delivery – becomes impossible to sustain. Students simply do not have the time to agonize.

Third, students learn to write for a real audience. Students often enter college with the sense that they should write using language that is as dry and complex as possible, for an audience of one: the teacher (or maybe even an audience of zero, depending on whether the student receives feedback). The student's purpose in writing, from this perspective, is not to communicate an idea, but to seem as smart and knowledgeable as possible in order to earn a good grade. This attitude is particularly reinforced by such things as the SAT Writing Test, which rewards the use of complex sentences and elevated language over clarity, simplicity, and accuracy of expression. Students who excelled in high school writing are often confused when they arrive at college and are expected to "learn to write," for they thought they had already mastered writing. However, students do not realize the many contexts in which clear, concise, and reasoned writing will be demanded of them in their various classes as well as in the cover letters, internship and scholarship applications, grant proposals, reports, and correspondence they will be writing in the years to come. Learning how to write for different audiences and purposes is at the heart of the curriculum, as students are tasked not with writing *to* their instructor but rather *for* their peers. They begin this work in the course blog, which "humanizes" their audience; this sense of a salient readership informs the scholarly work they do for the course, helping them to realize that they are writing to the same people they are joking and commiserating with on the blog. This enriched understanding also informs their peer reviews. Their task is to bring something new to their peers, to write in ways that will create or sustain a scholarly conversation. They write to *communicate*. This practice prepares them to write for the very people with whom they will be communicating for the rest of their lives: their peers.

Lastly, we teach students that written communication is a two-way street. It demands a careful reader—one who pays attention to what a writer is saying and doing—and a careful writer who knows his or her audience and purpose, has something of value to say, and chooses language and arrangement with an awareness of that purpose and audience. The writers learn that it is essential for them to share their writing with others and to receive feedback on the success of that communication. Writers in the course learn to take seriously the feedback they receive from

readers, from evaluation of the work's inventiveness to strengths and weaknesses of the logic, evidence, and clarity of expression. This substantial form of peer review teaches students that while presentation (grammar, clean sentences) is part of an effective piece of writing, far more important are the invention, substance, clarity of reasoning, and arrangement of written texts to readers who are genuinely engaged with the material.

Penn's writing curriculum contains numerous other components, but these goals are at the heart of the program. While we are sure that instructors interested in offering a writing course on happiness could use any number of other frameworks, we offer ours as a potential approach that has worked successfully for us at Penn and later at Hiram College (where the first author now teaches). It is worth noting that these two institutions are different in a number of ways; whereas Penn is a large university with an acceptance rate of 12%, an average incoming GPA of 3.9, and a student body that is largely well-prepared for college, Hiram is a small liberal arts school with an average incoming GPA of 3.29, and a long tradition of serving first-generation college students and other disadvantaged groups. That the above-described course design is able to effectively serve these two very different student populations suggests that it makes a solid foundation for anyone preparing such a course for the first time.[2]

The writing seminar on happiness

The writing seminar on happiness was developed by the first author in collaboration with the Critical Writing Program. The course began as one that was primarily psychology-based, but over time, with the encouragement of the writing program, grew into something more interdisciplinary. Here was the final course description that we agreed upon:

> "The Declaration of Independence states that individuals have an inalienable right to pursue happiness. But what is happiness, why is it important, and is it a worthwhile goal? In this class, we will explore psychological theories of happiness, and review research on the benefits of being happy and the ways individuals might become happier. We'll consider the views of philosophers and examine articles from the popular media. And we will consult our own personal experiences and reflect on our reactions to films and TV shows that make claims about the nature of happiness. Is happiness "real," or must one delude oneself in order to be happy? Throughout the semester, you will engage in debates both in class and on online forums, try your hand at opinion pieces, summarize and critique research findings, and learn to write compelling narratives about your life – all with the goal of creating a final portfolio of your writing."

Students begin writing short papers about the nature and value of happiness, based on their personal knowledge and experience of happiness In these initial assignments, they are introduced to devising and supporting reasons through their first main writing assignment, the "Two

Reasons" exercise (see Table 1). At first, students write only the body paragraphs of their essays. A person cannot introduce someone she has not met, and so it is our philosophy that a student cannot write an introduction without first having an essay to introduce. Predicated upon pre-writing of some sort, one of the earliest assignments asks students to write their proposition first, then two body paragraphs, each devoted to developing one reason in support of the proposition. They write the introduction last and, at this early stage, do not write a conclusion.

Students continue to build their knowledge of the topic through a series of increasingly complex readings. They begin with an introduction to the idea of positive psychology – the opening chapters of Peterson's *Primer in Positive Psychology* ("What is Positive Psychology?" and "Happiness"), and excerpts from the beginning of Seligman's *Authentic Happiness* (preface, "How Psychology Lost Its Way and I Found Mine," and "Why Bother to Be Happy?"). Instructors who do not wish to ask students to buy copies of these books, or whose library does not possess copies to put on reserve, there are primary source articles that contain similar information (Seligman & Csikszentmihalyi, 2000; Gable & Haidt, 2005; Lyubomirsky, King & Diener, 2005). We chose to use the Peterson and Seligman readings because they are more accessible to incoming freshman, who may be just developing the reading skills to digest scientific articles. In the initial weeks of class, the goal is not to stretch students' reading skills to their limits – that comes later – but to simply inspire students to start writing. It is our experience that students are often anxious enough about writing without the additional pressure of writing about something dense and complex.

Students then move on to the first of two books around which the course is based: Haidt's *The Happiness Hypothesis* (Haidt, 2006). Haidt (2006) takes an interdisciplinary approach, bringing both ancient philosophy and psychology to bear on many of the most fundamental issues in the study of happiness.[3] As students progress through this additional source – which is full of interesting ideas and evidence for those ideas – they expand their understanding of the discourse of happiness and have a stronger basis for making a more complex argument, using several reasons and ordering those reasons strategically to make the most compelling argument possible ("Nestorian Order" rhetorical form, see Table 1).

By the end of the 5th week, students have finished reading *The Happiness Hypothesis,* and they have started to experiment with a different type of essay – one in which the writer pits their own argument against a dissenting argument ("Refutation" rhetorical form, see Table 1). Here, the student may start to consider the ways in which her own experiences relate to the knowledge gained from the readings, perhaps exploring the benefits and limits of personal experience, as compared with scientific evidence, when making an argument. Students' argumentative abilities are pushed further still by the addition of a provocative

piece by philosopher Ziyad Marar, *The Happiness Paradox* (Marar, 2003). Student reactions to Marar's brief book vary from enthusiastic assent to fervent disagreement, but without fail, all students have a strong reaction, and that spurs them to write. It is with this reading – which polarizes students – that we introduce the idea of a "Concession" essay (see Table 1). Students must examine a viewpoint with which they strongly disagree, and then find some aspect that they can concede as valid. This is the last rhetorical strategy that students practice.

Once students have reached basic proficiency in argumentation as well as sufficient immersion in the topic, we turn to the writing of a conclusion. Students often mistake conclusions as a place to summarize and restate their argument – or worse, to state their argument for the first time! Students, therefore, are not allowed to write a conclusion until they have demonstrated that they are able to write an essay that stands alone. They are then introduced to the various uses of a conclusion, including: discussing caveats or exceptions to the proposition; revising the initial proposition in light of counter-evidence presented in the paper; proposing further topics of inquiry; and suggesting implications or practical applications of the proposition.

In the second half of the course, students turn their focus from the intellectual ("What is happiness and why is it important?") to the practical – they begin reading *The How of Happiness* (Lyubomirsky, 2008), which focuses on the idea of how happiness can be intentionally cultivated by an individual. Each student reads the opening chapters of Lyubomirsky (2008), then selects one of four categories of happiness activities featured in the book to emphasize for the rest of the class ("Practicing Gratitude and Positive Thinking," "Investing in Social Connections," "Managing Stress, Hardship and Trauma," or "Living in the Present"). They then spend the remainder of the term examining this topic from a variety of angles: 1) scientific, 2) popular culture, 3) personal experience, and 4) the experience of others. They write a short paper from each of these perspectives. For example, a student who chooses gratitude might read seminal papers on gratitude (e.g. Emmons & McCullough, 2003), watch *Pollyanna*, practice Lyubomirsky's "expressing gratitude" activity, and then interview two other students who tried to increase their optimism. A student who chooses living in the present might do readings on mindfulness (e.g. Brown, Ryan & Cresswell, 2007), watch *American Beauty*, do a savoring activity, and interview students who tried to increase their flow experiences. Students then work to integrate these smaller papers into a single, cohesive final paper that revolves around their chosen topic.

By the end of the course, students have learned about happiness as a theoretical concept, and they have examined their own attitudes towards happiness through self-reflection, hands-on experience with happiness strategies, and a reconciling of these personal experiences with empirical research.

Happiness as an ideal cornerstone of the first-year college experience

In Fall 2008, the Happiness writing seminar was the most highly requested of any other writing seminars that year, with over 200 students vying for 16 spots. This suggests that the topic of happiness was, in itself, one that excited students. Following the success of the two seminars on happiness in 2008-2009, the Critical Writing Program at Penn introduced in Fall 2012 a cluster of seminars taught by instructors from across the disciplines and devoted to this topic. Martin Seligman's *Flourish: A Visionary New Understanding of Happiness and Well-Being* (Seligman, 2012) is their shared text, while each instructor chooses other materials on the topic that are drawn from their own disciplines. While too early to tell, the collaboration promises to be quite successful.

While, in this chapter, we have focused on using happiness as the topic of a first-year writing course, other institutions use different models for freshman orientation, and we believe that happiness can be relevant in those contexts as well. The most popular alternative approach is the "common experience" model – in which the freshman experience is organized around some central theme, or set of topics. At some places, the topic varies over time. For example, Hiram chooses an ethical issue each year, assigns a common reading on the topic, and then offers guest speakers, as well as an interdisciplinary "ethics teach-in" where professors from all across the college weigh in on the topic's relevance to their discipline. Other institutions have a common course that freshmen take together – like Reed College's Humanities 110 – which sets the tone for the student's entire intellectual experience in college. In both of these contexts, there is a potential role for self-examination in general, and for an exploration of the meaning of happiness across disciplines and to oneself. Even institutions that do not offer a cohesive freshman experience have some sort of orientation process in which the topic of happiness might be included.

When implemented on a large scale, an exploration of the topic of happiness has the potential to transform students' lives beyond the classroom. As studies of happiness have suggested, it's a contagious emotion, one that improves the quality of life not just for the individual but for the social network in which those individuals are embedded (Fowler & Christakis, 2008). By introducing students to the sorts of skills and understanding attendant upon the study of happiness, we promote a positive engagement with their studies, their peers, and their professors, which in turn reduces stress, increases academic performance, and enhances retention and institutional loyalty. More importantly, we equip them to be citizens of a world that needs people who are both intellectually and emotionally prepared to meet the profound challenges of the 21st century.

Notes

1. We should note in passing that this blog is password-protected, so that students do not have to fear that one day they will regret something they wrote when they were 18.
2. Penn's writing curriculum, like any thoughtful academic program, is constantly evaluating itself and changing for the better. The present article provides a snapshot of the program as it was in 2008-2009, but the program continues to develop. For example, below we describe a progression between the four rhetorical strategies that has been somewhat revised in the current curriculum. Students also now spend more time explicitly working with analysis of rhetorical strategies in scholarly work, as well as synthesis and advanced research methods as they build longer research papers in "chunking" fashion. For up-to-date information on the current writing curriculum, please contact Dr. Parks (parksac@hiram.edu) and/or Dr. Ross (vross@writing.upenn.edu).
3. An annotated table of contents of The Happiness Hypothesis can be found online at http://www.happinesshypothesis.com/chapters.html

References

Brown, K.W., Ryan, R.M. & Creswell, J.D. (2007). Mindfulness: Theoretical foundations and evidence for its salutary effects. *Psychological Inquiry, 18,* 211–237.

Bruffee, K. (1972). A short course in writing. Cambridge: Winthrop Publishers.

Carini, R.M., Kuh, G.D., & Klein, S.P. (2006). Student engagement and student learning: Testing the linkages. *Research in Higher Education, 47,* 1–32.

Emmons, R.A. & McCullough, M.E. (2003). Counting blessings versus burdens: An experimental longitudinal investigation of gratitude and subjective well-being in daily life. *Journal of Personality and Social Psychology, 84,* 377–389.

Fowler, J.H. & Christakis, N.A. (2008). Dynamic spread of happiness in a large social network: Longitudinal analysis over 20 years in the Framingham Heart Study. *British Medical Journal, 337,* a2338.

Fredrickson, B.L. (2009). *Positivity.* New York: Crown.

Gable S.L. & Haidt, J. (2005). What (and why) is positive psychology? *Review of General Psychology, 9,* 103–110.

Goldberg, A.B., Fillmore, N., Andrzejewski, D., Xu, Z., Gibson, B., & Zhu, X. (2009). May all your wishes come true: A study of wishes and how to recognize them. In *Human language technologies* (pp. 263–271). Boulder, CO: Association for Computation Linguistics.

Haidt, J. (2006). *The happiness hypothesis: finding modern truth in ancient wisdom.* New York: Basic Books.

Lyubomirsky, S. (2008). *The how of happiness: A new approach to getting the life you want.* New York: Penguin Books.

Lyubomirsky, S., King, L.A., & Diener, E. (2005). The benefits of frequent positive affect. *Psychological Bulletin, 131,* 803–855.

Macdonald, S.P. (2010). *Professional academic writing in the humanities and social sciences.* Carbondale: Southern Illinois University Press.

Marar, Z. (2003). *The happiness paradox.* London: Reaktion Books.

McLeod, S.H. & Soven, M.I. (Eds.) (2006). *Composing a community: A history of writing across the curriculum.* Anderson: Parlor Press.

Nelson, J.S. (1990). *Rhetoric of the human sciences: Language and argument in scholarship and public affairs.* Madison: University of Wisconsin Press.

O'Neill, P. (2002). *A field of dreams: Independent writing programs and the future of composition studies.* Logan: Utah State University Press.

Parks, A.C. & Biswas-Diener, R. (2013). Positive interventions: Past, present and future. In T. Kashdan and J. Ciarrichi (Eds.), *Bridging Acceptance and Commitment Therapy and Positive Psychology: A Practitioner's Guide to a Unifying Framework.* Oakland, CA: New Harbinger.

Russell, D.R. (2002). *Writing in the academic disciplines, second edition: A curricular history.* Carbondale: Southern Illinois University Press.

Seligman, M.E.P. (2010). *Flourish: A visionary new understanding of happiness and well-being.* New York: Free Press.

Seligman, M.E.P. & Csikszentmihalyi (2000). Positive psychology: An introduction. *American Psychologist, 55,* 5–14.

Wilner, A. (2005). The challenges of assignment design in discipline-based freshman writing classes. *Composition Forum, 14.2.* Available online at *http://compositionforum.com/issue/14.2/wilner-assignment-design.php*

The moral of the story: The importance of applying an ethics lens to the teaching of positive psychology

Dianne A. Vella-Brodrick

School of Psychology and Psychiatry, Monash University, Wellington Road, Clayton 3800, Australia

In a short-time positive psychology has progressed into a scientific and multidisciplinary field of enquiry. It is now necessary for positive psychology to develop clear practice standards which will be collectively endorsed and upheld by members and those undergoing training in positive psychology. Teachers of positive psychology are in a prime position to disseminate ethical knowledge. Moreover, the objectives of ethics and positive psychology are closely aligned in their focus on achieving optimal outcomes; hence, the pairing of the two is ideal. Consequently, it would be ironic if positive psychology did not explicitly embrace ethical standards in guiding those training for a future in positive psychology. As a professional entity, positive psychology needs to provide more direction and encouragement for teachers, students, scholars and practitioners of positive psychology, and in time, this should be codified and discussed in positive psychology university degrees to promote consistency among its future members.

'A good profession seeks to advance the knowledge base on which it draws and continually assesses the validity of its practices. It is not a closed system' (O'Gorman, 2007, p. 16).

Introduction

Positive psychology as a psychological framework and a useful partner to many professions, should not be immune to the fundamental ethical process of self-review, and this responsibility to examine ethical aspects also needs to surface in the teaching of positive psychology.

My teaching of positive psychology has been within the School of Psychology and Psychiatry at Monash University in Australia. I have developed and taught two positive psychology-based subjects for advanced undergraduate students. The first subject, which has been taught since 2006, requires psychology majors to undertake a minor research project focused on positive constructs or interventions. The second subject, which has been taught since 2009, is a positive psychology elective introducing students from a wide range of courses to the main concepts, methods and findings of positive psychology. Both subjects are semester long (delivered over 12 weeks) and involve 2 and 3 hours, respectively, of class contact per week. I have also been teaching ethics and professional practice classes to fourth year and Masters level psychology students for over a decade. This teaching experience has enabled me to recognise that the underlying concepts of both positive psychology and ethics are similar in many respects, and that an integration of these two frameworks can communicate poignant and effective messages, and raise important questions for contemplation by positive psychology students.

In this article, I will argue that ethics is fundamental to the practice of positive psychology and should be included in positive psychology curricula. First, some of the key concepts underlying ethics and positive psychology and how these dovetail, will be presented. Second, the rationale for adopting an ethical lens to the teaching of positive psychology will be provided. Third, some practical examples of how ethical concepts can be integrated into the teaching of positive psychology will be included, and finally, recommendations for maintaining these standards will be made.

Positive psychology: A psychological framework with professional and ethical responsibilities

Positive psychology originated in response to psychology's preoccupation with repairing what is wrong. In an attempt to redress this negative bias, positive psychology has promoted strength-based approaches which involve the identification and development of positive qualities (Seligman & Csikszentmihalyi, 2000). Proponents of positive psychology have also promoted this field of study as being scientifically grounded (Seligman & Csikszentmihalyi, 2000). Furthermore, the formation of the International Positive Psychology Association (IPPA) formalizes positive psychology as a professional entity. This therefore means that just like psychology or any other scientifically based *profession*, quality standards need to be identified and developed for scholars, practitioners and students of positive psychology to follow. Although positive psychology is making excellent and rapid progress with its scientific missions, as evidenced by the development of a dedicated journal, the establishment of a professional association and the hosting of international meetings, it is now timely for positive psychology to examine more closely its ethical responsibilities. Although some regulations around IPPA membership are currently in place, the importance of professional ethics needs to be communicated more explicitly to its membership and to those being trained in the field so that professional standards can also be upheld. There is also empirical support that an understanding of ethics can enhance critical thinking (Allegretti & Frederick, 1995) and moral reasoning (Self & Olivarez, 1996), both desirable qualities for those working in positive psychology.

Professional ethics is concerned with the governance of conduct associated with professional services provided to members of the public. One distinguishing feature of a profession is that it has a code of ethics (O'Gorman, 2007), which aims to promote best practice standards using guiding principles endorsed and regulated by the members of the profession at large. For example, the Australian Psychological Society endorses eight common principles, namely (1) respect for the dignity and rights of people, (2) justice, (3) autonomy, (4) nonmaleficence (to do no harm), (5) beneficence (to do good), (6) veracity, (7) fidelity and (8) responsibility (see Allan & Love (2010) for a description of each of these principles). These broad principles are believed to encapsulate the spirit of ethical practice and are commonly embedded within ethical codes from different nations (e.g. American Psychological Association – Appendix) and from a wide range of disciplines including medicine and allied health (albeit in various combinations or under slightly varied labels).

Why are ethical concepts relevant to the teaching of positive psychology?

In brief, best practice is the cornerstone of being a 'professional' (O'Gorman, 2007) and ethical standards

serve important functions. First, ethical codes guide their members with the standards for appropriate conduct with which to serve their clients. Second, they promote transparency and hence, accountability to consumers and the public. Third, they enable the profession to 'take stock' and evaluate how the field in general is progressing with the view to improving aspects such as service quality, public image, knowledge, interdisciplinary collaboration, skills and training. These points are particularly relevant to the field of positive psychology given it is relatively new and members can come from diverse professional backgrounds. One of the challenges, therefore, is for professional standards to be consistent across the various members. Positive psychology has been scrutinised in the past (Held, 2004) and would benefit from the implementation of a thorough process of conduct and evaluation, starting from the training phase. Indeed, scholars of positive psychology have, some years ago, made a call for this careful monitoring to be more pronounced among its membership:

> In the excitement that may be associated with this new and invigorating approach, it may be tempting to over-extrapolate so as to convey a sense of the progress that is being made...Contrary to this "breakthrough" mentality, however, science typically advances in the context of slow, incremental increases in knowledge. Therefore...researchers must be very careful to make appropriate inferences from their data. Claims that go beyond the data are never appropriate, and they can be especially damaging to the credibility of a new field. When one positive psychologist makes an unwarranted claim, this undermines the trustworthiness of all positive psychologists and the "movement" more generally. Accordingly, we must carefully monitor both our colleagues and ourselves (Snyder & Lopez., 2002, pp. 754–755).

This mindset, across all positive psychology practices (not just research), in a more formalised package, consistent with other established professions is needed. Positive psychology courses should involve some level of ethics training and it is possible that some already do, but many do not. Even when ethics is being delivered as part of a positive psychology programme, there may be issues of consistency of information as there is no predetermined or codified standard of practice endorsed by those in positive psychology at present. Most professions, including psychology, are mandated by accreditation bodies to provide specific ethics training throughout their accredited degrees with ethics being viewed as a core subject that is integral to best practice.

As previously noted, the study of positive psychology can straddle many disciplines including business, law, economics and politics. There is no questioning that interdisciplinary perspectives on methods for achieving fulfilling lives, and the corresponding implications, can provide rich insight and should be encouraged. However, this lack of explicit affiliation with any one specific discipline means that best practice standards may become confused, diluted or even exempt and may vary according to the level of professional training and background the practitioner or scholar of positive psychology has received. One way of addressing this issue is to draw on principles commonly endorsed by other well-respected disciplines, such as medicine or psychology. In particular, the standards and ethical principles employed by psychologists seem most relevant to positive psychology (e.g. the APA principles in Appendix) and are worth pursuing for use among scholars, practitioners and students of positive psychology.

How to apply an ethics lens to the teaching of positive psychology

Those of us who teach positive psychology are in an ideal position to instil these important ethical standards and principles to potential scholars and practitioners of positive psychology. While teaching or studying ethics may not have instant appeal, there are many creative and interesting ways to deliver ethical material, particularly when combined with positive psychology content. These methods can include experiential activities, case studies, role plays and debates. Moreover, many concepts such as beneficence, competence, integrity, autonomy, justice and compassion, while ethical in nature, are also consistent with the fundamentals of positive psychology (i.e. flourishing and aspiring to meet one's full potential and to use these strengths to serve the broader community). Hence, amalgamating the two areas of study should not be particularly difficult or onerous, and this fusion should appear seamless and feel natural to both teachers and students.

In my positive psychology teaching, I integrate ethical concepts where ever relevant. For example, if I am discussing with students the empirical findings on the strengths most and least highly correlated with life satisfaction, I will also raise for discussion the implications of these findings from an ethical and moral lens. I ask students questions like: is life satisfaction an ideal outcome variable? What if we replaced life satisfaction with eudaimonic or collectivist outcomes such as prosocial and altruistic behaviours and attitudes – might we find different correlates of strengths Also, are the least commonly used strengths therefore the least valuable strengths (e.g. prudence and self-regulation are among the lowest strengths but does this mean they are not important for mental health and community cohesion)?

Specific activities that accentuate some of the ethical issues inherent in the practice of positive psychology are also used in my teaching. What follows are some examples which serve to illustrate the logical connection between ethics and positive psychology and how the dual perspectives can create increased depth and interest to an activity or concept. The *primary* ethical concept being integrated into each of the positive psychology activities is identified. Key questions, a brief description of the activity, points for discussion and the general objective for each activity are also summarised.

Fidelity and responsibility

Key questions

What do we do with the knowledge gained from positive psychology? Do we need to consider servicing the broader community? Do we have a role to play in guiding for example, education and health policy? How much information is needed before we can act effectively as advocates for including positive psychology findings into public health policy?

Activity

Write a letter to government recommending a new education or health policy based on positive psychology research findings.

- Example (in brief):

  Volunteering has been found to produce positive outcomes both for the recipient and for the giver; so, we ask you as the health minister, to consider granting all government employees approximately 2 days of paid leave per year to undertake voluntary work for a not for profit community organisation.

Further points for class discussion

If empirical research findings are supporting the health benefits of particular actions (such as volunteering), then to what extent are proponents of positive psychology expected to convey this information to relevant authorities? Who might these authorities be? Who specifically, should act as these advocates? What if the research findings were suggesting that a positive intervention was not effective, would you be equally active in ensuring it is *not* adopted by others?

General objective

This activity encourages students to contemplate how far they can and should take the knowledge acquired from positive psychology for the good of the wider community, the mediums that are available for doing this, and what motives and role they might have in doing so. Positive psychology is focused on fostering well-being and has widespread applicability; so, the scope for promoting the knowledge gained in high impact contexts is considerable and should not be neglected.

Nonmaleficence, responsibility and integrity

Key questions

What messages are we conveying to potential consumers about our findings in positive psychology? Is there the tendency to over-generalise or exaggerate the significance of research findings or to endorse certain practices without sufficient supporting evidence?

Activity

Identify a significant research finding in positive psychology and develop a marketing campaign around this finding and its implications.

- Example (in brief):

  "Write down three good things and why you think they happened every day for a week and your well-being will increase and depression decrease, six months later". (omission in example campaign: many study participants completed this activity beyond the week, hence it may be misleading to suggest that one week of the 'three good things' activity will suffice for positive effects to last six months (Seligman, Steen, Park, & Peterson, 2005)).

Further points for class discussion

Can the message behind your campaign be interpreted in different ways? How could the message have been promoted more accurately? Were there any clauses that needed to be mentioned? Is there potential for harm when messages are oversimplified? How can we prevent this from occurring? Do we have a responsibility to explore whether the findings from other fields align with our findings (e.g. what do we know about health behaviour change from the field of health psychology)? If there are inconsistencies, how do we reconcile and communicate these?

General objective

This activity served to highlight to students how narrowly focused and close to the subject matter, we can all become and that often miscommunication or omission of important detail is unintentional. Nevertheless, these miscommunications can adversely impact others (e.g. instil false hope). As positive psychology has such widespread appeal, we need to take care to educate the public with accurate and realistic information about how they can apply positive psychology for optimal gains. Hence, an exploration of methods for remaining objective and communicating accurate information is central to this activity.

Respect for people's rights and dignity, autonomy

Key question

Are individuals able to make effective decisions about their health and well-being and should they be free to choose whatever actions they wish, even though there may be evidence gained from studies in positive psychology indicating that their actions are generally contrary to good psychological health?

Activity: Case study

Mary, a 26-year old who works as a 'temp', likes to live life 1 day at a time and refuses to plan and work towards a future. Mary enjoys the out of body sensations, she experiences when she takes lysergic acid diethylamide which she takes a couple of times a week generally before or after she goes out dancing at nightclubs. She enjoys shopping for clothes and derives great pleasure from going on occasional but extravagant shopping sprees. Mary is not in a steady relationship but prefers to play the field and enjoys 'experimenting' with a variety of sexual partners. She has numerous friends, but is not very close to her family. Mary will often strike up conversations with strangers and loves meeting new people. Mary shares a small apartment with five flatmates and although the place is crammed, it is across the road from the ocean, where she often enjoys swimming and late night skinny dipping. Mary's friends describe her as a bubbly, wild and energetic person who just loves to have fun. At times, particularly when home alone, Mary feels empty inside, but most of the time she describes her life as being a 'blast'?

Further points for class discussion

- Under what circumstances should Mary's life be evaluated, if at all?
- What knowledge has been gained in the field of positive psychology about how to live the good life or full life, and how does Mary's life compare with this? Aspects to consider include:
  - Self-concordant motivation (Sheldon & Houser-Marko, 2001).
  - Self-determination Theory (Deci & Ryan, 1985).
  - Orientations to happiness framework (Peterson, Park, & Seligman, 2005)
- Does Mary have the right to choose how she lives her life, even if it is not consistent with some of the positive psychology findings about how to live the good life?
- Is Mary the only one being affected by her lifestyle? What are the potential consequences

of Mary's lifestyle to others and the community at large? Are these questions relevant?

- What are some of the ethical issues raised by this case?

  ○ Autonomy *versus* duty of care/beneficence

- What changes, if any, would you recommend to Mary and why?

General objective

The purpose of this activity is to illustrate the importance of treating people with respect and dignity and as authorities on, and decision-makers of, their own lives. Students are asked to contemplate their role as positive psychologists in such scenarios and the impact their personal values can have on their professional decision making. This scenario also demonstrates that principles can sometimes clash (e.g. autonomy *vs.* beneficence) and that we need to justify why we have prioritised one principle over another in our decision making – is empirical knowledge sufficient? The issue of prescription *versus* description, in terms of what we do with information gained from positive psychology, is also discussed in this activity.

Summary and conclusion

I have argued that ethics is the perfect partner to positive psychology and that its inclusion in training programs will contribute to positive psychology's sustainability and reputation as a worthy field of scientific study. The positive psychology classes to which I refer in this article have received favourable feedback from students to the extent that the Deputy Vice Chancellor (Education) at Monash University has commended the positive psychology elective, also taught by Jacolyn Norrish, for having received student ratings in excess of 4.7 out of 5. This is testament that ethical principles can be successfully embedded in the teaching of positive psychology without sacrificing student engagement and enjoyment in the learning process. For example, students in anonymous evaluations of these positive psychology classes commented that the 'interactive teaching method really allowed me to grasp concepts well and made classes interesting' and how they 'appreciated variation in teaching tools and methods used' and that the material was presented 'thoughtfully and critically'.

Consequently, I encourage all positive psychology teachers to include ethical concepts in their teaching of positive psychology. Indeed, if the mission of positive psychology is to be grounded in science and to endorse best practice standards, akin with the aspirations of other more established and respected professions, then

an ethical component, whether explicit or implicit, is necessary. Perhaps in the near future, some negotiation and more regulated monitoring of the ethical content to be delivered under the auspices of positive psychology may be more plausible.

Although many of the ethical issues raised in the example teaching activities provided in this article are not exclusive to positive psychology, and it is likely that ethical concepts like the ones noted in the examples are already being taught in some positive psychology classes, a more strategic and deliberate approach to embedding ethical standards in positive psychology curricula is needed, so that positive psychology can remain open to critically assessing the quality and value of its own contributions. Indeed, positive psychology is in a prime position to adopt an ethical lens to teaching positive psychology as the objectives of the two fields are very similar and much of what is espoused in positive psychology is closely aligned with ethical and humanitarian standards. Consequently, it would be ironic if positive psychology did not explicitly embrace ethical standards in the training of future positive psychology professionals and to provide encouragement, guidance and resources to teachers in this pursuit.

References

Allan, A., & Love, A. (Eds.). (2010). *Ethical practice in psychology: Reflections from the creators of the APS Code of Ethics.* West Sussex: John Wiley and Sons.

Allegretti, C.L., & Frederick, J.N. (1995). A model for thinking critically about ethical issues. *Teaching of Psychology, 22*, 46–48.

Deci, E.L., & Ryan, R.M. (1985). *Intrinsic motivation and self-determinaton in human behaviour.* New York, NY: Plenum.

Held, B.S. (2004). The negative side of positive psychology. *Journal of Humanistic Psychology, 44*, 9–46.

O'Gorman, J. (2007). *Psychology as a profession in Australia.* Bowen Hills, QLD: Australian Academic Press.

Peterson, C., Park, N., & Seligman, M.E. (2005). Orientations to happiness and life satisfaction: The full life versus the empty life. *Journal of Happiness Studies, 6*, 25–41.

Self, D.J., & Olivarez, M. (1996). Retention of moral reasoning skills over the four years of medical education. *Teaching and Learning in Medicine, 8*, 195–199.

Seligman, M.E.P., & Csikszentmihalyi, M. (2000). Positive psychology: An introduction. *American Psychologist, 55*, 5–14.

Seligman, M.E.P., Steen, T.A., Park, N., & Peterson, C. (2005). Positive psychology progress: Empirical validation of interventions. *American Psychologist, 60*, 410–421.

Sheldon, K.M., & Houser-Marko, L. (2001). Self-concordance, goal attainment, and the pursuit of happiness: Can there be an upward spiral? *Journal of Personality and Social Psychology, 80*, 152–165.

Snyder, C.R., & Lopez, S.J. (2002). The future of positive psychology: A declaration of independence. In C.R. Snyder & S.J. Lopez (Eds.), *Handbook of positive psychology* (pp. 751–767). New York, NY: Oxford University Press.

Appendix: American Psychological Society Code of conduct – ethical principles (amended 2010)

Source: http://www.apa.org/ethics/code/index.aspx

Principle A: Beneficence and nonmaleficence

Psychologists strive to benefit those with whom they work and take care to do no harm. In their professional actions, psychologists seek to safeguard the welfare and rights of those with whom they interact professionally and other affected persons, and the welfare of animal subjects of research. When conflicts occur among psychologists' obligations or concerns, they attempt to resolve these conflicts in a responsible fashion that avoids or minimises harm. Because psychologists' scientific and professional judgements and actions may affect the lives of others, they are alert to and guard against personal, financial, social, organisational or political factors that might lead to misuse of their influence. Psychologists strive to be aware of the possible effect of their own physical and mental health on their ability to help those with whom they work.

Principle B: Fidelity and responsibility

Psychologists establish relationships of trust with those with whom they work. They are aware of their professional and scientific responsibilities to society and to the specific communities in which they work. Psychologists uphold professional standards of conduct, clarify their professional roles and obligations, accept appropriate responsibility for their behaviour and seek to manage conflicts of interest that could lead to exploitation or harm. Psychologists consult with, refer to, or cooperate with other professionals and institutions to the extent needed to serve the best interests of those with whom they work. They are concerned about the ethical compliance of their colleagues' scientific and professional conduct. Psychologists strive to contribute a portion of their professional time for little or no compensation or personal advantage.

Principle C: Integrity

Psychologists seek to promote accuracy, honesty and truthfulness in the science, teaching and practice of psychology. In these activities, psychologists do not steal, cheat or engage in fraud, subterfuge or intentional misrepresentation of fact. Psychologists strive to keep their promises and to avoid unwise or unclear commitments. In situations in which deception may be ethically justifiable to maximise benefits and minimise harm, psychologists have a serious obligation to consider the need for, the possible consequences of, and their responsibility to correct any resulting mistrust or other harmful effects that arise from the use of such techniques.

Principle D: Justice

Psychologists recognise that fairness and justice entitle all persons to access to and benefit from the contributions of psychology and to equal quality in the processes, procedures and services being conducted by psychologists. Psychologists exercise reasonable judgement and take precautions to ensure that their potential biases, the boundaries of their competence and the limitations of their expertise do not lead to or condone unjust practices.

Principle E: Respect for people's rights and dignity

Psychologists respect the dignity and worth of all people, and the rights of individuals to privacy, confidentiality and self-determination. Psychologists are aware that special safeguards may be necessary to protect the rights and welfare of persons or communities whose vulnerabilities impair autonomous decision making. Psychologists are aware of and respect cultural, individual and role differences, including those based on age, gender, gender identity, race, ethnicity, culture, national origin, religion, sexual orientation, disability, language and socioeconomic status, and consider these factors when working with members of such groups. Psychologists try to eliminate the effect on their work of biases based on those factors, and they do not knowingly participate in or condone activities of others based upon such prejudices.

Index

Page numbers in **bold** type refer to figures
Page numbers in *italic* type refer to tables